PRO FOOTBALL
STRATEGY

— What the Sunday fan should know to be a Monday quarterback.

Jim Hopkinson

Knowledge Builders, Inc.

Lake Forest, Illinois

Copyright © 1982 by James E. Hopkinson

All rights reserved. No portion of this book may be reproduced — electronically, mechanically, or by any other means, including photocopying — without written permission of the publisher.

Published by: Knowledge Builders, Inc.
744 E. Green Briar
Lake Forest, Illinois 60045

Printed by: The D.B. Hess Company
Woodstock, Illinois 60098

Library of Congress Catalog Card Number: 81-83104
International Standard Book Number: 0-940950-00-6

CONTENTS

Chapter 1	**INTRODUCTION (Our Game Plan)**	1
	Explanation of Diagrams	6
Chapter 2	**MISCELLANEOUS INFO**	9
Chapter 3	**FORMATIONS**	15
	BASIC CONSIDERATIONS	16
	OFFENSIVE FORMATIONS	21
	Constraints	
	Basic Formations	22
	The Pro Set	
	Variations of the Pro Set	25
	Halfbacks & Fullbacks	27
	I Formation	28
	Slot Formation	29
	Double Wing	30
	2 Tight Ends (Double Tight)	31
	3 Wide Receivers	
	The Shotgun	32
	Man in Motion	33
	Offensive Shifts	34
	DEFENSIVE FORMATIONS	35
	Constraints	
	Positioning of Players	
	Deception vs. Execution	36
	Basic Formations	
	4-3 Defense	
	3-4 Defense	39
	Variations of the 4-3 & 3-4	41
	Overshift	
	Undershift	
	Gap Defense	
	Stack Defense	
	The Flex Defense	42
	Nickel Defense	43
	Goal Line Defense	44

Chapter 4   PLAYS   45

OFFENSIVE RUNNING PLAYS   46

    Off-Tackle Power Play
    Quick Trap   50
    Misdirection Play   52

DEFENSIVE PLAYS   56

    Slant
    Pinch
    Inside Charge   57
    Outside Charge
    Stack
    Key Defense
    Blast (Charge)   58
    Linemen & Linebackers
    Containment of End Run   59
    Pursuit   60
    Stunts   61
    Blitz   63

PASS PLAYS   64

    Pass Blocking
    Wide Receiver Pass Routes   68
    Tight End Pass Routes   70
    Running Back Pass Routes   71
    Pass Patterns   72

PASS DEFENSES   73

    Man-to-Man Coverages   74
       Linebacker Short Zones
       Free Safety Defense   75
       Double Coverage on Split End   76
       Double Coverage on Both Wide Rec'rs
       Heavy Blitz (3-4 Defense)   77
       Nickel Defense

    Zone Defenses   78
       Strong Side Zone
       Strong Side Inverted Zone
       Strong Side Linebacker Zone   79
       Weak Side Zone   80
       Double Zone
       5-Under, 3-Deep Strong Side Zone   81

    Combination Coverages
       Man Under a 2-Deep Zone
       Mombo Coverage   82
       Zone with Designated Chaser

Chapter 5	**PASSING ATTACKS**	**83**
	Throw Away from Rotation	84
	Stretching Zones	85
	Flooding Zones	86
	Using a Slot	87
	Controlling Linebackers	89
	Throwing Underneath	
	Which Way to Rotate?	90
	Throw Away from Free Safety	
	Tight End vs. Double Coverage	91
	Offensive Line's Role	
Chapter 6	**THE PLAYERS**	**93**
	OFFENSIVE LINEMEN	95
	Blocking	101
	RUNNING BACKS	103
	WIDE RECEIVERS	109
	TIGHT ENDS	115
	QUARTERBACKS	121
	DEFENSIVE LINEMEN	131
	Holding	141
	LINEBACKERS	143
	CORNERBACKS	149
	SAFETIES	155
	KICKERS	163
	PUNTERS	169
	Average Player Characteristics	174
Chapter 7	**PLAY CALLS**	**175**
	DIFFERENT SYSTEMS	176
	OFFENSIVE PLAY CALLS	
	LINE CALLS	190
	DEFENSIVE CALLS	193

Chapter 8	**IN MOTION**	**199**
	Is He Leaning?	200
	Line Splits	201
	Running Backs & Tight Ends	202
	How Informative are Keys?	
	Offensive Keys	203
	Personal Traits	205
	Other Keys	
	Adjusting to Counter a Blitz	206
	Finding Best Opening	207
	Throws into the Middle	209
	Altering a Pass Route	210
	Looking into Backfield	211
	Looking Downfield	
	Blocking for Short Passes	212
	Scrambling & Blocking	
	DEFENSIVE COUNTERS	213
Chapter 9	**SPECIAL TEAMS**	**219**
	KICKOFFS	220
	PUNTS	223
	FIELD GOALS & EXTRA POINTS	226
Chapter 10	**STATISTICS**	**229**
	LEAGUE STATS	230
	TEAM STATS	233
	INDIVIDUAL PLAYER STATS	238
Chapter 11	**WATCHING & KEEPING SCORE**	**245**
Chapter 12	**CONCLUSION**	**255**
	INDEX	**258**

CHAPTER 1

INTRODUCTION
(Our Game Plan)

Welcome

Welcome to *PRO FOOTBALL STRATEGY — What the Sunday fan should know to be a Monday quarterback.* This is a book for the average fan who has watched football games in the past and will watch many more in the future. The objective is to help the fan become more knowledgeable about football strategy, thereby making the game more interesting to watch.

Football is not a sport of continuous action. It is a series of strategic moves which gives the fan the opportunity to observe the tactical decisions as they are made and executed. Play selection, action, stop. The game moves stepwise from beginning to end. More so than sports of continuous action, football lends itself to strategic analysis.

The sheer number of players on each side makes at least some analysis necessary for a true understanding of the game. All 11 have specific assignments which complement one another. The strategies, both offensive and defensive, must be detailed and well-conceived. You may have heard how rookies spend hours learning their assignments and understanding the terminology. The tactics are complex, but not inscrutable.

The purpose of this book, then, is to provide the average fan with some insight into the strategies used. At the same time we've tried to make a somewhat complicated subject as uncomplicated as possible. The approach used is direct. And we've also tried to keep it interesting. The main point is that if you are likely to watch at least a few pro football games each season, spending some time with this book should make those games more enjoyable.

What You'll Get & What You Won't

Let's start with some "won'ts" first. The book will not make you an expert. That would require more than reading this book — or at a minimum a much bigger one. On the other hand, we assume you have watched games in the past and know the rudiments: 11 players on each side, 4 downs to make a 1st down, teams usually pass on 3rd down and long, and so on. We are not going to bore you with that.

Rather, the book explains many of the tactics and techniques commonly employed by professional football teams. During each game the sportscasters use a lot of football terms. The meanings are sometimes self-evident, but often are not. If you are a regular fan, you probably have a pretty good idea of what they are saying. But you may also ignore some of the comments as well as some of the action, and simply concentrate on what you do understand.

This book is not an encyclopedia of basic football. No attempt has been made to cover everything in any particular area. To the contrary, the content has been selected largely on the basis of what would be interesting and informative to the average fan. At the same time, all the major areas of football play are discussed to some extent, so the fan is given a rather comprehensive overview of the game. The approach is outlined below.

Format of Book

- Miscellaneous Info

Some terms, a few rules, a fact or two — facets of every game worth knowing.

- Formations

Why are formations multiplying, and which ones, offensive and defensive, should the fan recognize? Plays start with formations and so will we.

- Plays

Ever draw up a play? We do here. We look at three plays in detail, how they're supposed to work, what each player does. From there it's on to containment, check thru's, combo coverages, 2-deep zones, and more, all in summary fashion.

- Passing Attacks

Basic passing strategy. Some offensive maneuvers employed to get around defenses commonly encountered. (Hint: Throw away from the rotation.)

- Players

What qualities do you look for in a center? What techniques does he use and what are some problems he must cope with? Same for guards, tackles, running backs, wide outs, tight ends, quarterbacks, nose tackles, defensive ends, linebackers, cornerbacks, safeties, kickers, punters.

- Play Calls

From "Two 84" to "Sam Slam" to "Ball, Ball, Ball". It's not just the quarterback making calls.

- In Motion

Part 1: What happens when the ball is snapped? Well, for one thing, the pass route a receiver runs may bear little resemblance to the one called in the huddle.

Part 2: Consider 10 offensive plays and attempt (quickly) to come up with a good defense for each. Paper games? Sure, but at least it's a start.

- Special Teams

Special teams are important. They involve special rules, formations, and overall considerations.

- Statistics

How many plays does a team normally have to run, pass, punt, or attempt a field goal? Which correlates better with winning teams — passing offense or quarterback sacks? How is a quarterback's NFL rating actually calculated?

- Watching & Keeping Score

Halfway through a game, ever wonder how many passes were thrown to the tight end? Whether the opposition is running right or left most of the time? How often your team threw on 1st down? A lot of baseball fans keep track of baseball games. Football fans can do the same.

Diagrams

Diagrams are presented to help clarify the text. Where they appear, they go right along with the subject being covered. Using both the text and the diagrams, the reader should be able to get a good idea of everything being discussed. And the diagrams make referring back very easy.

It's important to note that a standard format is used in all the diagrams. That format is explained on two pages following this chapter.

Our Hypothetical Fan

Learning through experience can be quicker, more interesting, and certainly offer more insight. However, pro football fans cannot play a few downs in the National Football League to find out how things really are. We hope, therefore, to infuse some knowledge quickly and concisely by employing a hypothetical situation on and off throughout the chapters.

What we are going to do, on a hypothetical basis, is let Joe, an average fan, attend the practice sesssions of an NFL team. He will be able to meet with a few of the coaches and players to ask some questions and get the benefit of their insights. We hope that the discussions which result are along lines that you find informative.

> [*Ed. note:* There is no requirement that the chapters be read in order (though we suggest it), or even that the book be read in its entirety. It was designed so that each part would be informative to the fan on the topic covered. So if you want to read about certain subjects, you should be able to zero in on them.
>
> One final comment for those reading through. The avid fan will be intrigued by Chapters 3, 4, and 5. The casual fan may think they're too technical and skip to Chapter 6. Resist the

temptation! Even a quick reading of those chapters is bound to give a whole new perspective on the game. And there's sure to be some things you'll remember when watching games in the future.]

Explanation of Diagrams

To avoid excessive detail in the diagrams a standard format and series of symbols are used. The individual players will not always be labelled, except when initially explaining the formations or where space permits. In the latter cases, only the key players in each diagram will be denoted.

In order to easily follow the diagrams throughout this book, the points listed below should be clearly understood:

Defense on Top, Offense on Bottom

When both teams are shown:
- the defensive team is always at the top of the diagram;
- the offensive team is always at the bottom.

Symbols Used

○ — All offensive players (except the center) are designated with small circles.

◇ — The center is indicated with a diamond in order to provide a reference point for the middle of the offensive formation.

▽ — All defensive linemen (tackles and ends) are shown by triangles with the points toward the offense since they charge in that direction.

□ — All linebackers (middle linebacker, inside linebackers, and outside linebackers) are designated with squares.

△ — All defensive backs (cornerbacks, strong safety, and free safety) are shown by triangles with the points directed downfield since they usually defend in that area.

Refer Back to This Page

In the event you are uncertain as to which symbols represent which players in any particular diagram, refer back to this and the accompanying page. That page shows how the players line up in the basic offensive formation (pro set) and basic defensive formation (3-4 defense). Despite the fact that the positions of certain players will vary in some diagrams, by checking the symbols used the category of each player can easily be determined.

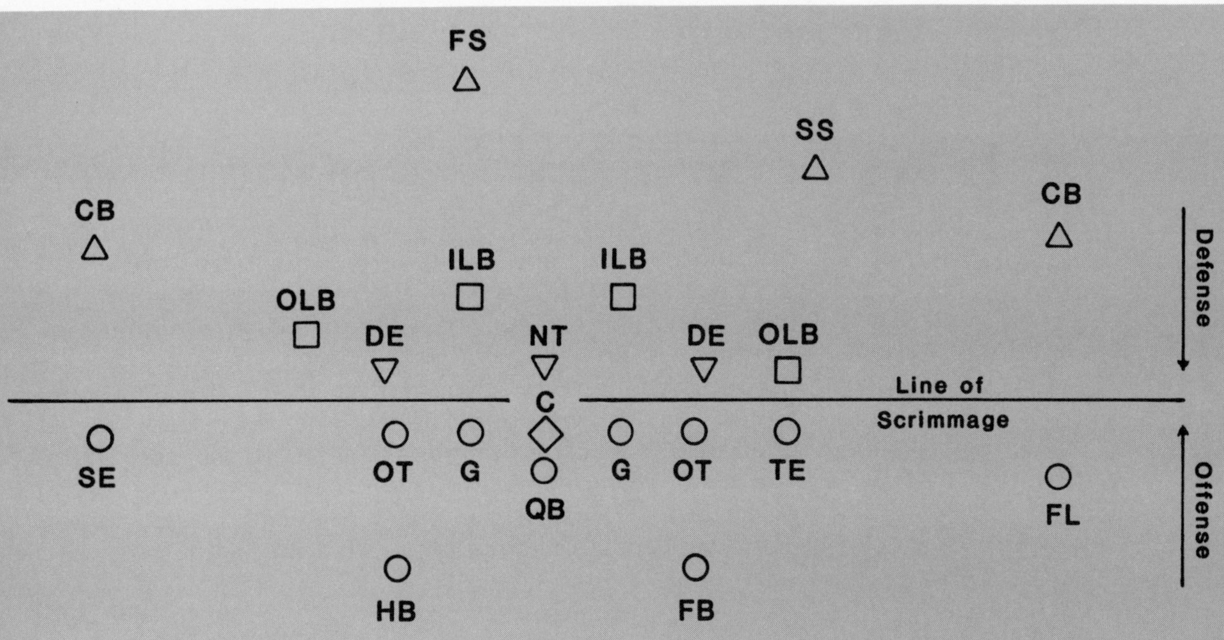

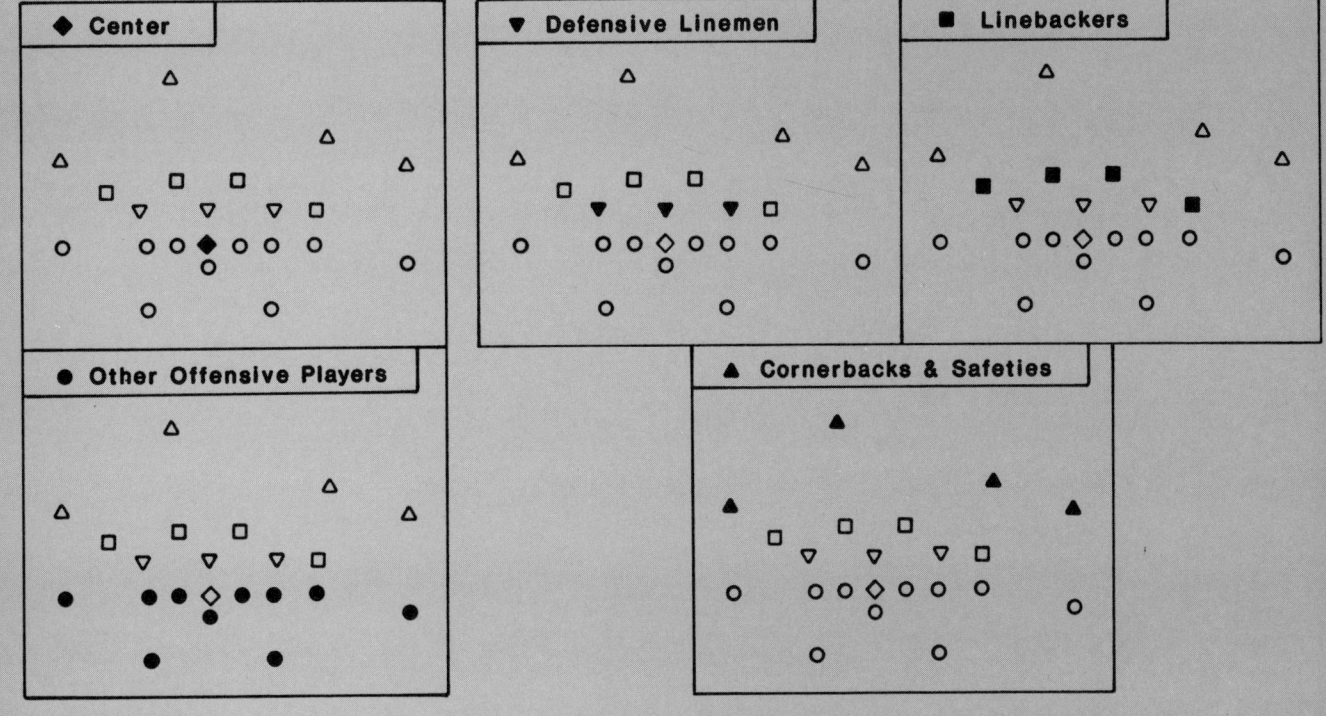

OFFENSE

◇ — C: Center

○ — G: Guards (2)
OT: Offensive Tackles (2)
TE: Tight End
SE: Split End
FL: Flanker
QB: Quarterback
HB: Halfback
FB: Fullback

SSB: Single Set Back *
SB: Slotback *
WB: Wingback *

DEFENSE

▽ — NT: Nose Tackle
DT: Defensive Tackles (2)*
DE: Defensive Ends (2)

□ — ILB: Inside Linebackers (2)
MLB: Middle Linebacker *
OLB: Outside Linebackers (2)

△ — CB: Cornerbacks (2)
SS: Strong Safety
FS: Free (or Weak) Safety
NB: Nickel Back *

* Not shown (used in other formations)

Ed. note: You may note that numbers under 10 are not spelled out in many places throughout the text. The use of single digit numerals, rather than words, in such instances is recognized as a departure from the conventional rules of grammar. The purpose is to highlight such numbers and thus facilitate reading comprehension of a text involving numerous groupings of players and many measurements of time and distance.

CHAPTER 2

MISCELLANEOUS INFO

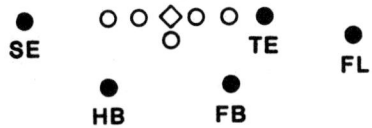

● - Eligible Receiver

Many different formations are used on offense. But one basic requirement is there be at least **7 men on the line of scrimmage**. Aside from the quarterback, there are never more than 3 offensive men behind the line.

Only those players at either end of the offensive line and those in the backfield are **eligible receivers**. This is the reason that one of the wide receivers is generally 1 yard behind the line so he is considered in the backfield and thus eligible as a receiver.

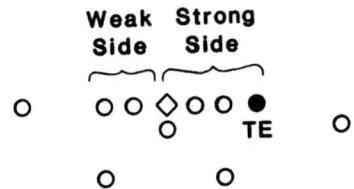

In most pro offensive formations there is only one tight end. The side with the tight end is called the **strong side**. The side of the offensive formation without the tight end is called the **weak side**. The strong side can be either the left or the right and generally changes many times during a game.

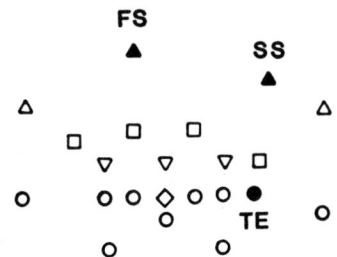

There are two safeties on the defensive team. The one who lines up opposite the strong side of the offense is called the **strong safety**. The one who lines up opposite the weak side of the offense is called the **weak safety** or **free safety**. The latter designation arises because in many man-to-man pass defenses the weak side safety has no particular receiver to cover and thus is "free" to help where needed.

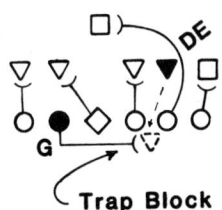

In a **trap play** one of the offensive linemen will vacate his normal blocking area or otherwise let a defensive lineman come across the line of scrimmage. Simultaneously, the offensive guard or tackle on the other side of the center pulls from his position to block the defensive man from the side. It's used to surprise a hard-charging defense man and give the blocker a good angle (from the side rather than head on).

A <u>**crackback block**</u> involves a wide receiver who comes back toward the center of the field to block. Because of the angle a receiver often has in making this block, a crackback must be executed above the waist to avoid injury to the defense man. Tight ends are subject to this rule if they line up more than 2 yards outside their offensive tackle. And running backs fall under a similar rule once they go 2 yards outside an offensive tackle. The illegal crackback zone is 5 yards on either side of the line of scrimmage.

Blocking an opponent from behind is a <u>**clip**</u>. Clipping <u>is allowed</u> in "close line play". Specifically, this is the area within 3 yards on either side of the line of scrimmage and between the two offensive tackles. Beginning in 1981, blocking from behind but above the waist became illegal use of hands, not a clip. (This reduces the penalty from 15 to 10 yards.)

There are 7 <u>**officials**</u>. In 1929 there were 4: the referee, umpire, head linesman, and field judge. The other 3 officials (back judge, line judge, and side judge) were added over the years after 1946. Here's what the original 4 do now. The <u>**referee**</u> has overall control and is the final authority regarding interpretations of the rules. His position is in the offensive backfield about 10 yards behind the line of scrimmage. The <u>**umpire**</u> is about 5 yards on the other side of the line behind the defensive linemen. His main responsibility is to watch line play (and not get himself caught in the action). The <u>**head linesman**</u> is on the line of scrimmage near one sideline. He looks for infractions prior to the snap, rules on plays in his area, assists in determining forward progress, and is in charge of the chain crew. The <u>**field judge**</u> positions himself about 25 yards downfield. He watches the tight end and defenders. From his deep position he makes decisions on pass catches, interference, fumbles, and with the back judge rules on field goals.

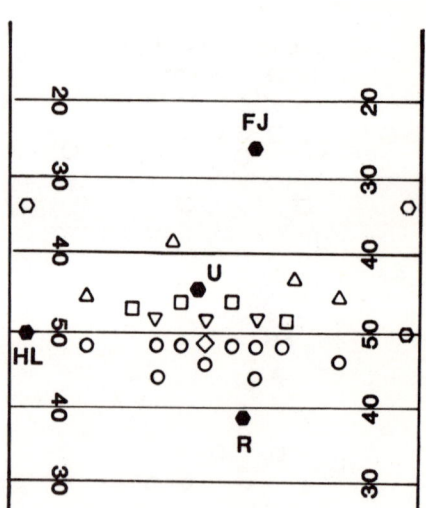

The stadium clock is the <u>**official time**</u>. Only if it stops or is operating incorrectly does the <u>**line judge**</u> take over official timing. Otherwise, he keeps time simply as a backup to the stadium clock. If a 30-second clock becomes inoperative, the <u>**field judge**</u>, who calls the delay-of-game penalties, takes over official 30-second timing.

How **wide** is the field? About 53 yards (160 feet). That means a short sideline pass travels about the same distance as one thrown 20 yards downfield. And the **hashmarks** are only about 3 yards to either side of the center of the field. (The ball is spotted at the closest hashmark from where last downed, unless that was between the hashmarks.) Thus, the wide side versus the short side for any play is at most 30 yards versus 23 yards. Incidentally, the hashmarks are in line with the uprights of the goal posts.

On passing plays, **ineligible receivers** cannot go beyond the line of scrimmage. Thus, the center, the guards, the tackles, and the quarterback must not go downfield. (An offensive lineman may drive an opponent beyond the line, provided the initial contact was made within 1 yard of the line of scrimmage.) In addition, ineligible receivers must not catch or even accidentally touch a forward pass.

Penalties:

Ineligible man downfield — 10 yards

Ball touched by ineligible man <u>on or behind</u> the line:
Accidentally — loss of down
Intentionally — loss of 10 yards

Ball touched by ineligible man <u>beyond</u> the line:
Accidentally or intentionally — loss of down or 10 yards.

That's why you'll sometimes see ineligible receivers dodging forward passes. However, once a pass is touched by an eligible receiver or any defender, all offensive players become eligible receivers.

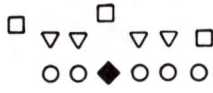
Even Defense

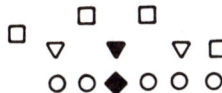
Odd Defense

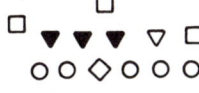
Gap Defense

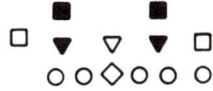
Stack Defense

An **even defensive alignment** means that there is no defensive lineman playing directly across from the offensive center. An **odd defensive alignment** means that there is someone directly over the center. In a **gap defense** one or more of the defense men line up in the gaps between the offensive linemen. In a **stack defense** linebackers are directly behind defensive linemen. Each alignment positions the defense to react somewhat differently. For example, against a stack defense the offensive linemen don't know which way the defensive lineman and linebacker in each stack will go.

11

Since offensive players are not allowed to block opponents downfield on a pass play, an eligible receiver cannot interfere with a defender covering another receiver. On a **pick play** the receiver attempts to "accidentally" shield off a defender by running in a path which crosses or is close to the path of another receiver. However, if the receiver intentionally makes contact which disrupts the defender, pass interference will be called.

Before the introduction of **rule blocking**, the offensive linemen used to block according to the defensive formation they faced. With rule blocking each lineman has an assignment regardless of what defense he faces. For instance, the rule for an offensive guard on a running play could be: cut off the man over him; if there is none, release to seal off the first inside linebacker.

When the normal blocking for the play called in the huddle won't work because of the defensive alignment, the offensive linemen affected can use rule blocking. Another way to make blocking adjustments is through **line calls**. Up at the line, after they see how the defensive linemen are positioned, the offensive linemen use code words to designate the overall blocking pattern or to make specific adjustments.

Option blocking allows the blocker to take his opponent in the direction he wants to go. There is no predetermined side to which the blocker must move his assigned man. If the defender wants to go inside (toward the center), the blocker moves with him in that direction. If he wants to go outside (away from the center), the blocker goes that way. It is up to the runner to see in what direction the block is going and to cut behind it.

A defense man **can't tackle or hold** any offensive player unless he is the ball carrier. Exception: a player faking possession or to whom a fake handoff was made can be tackled, but only if he is crossing the line of scrimmage between the normal positions of the offensive tight ends.

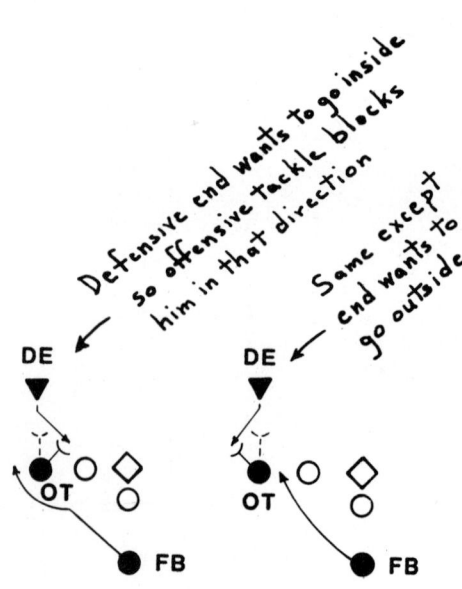

Option Blocking

(Fullback cuts behind block — no predetermined side)

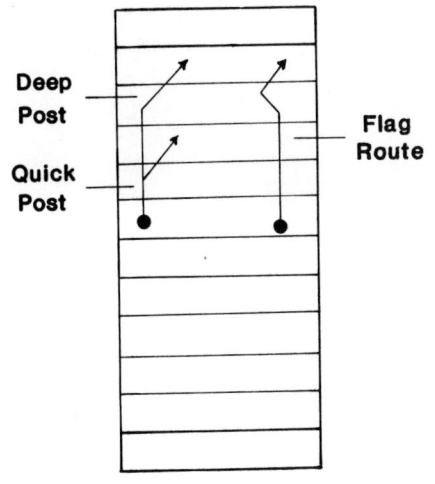

When a receiver runs a <u>post route</u> he is aiming toward the goal post. On a deep post the receiver goes fairly deep before making his move to the middle. On a quick post he cuts much sooner. A <u>flag route</u> means the receiver is heading toward a corner of the end zone (the corners used to be marked by small flags).

The <u>use of hands</u> to grasp, push, or otherwise fend off an opponent <u>is not allowed</u> for offensive players except when carrying the ball or pass blocking. The latter exception is limited — the pass blocker can use hands only to push off an opponent. Technically, the hands must be inside the blocker's elbows and below the opponent's neck. Thus, pushing with extended arms is permitted only for pass blocking, but grasping or encircling a defense man is not.

Defenders can <u>use their hands</u>. They can push or pull blockers on the line of scrimmage, and when attempting to get at a runner or a fumble. This gives the defense an advantage in one-on-one confrontations. However, the offensive men do know two things the defenders don't: when the play will begin and where it is going.

<u>Eligible receivers</u> get special treatment. They <u>cannot</u> be blocked below the waist. As usual there is an exception: receivers lined up within 2 yards of an offensive tackle <u>can</u> be blocked below the waist but only until they cross the line — then it must be above the waist just like the general rule.

Unless a play is clearly a running play, each defense man may contact an eligible receiver only once within 5 yards beyond the line of scrimmage. After an eligible receiver is more than 5 yards from the line, defensive players may only defend against contact caused by the receiver. This is the <u>one-chuck rule</u> which frees the receiver from defensive contact downfield until the ball is thrown to him.

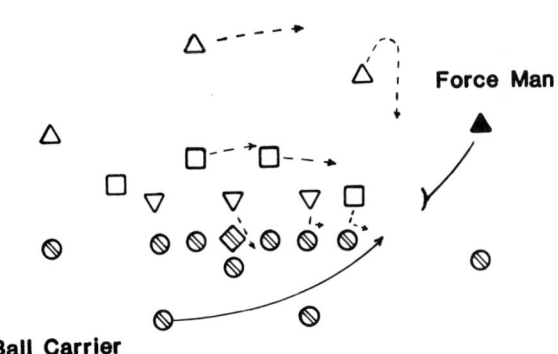

Containment

<u>Containment</u> is an integral part of <u>pursuit</u>. The contain or <u>force man's</u> primary responsibility is to prevent the ball carrier from getting outside and to pressure him back toward the middle if he cannot tackle him. In other words, he forces the runner back toward the pursuing defenders. If the ball carrier gets outside the contain man, he can go for big yardage since only one or two defenders may be in a position to catch him.

13

Clubs must assign **numbers** according to positions:

- 1-19: Quarterbacks and kickers
- 20-49: Running backs and defensive backs
- 50-59: Centers and linebackers
- 60-79: All offensive and defensive linemen (centers may be included)
- 80-89: Wide receivers and tight ends
- 90-99: Defensive linemen

Note: If a player with a number for a normally ineligible receiver wants to be an eligible receiver for a given play, he must inform the referee and line up appropriately; the referee will alert the defensive captain.

Note: Players in the NFL before 1973 who are still active may retain their numbers if not in accord with this classification scheme.

On a **kickoff**, the ball is live once the ball travels 10 yards or is touched by the receiving team. That means whichever team, kicking or receiving, recovers the ball gets possession. (But if the kicking team recovers, it cannot advance the ball.) So the receiving team must attempt to get possession. However, on a **punt** the ball cannot be recovered beyond the line of scrimmage by the kicking team. Therefore, the receiving team can let the ball roll dead if it wishes.

There is a difference between a **fumble** and a **muff**. When a player fumbles, he loses possession of the ball. When a player muffs, he touches a loose ball while unsuccessfully attempting to obtain possession. Example: On a kickoff the kick returner muffs it and the kicking team recovers. It is their ball, but it <u>cannot</u> be advanced (because it is a kickoff). However, if the kick returner caught it, fumbled, and the kicking team recovered, the ball <u>can</u> be advanced. The defense can advance recovered fumbles.

After a **fair catch**, the receiving team may elect to place the ball in play with a **free kick**. (The opposing team must line up at least 10 yards away.) The kick may be either a punt or a placekick without a tee. If the ball is placekicked and goes through the uprights, a field goal results. Usually this is done only immediately before halftime or the end of the game because the ball goes over to the defense if they recover it.

14

CHAPTER 3

FORMATIONS

Formations deal with the placement of players. Formations don't win ball games, but they can position the players so the plays have the best chance of succeeding. This chapter begins with a brief discussion of current trends in strategy and a few basic considerations as to alignment of players. It then covers the most frequently used offensive and defensive formations.

BASIC CONSIDERATIONS

Current Trends: Passing & Substitution

Pro football strategy is in flux. Recent NFL rule changes have made it easier for linemen to pass block and for receivers to get downfield. As a result there is greater emphasis on passing. How much emphasis? Some coaches sigh and mutter something about throwball, not football. In any event, it just goes to show that football, and the way it is played, continues to evolve.

Over the years, specific strategies were tried, rose in favor, became standard fare, only to be outmoded as offensive or defensive counters were formulated, the rules were changed, or players became more physically talented. Currently, the offense has the edge as defensive coaches devise plans to throttle down the new passing attacks.

Situation substitution is another accelerating trend going to the heart of football strategy. For years starting lineups on offense and defense remained substantially unchanged throughout the game, except for offensive players bringing in plays. Now, substitutions are made on almost every series of downs, if not on every down. In passing situations, the best rushing linemen are inserted, linebackers come out in favor of pass-oriented defensive backs, and even good running backs are pulled for ball carriers who are better receivers. In running situations, the whole process is reversed. So, as in the rest of life, football players are becoming specialists. There are fewer second string players who just ride the bench. More and more are "regulars" on a special offense or defense.

One by-product is a reduction in individual matchups. And some say great running backs can't be the dominant force they once were; you must build your attack on passing, not running. Maybe the rules do favor increased passing, but no one is declaring the running game dead. A one-dimensional approach is rarely successful. Consistent winners display some balance between passing and running.

One thing is for certain — there is more than one way to succeed in the NFL. Some teams play percentage football. They determine what play, what defense, what tactic has the best chance of succeeding. On offense they try to move the chains, progress steadily down the field. Other teams play pressure football. They don't care about a strong ground game or precision passing, just go deep and score. Enough big plays will win most games. Some say take what the defense gives you. Others say dictate to the defense. Over the years, the Super Bowl teams have had many contrasting styles.

Multiple Formations & Complexity

The overall trend in strategy is toward more complexity. And human nature being what it is, the trend will probably continue until some coach resorts to simplicity and succeeds. Multiple formations are all part of this. On the one hand, formations position players so they can best execute the plays called. On the other hand, formations can't disclose exactly what the offense or defense plans to do after the snap. Add to that the fact that special players are being used on certain downs and formations were bound to proliferate.

There is another aspect to this. The basis of any game plan involves tendencies — what the opposition does in a given situation, and more to the point here, what they do out of given formations. For each game, coaches will study the opposition's last three game films and formulate their own game plan based on what they see. The more complex a team's offense or defense is, the harder it is for the coaches to figure it out, and the more time it takes to formulate an effective game plan. Time not only in the projection room, but also on the practice field. Time is a precious commodity. There is only one week between games, and the more time the offense spends working against the opposition's stunts and coverages or the defense has to practice against the opposition's multiple formations, the less time can be spent polishing their own plays or adding new wrinkles.

Aside from the practical aspect of preparing for the game, complexity makes recognition more difficult. Each player on every play has certain alternative assignments. What he does depends on what the opposition does. He'll have certain keys. Take a defensive back who keys a wide receiver: if the receiver runs down the sideline, the back does one thing; if the receiver blocks a defender, the back does another. When the oppposition lines up in an unusual formation and then starts moving people around, the recognition process slows. It takes the defense a split second longer to read and react to the offense, and, conversely, longer for the offense to find the sweet spots in a shifting defense.

Anyway, that's the conventional thinking. Out of the myriad of formations being used, the plays themselves are often quite simple, stuff that's been used for years. But new techniques are being added. To many, the object is to play percentage football (go with the odds), but still remain as unpredictable as possible. Reconciling these conflicting objectives is probably what NFL coaches have always been doing. Still, if you use a straightforward, predictable attack, you have to have a lot better personnel. And given the parity brought about by the drafting system, overall quality is not that uneven among the 28 teams.

Strategy & Personnel

We do not mean to imply that every team starts with more or less the same stock of players. Fans are aware of the game's superstars. Some teams have them and some teams don't. But one or two stars don't make a team. The offensive and defensive strategies employed have to be the ones that best fit the top 12 or 13 players on the offensive and defensive rosters. That means incorporating variations and doing things differently than other teams. These differences are sometimes apparent, but often are subtle. If you're not already aware of that, you will be when you're through with this book.

No matter what scheme is used, it's up to the players to make it work. An elementary fact. Nevertheless, the attitude of the players toward the techniques being used is rarely discussed. Not just the overall plays, but things very personal to the individual players such as the way linemen block or how defensive backs cover receivers. Suppose you're an offensive lineman and you don't like the way the assistant coach has you blocking on a particular play. You don't think it will work. Well, before anybody shows up for Sunday's game, that play is in trouble. In addition to guiding the players through their individual assignments, the coaches have to win their confidence in the plays themselves. If the players think they'll work, they generally will.

All the new complicated schemes have not made life easier for players. It's more of a brain game than in the past. Each week there is a final exam. And you better believe there are a lot of mental mistakes over the course of the season. It's just that most of them aren't that visible, like a likebacker pursuing the wrong way or a lineman missing a blitz. But they're there and they hurt.

Time of the Essence

Plays in the NFL on the average take about 5 seconds from start to finish. That includes both short and long runs, passes, kickoffs, and punts. A short run takes less than 3 seconds. A long pass may take 8 or 9 seconds. The point is that plays are over very fast.

While watching games, it is easy to lose track of just how fast things are going. A simple running play involves the following: the ball is snapped, the running back starts, the linemen block, the quarterback pivots and hands off, the running back hits the hole, the defense tackles, and the official whistles the play dead. Elapsed time: 3 seconds. This is why coaches talk in terms of 10ths of seconds. For instance, 0.3 second may seem like so short a time it wouldn't matter one way or the other. But on a 3-second play, it represents 10% of the total interval involved. Almost all passes are thrown within 3.5 seconds of the snap, and most are gone by the 3.0 mark. So coaches are concerned if a quarterback takes more than 1.9 seconds to drop back and set up. Similar considerations dictate that the snap to the punter take no longer than 0.9 second and that the field goal unit get the kick off, start to finish, in 1.3 seconds.

Play the Angles

Angles are another important dimension in football. Imagine that your assignment is to block the man in front of you. As he lunges forward, you collide head on attempting to neutralize his charge and then turn him to one side. Now imagine that instead of being directly across, he is positioned to one side. As he charges the line, you now have an easier time knocking him to one side because he is less stable laterally and you're not absorbing the full force of his charge. That is why offensive linemen attempt to get even a small angle on their defensive counterparts.

Plays and blocking schemes are drawn up with this in mind. The handoff, probably the lowest form of fan stimulation, must occur where it gives the running back the best angle of approach to the point of attack. Angles apply to the defense also. For example, the whole pattern of pursuit to the ball carrier is premised on several players taking different angles to minimize the chance of the runner breaking clear.

Synchronizing the Players

Given the short intervals involved, the play designer must closely coordinate the assignments of all 11 players. On a running play, the offensive linemen must be able to make and hold their blocks long enough to allow the ball carrier to break the line of scrimmage. Blocks cannot be sustained very long, and a hole that is opened, will close very fast because of the defenders beyond the line who are not blocked. This means that a well-conceived running play will have the blockers and ball carrier timed up appropriately.

The difference between a quick-hitter and a slow-developing play should be noted. If a running back hits straight ahead, he travels about 5 yards to the line (fast). If he goes from one side of the backfield to the other, he covers about 10 yards (slow). If he sweeps wide, he can run 20 yards before crossing the line (slower). The objective in all is the same — get the ball carrier across the line. However, the dynamics of the various running plays can be quite different.

Reaction & Overreaction

All plays are based on the expected reaction of the opposing players. But coaches often design in movements to prompt overreaction. Play action (the quarterback fakes a running play before passing) is aimed at holding the defense up while they ascertain what the play is. Misdirection (the running back starts one way and cuts back the other) is designed to get the defense moving in the wrong direction. So while one tries to get the defense to hesitate, the other attempts to get them running in the wrong direction.

Offensive coaches know what defensive players are watching for and have to work out tactics to get the desired reaction. On a reverse (the running back starts running in one direction, then suddenly hands off to a player running in the opposite direction) timing and faking are critical. If the reverse handoff comes too fast, the play won't work. The offense is spending a lot of time in the backfield, and the defense can easily stop it unless they are all flowing in the wrong direction. So the offense can't hurry it.

Good offensive strategy is not based on fooling the defense. To be effective, deception must be used judiciously. It is not a major factor in most plays. Execution is the key. Eleven men carrying out their assignments against a defense which doesn't know exactly what to expect.

OFFENSIVE FORMATIONS

Constraints

The rules require that the offensive team have at least 7 men on the line of scrimmage. Except for some short-yardage or goal-line situations, more than 7 men are rarely placed on the line. The reason relates to another rule, the one concerning eligible receivers. Only the players at either end of the offensive line and those in the backfield (other than the quarterback) are eligible receivers. To be in the backfield, the player must be at least 1 yard behind the line of scrimmage. So in order to maximize the number of eligible receivers, the offense keeps as many men as possible in the backfield (3, excluding the quarterback).

In almost all offensive formations 6 players are in the same position: the center, the guards, the offensive tackles, and the quarterback. (An exception is the shotgun where the quarterback is about 5 yards behind the center.) Thus, the offensive formations vary only in how the remaining 5 players are positioned.

Basic Formations

[Our fan, Joe, has spotted one of the offensive coaches in the coffee shop near the practice field. After introducing himself to the coach, the coach asks Joe to join him for breakfast. (In the following dialogue "C" refers to the coach and "F" refers to the fan.)]

The Pro Set

C. Yeah, I heard about you. They said you'd be watching the practices and asking some questions. I'll be happy to explain anything I can.

F. Well, first I'd better tell you that I never played football. I've watched games for years and I'm becoming more interested in what is going on. Perhaps you can explain something about the various formations used.

C. Okay, but rather than go over a lot of things you may already know, why don't you start off by diagramming an offensive formation (as he pulls out a blank sheet of paper from his large notebook on the table).

F. All right, but some of this may sound rather dumb.

C. Don't worry. We run into a lot of nonfootball people who think they are experts. But they can sure come up with some pretty dumb statements.

F. (Starting to draw) The center is over the ball. And there's an offensive guard on either side of the center. Then comes an offensive tackle on the outside of each guard. And the quarterback is behind the center.

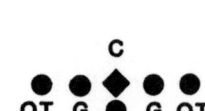

Offensive Linemen & Quarterback

C. Fine, you've got 6 players so far, which is more than half the offense. Except for line splits, almost any offensive formation will have those 6 in the same position you have drawn them.

F. Line splits?

C. That refers to spacing. The center, the offensive guards, and the offensive tackles normally line up about 3 feet apart. Some of those splits may be narrower or wider to improve blocking angles or otherwise facilitate the play. But let's not get into that at this point.

F. Now it gets a little tougher. I know that there is usually one tight end because the sportscasters remark when two tight ends are in. I'll put him on the right side. And there are generally two running backs somewhere in the backfield, so I'll show them next to each other a little behind the quarterback.

Let's see, that's 9 players. Adding a wide receiver at either end of the line makes 11.

C. (Smiling) Good. You've just diagrammed the basic formation of pro football today. It's called the **pro set** or **open set** or a couple of other names. We'll use pro set. However, the wide receiver on the same side as the tight end in your drawing should be 1 yard back from the line of scrimmage, so he is in the backfield. That makes the tight end an eligible receiver.

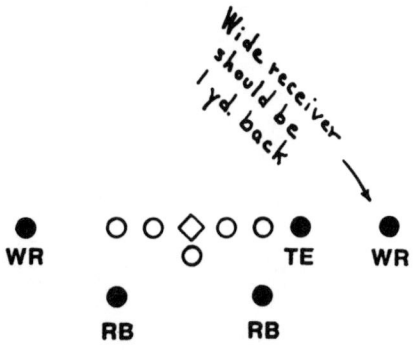

Tight End, Wide Receivers & Running Backs

F. Why is that?

23

C. The man on either side of the line is an eligible receiver and so is anyone in the backfield except the quarterback. The way you drew it, only the 2 wide receivers and 2 running backs would be eligible.

F. I see, by pulling the wide receiver back, the tight end becomes the man at the end of the right side of the offensive line. So he is an eligible receiver and so is the wide receiver because he is in the backfield.

Do they ever put the tight end a yard back and leave the wide receiver on the line?

C. That would make both of them eligible receivers, but it is usually not done because it would hamper the tight end's blocking. On running plays the offense needs his block on a linebacker or defensive lineman, and putting the tight end on the line of scrimmage enables him to do this best.

Some teams are starting to line up tight ends in new ways — send them in motion, even put them in a wide receiver position or in the backfield. But that's rather rare. Occasionally you will see a sole tight end a yard back, and then the wide receiver on that side does have to move up to the line.

Incidentally, the wide receiver on the tight end side is called a **flanker** and the wide receiver on the other side is called a **split end**. Also, the side of the offensive line with the tight end is called the **strong side**, and the other side is called the **weak side**. That's because there's an extra blocker on the strong side.

F. Will the team always use the right side or the left side as its strong side?

C. No. It varies from play to play. In other words, on one play it could be the left side and on the next, the right side. Depending on the team's personnel and the defense they are faced with, there may be a preference to run particular plays to one side. But the strong side usually varies throughout the game.

F. Why is the pro set considered such a basic formation?

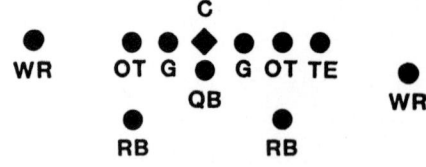

Pro Set

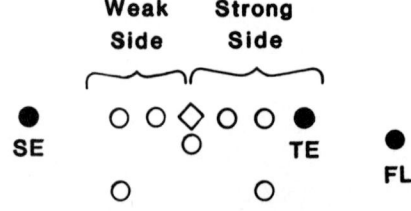

Pro Set, Strong Right

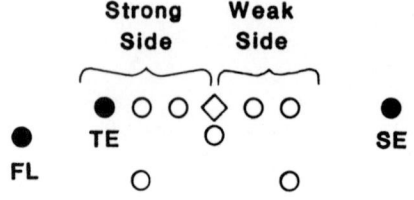

Pro Set, Strong Left

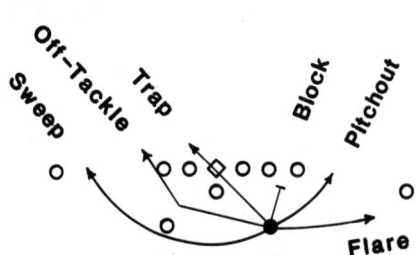

Pro Set - Right RB

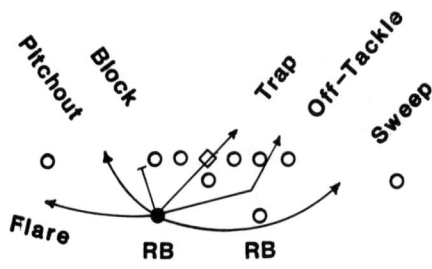

Pro Set - Left RB

C. Overall it probably offers about the best balance between pass and run. In other words, you can do a lot of things out of it.

There's a receiver split wide to each side; they are both away from that mass of humanity around the ball. This allows them to get down the field quickly. It also spreads the defense out and enables the receivers to take defenders out of a running play by simply going deep.

The two running backs in the backfield provide 2 potential ball carriers, 2 potential pass blockers (something which fans often overlook), or 2 eligible receivers. The running backs are positioned such that either can take a quick pitch and head outside, take a handoff and go off-tackle on the other side of the line, run a sweep in that direction, or perhaps run a trap up the middle. Alternatively, a running back can hit his side of the line fast as a blocker, helping to create a hole for the other running back carrying the ball.

As I mentioned, the running backs are well positioned to aid in pass blocking or can flare out toward the side for short passes if the other receivers aren't open.

The tight end provides extra blocking on one side, which coupled with the blocking of the running back on the same side allows for power plays in that direction. Also, the tight end is the third receiver on the line, good for passes up the middle.

F. Does the pro set formation have any major weaknesses?

C. Its main weakness is a lack of power for inside running.

Variations of the Pro Set

F. Are there variations of the pro set?

C. Sure, let's concentrate on the running backs. In the standard pro set the 2 running backs are about 5 yards behind the line and split about as wide as the offensive tackles. This is often referred to as **split backs**. If you start watching how the running backs line up during a game, you'll see several variations in the pro set. This gives the formation additional flexibility and makes it hard to type the kind of play and point of attack.

In a **strong side set**, or near formation, the running back on the same (or near) side as the tight end remains in a normal pro set position, behind the offensive tackle, or moves forward and in about $\frac{1}{2}$ yard. The other running back positions himself directly behind the quarterback.

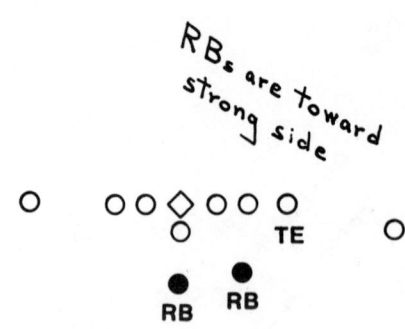

Strong Side Set

The **weak side set**, or far formation, is just the opposite. The running back on the side away (far) from the tight end remains in a normal pro set position, or goes forward and in about $\frac{1}{2}$ yard, while the other running back moves behind the quarterback.

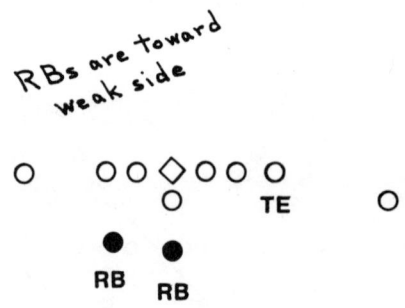

Weak Side Set

F. Do these adjustments favor any particular plays?

C. Unfortunately, I can't say just one or two plays are most likely to occur. That is one of the reasons we use the formations. With good people you can run several things from each. But let me try to narrow it down somewhat.

With the weak side set, the running back toward the weak side can run the plays I mentioned above since he is in the same position as in the standard pro set.

The other running back is now behind the quarterback. So he is closer to the weak side offensive tackle. That makes the off-tackle play quicker for him than with the standard pro set. Moreover, being right behind the quarterback positions him for runs up the middle and misdirections where he takes steps toward one side and then cuts the other way. Starting from a central location, the running back behind the quarterback doesn't sweep, but he can take a pitchout to either side.

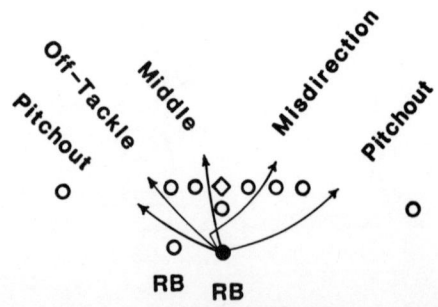

Weak Side Set

26

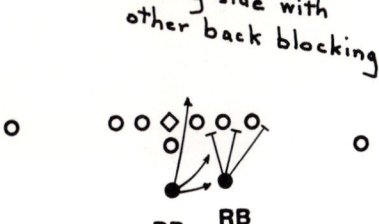

Strong Side Set

Good for runs to strong side with other back blocking

F. How about the strong side set?

C. You'll notice there is no tight end or running back on the weak side. So the blocking is limited for runs to that side. Actually, the strong side set concentrates the power between the middle and the strong side. It sets up runs to that area especially by the running back behind the quarterback because of the angle. Consequently, the strong side formation is often used for runs to that side in short-yardage situations.

Halfbacks & Fullbacks

F. You have been referring to running backs. Most sportscasters use that term too, but they also use halfback and fullback designations. I realize that "running back" is a generic term which includes halfbacks and fullbacks...

C. Just like "wide receiver" is a generic term which includes split ends and flankers.

F. Right. Now as I understand it the halfback is usually the smaller, quicker runner. Whereas the fullback is usually the bigger, more powerful runner and also the better blocker.

C. That's a fair description as long as you inserted "usually". If you look around the league, you'll find departures from the norm:

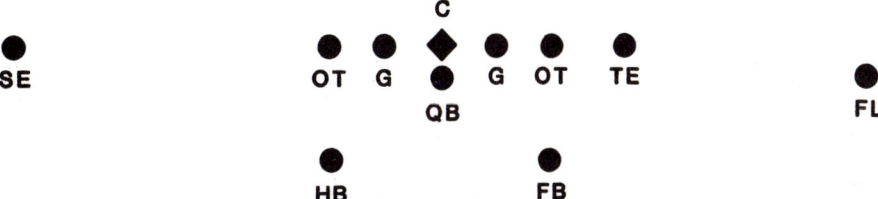

The Pro Set

some teams where the halfback is the better blocker than the fullback or where the fullback may be faster than the halfback.

F. Do halfbacks and fullbacks take different positions in the pro set?

C. With split backs, the fullback is traditionally the running back nearest the tight end in a standard pro set formation. That is the power side. In both the strong side and the weak side sets, the fullback is behind the quarterback. This sets up the quicker halfback for outside running and blocking, and the more powerful fullback for inside runs.

But teams will sometimes interchange the halfback and fullback positions, and have the fullback line up in the halfback position and vice versa. This gives the formation added flexibility.

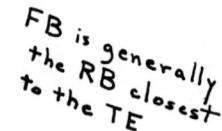
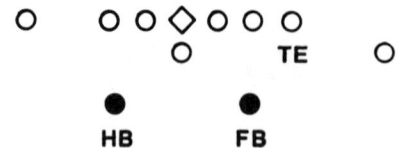

HB & FB Positions

I Formation

[Joe and the coach have finished breakfast and are on their second cups of coffee.]

C. Well, I have just about 10 minutes before I have to leave. I generally get to our training complex a little early to review a few things.

So let me quickly go over a couple of the other common formations. Let's start with the I formation.

F. That's where both running backs line up directly behind the quarterback.

C. Right. The first back (sometimes called the **upback**) is about 5 yards behind the line. The second back (called the **tailback**) is about 2 yards behind the upback.

F. If you move the running back deeper, it's going to take him longer to get to the line. Isn't the play slower in developing?

C. Yes. But coaches are willing to increase the time so the tailback can see how the blocking

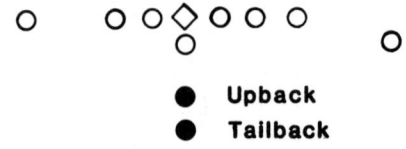

I Formation

28

is developing. This enables him to run to the best hole. And for this reason, the team's best runner, halfback or fullback, is usually placed in the tailback position.

In addition, the tailback takes a 2-point stance (hands on knees) rather than a 3-point stance (one hand on the ground) so he can see over the first running back.

F. What kind of plays does the I favor?

C. It facilitates inside runs and, as I said, the tailback is the primary carrier in this one. He is aligned behind the quarterback so the play can go to either side — just give him the ball and let him find a hole. The quarterback can also give to the upback for a quick hit.

The I is good against teams that pursue quickly. It sets up the ball carrier to cut back against the flow of the defense. The upback is important too. His faking and blocking are essential. Occasionally he is the ball carrier, and he must be able to slam into the line and pick up some yards.

F. What about passing?

C. The drawback for passing is that it takes longer for the running backs to get out into their routes. The alignment and extra depth used to set up the run works against getting the running backs out as potential receivers.

Slot Formation

C. The **slot** refers to the gap in the offensive line either between the split end and the offensive tackle or the flanker and the tight end. The basic slot formation places both wide receivers on the weak side. The split end is in his normal position and the flanker is now in the slot (and is sometimes referred to as a **slotback**). This sets up weak side passing and strong side running.

The wide receiver in the slot can get downfield quickly since he is still away from all the people around the ball. And more

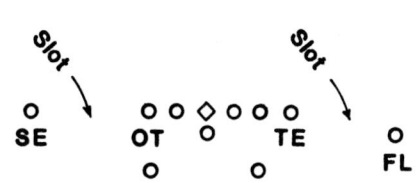

Slot Locations

important, because two wide receivers are on the same side, it's harder for the defense to use a straight zone against them. As a result, the formation is employed to help isolate at least one of the receivers on one defense man.

F. How do the running backs line up in a slot formation?

C. The positions of the running backs vary. For example, they can be split as in a pro set (formation is called a **pro slot**) or they can be lined up as in an I formation (making it a **slot I**).

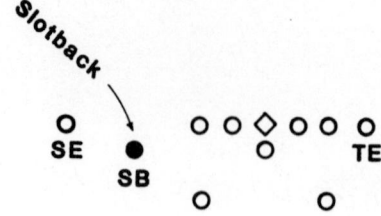

Pro Slot

Double Wing

C. In a double wing, one running back has moved up to a point about 1 yard outside the weak side offensive tackle and about 1 yard behind the line (so he remains an eligible receiver). In this position he is called a **wingback**. This allows the wingback to get quickly into a pass route. Alternatively, he can block to the inside.

F. Why is it called a double wing if there is only one wingback?

C. The name is really not descriptive of the actual formation. It's derived from some old formations. You can think of it in terms of two receivers being on each side of the center. If the wingback were placed on the other side of the line, next to the tight end, you would have a **triple wing** — three receivers to one side.

F. Which one of the running backs goes to the wingback position, is it the halfback or the fullback?

C. The better pass catcher is on the wing. The remaining back is referred to as a **single set back**, and he may be behind or to either side of the quarterback. A wide receiver or tight end can also be used in the wingback position. In any case, the double wing is primarily a passing formation.

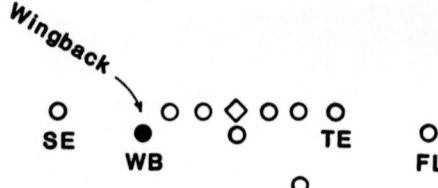

Double Wing

Triple Wing

2 Tight Ends (Double Tight)

F. Don't some teams use formations with two tight ends?

C. A tight end at each side of the interior line (the <u>interior line</u> is from offensive tackle to offensive tackle) provides extra blocking. They pressure the defensive line and force both outside linebackers to play in tight. Defenses are often more conservative against a double tight formation.

In order to use two tight ends, you have to give up a wide receiver or a running back. For short yardage, a team will generally eliminate one of the wide receivers.

Some teams which have a powerful or exceptional runner occasionally use two tight ends with only one running back, and let him pick the best hole. A problem with any formation having only one running back is that the defense can key on him regarding the run. But with increased emphasis on the pass, teams are using a lot of single set back formations. Surprisingly, the running can be pretty good. But it usually requires a good passing offense, so the defense can't concentrate on the run.

With both tight ends as eligible receivers and one or two wide receivers, the 2-tight end offense doesn't exactly give up the pass, but it is really more suited to a ball-control, running-type offense. I might add, we sometimes see that second tight end in a wingback position (on either side) which helps get him into the pass pattern.

F. Is there any strong side or weak side with two tight ends?

C. No, not in the double-tight formation.

3 Wide Receivers

C. Formations with three wide receivers are much more prominent with the new rules that favor passing. Generally, the additional wide receiver is in the slot.

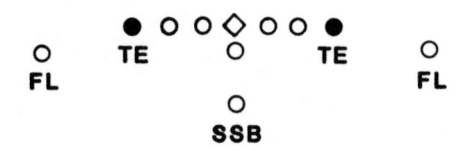

```
       ● ○ ○ ◇ ○ ○ ●
O      TE    O    TE      O
FL                        FL
             O
            SSB

       Double Tight
   (with Single Set Back)
```

F. Use of the extra wide receiver means elimination of either the tight end or a running back.

C. That's right. If a single set back is used, the wide receiver is typically slotted on the weak side. On the other hand, if the tight end is eliminated, there is no strong side per se, and the wide receiver may be slotted to either side.

The formation allows three wide receivers to get downfield quickly, which puts pressure on the pass defense. And, as I mentioned before, putting a man in the slot makes it harder to cover that side with a straight zone. By coordinating the routes of all three it is easier to isolate at least one wide receiver on one defender, as opposed to using two wide receivers and having both of them double covered.

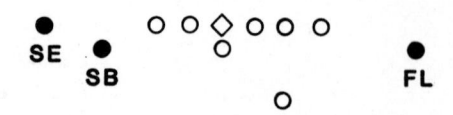

3 Wide Receivers
(with Single Set Back)

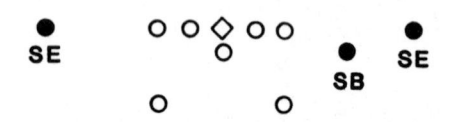

3 Wide Receivers
(with No Tight End)

The Shotgun

F. What about the shotgun? I know the quarterback is way behind the line in that one. As I understand it, the purpose is to position the quarterback so he can start watching his receivers right away and not have to turn and retreat from the line to set up.

C. Well, that's right, except that a quarterback usually looks first at how the defense is reacting; he knows where his receivers are headed. And the quarterback still does back up. If he lined up 7 to 9 yards deep, the chances of a bad snap would be too great. Because the center has to block immediately he snaps the ball back without looking. So the quarterback lines up about 5 yards deep which greatly reduces the risk of a bad snap.

Since the quarterback is already about halfway to the set-up spot, he doesn't have to turn his back to at least one-third of the field and retreat. Instead he backpedals about 5 yards with full view of the entire defense. He can see a breakdown in the blocking as well as any blitz immediately. However, unlike a normal formation, the quarterback has to initially look at the snap to catch it. This forces him to take his eyes off the first response of the defense at the snap, which can be important to reading the coverage fast.

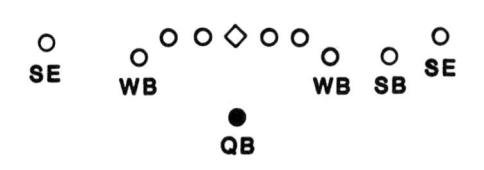

The combination and positioning of wide receivers, running backs, and the tight end can vary. One shotgun formation eliminates the tight end. It uses three wide receivers with two of them spread wide and one in a slot. And it places the two running backs in wingback positions just outside the offensive tackles on either side of the line. So there are five receivers spread across the field who can all quickly get into their pass routes.

One problem with this formation is that with no real threat of a run, the defense can concentrate on the pass, thus mitigating part of the advantage of having the quarterback deep. Some teams are running occasionally from the shotgun and we may see more of this. The running backs are split like wingbacks but are in the backfield about as deep as the quarterback. On the snap either back can cross in front of the quarterback for a handoff and sweep to the outside.

Man in Motion

F. You haven't discussed any man in motion. I know the basic rule. It allows 1 player in the backfield to be moving parallel with or angling away from the line immediately prior to the snap (he can't be moving toward the line). And as I recall, it generally involves a wide receiver.

C. The man in motion could be a wide receiver, a tight end, or a running back. It often involves a wingback who goes in motion to the other side, reaching the slot just as the ball is snapped.

Motion helps the receiver avoid being chucked by a defender at the line, thereby increasing the probability for a quick release.

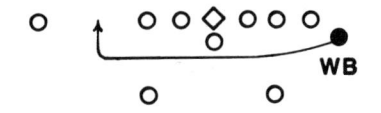

The theory behind motion is that it forces the defense to adjust, since it occurs after the offense and defense are initially set. You can

33

get a cornerback to run with a wide receiver across the field or put a tight end in motion and shift the strong side to the opposite end. Motion is being used a lot in order to keep the defense off balance. And if the defense goes into certain standard coverages against motion, it makes it easier for the quarterback to read.

Motion is used not only to set up a pass, but also to help a run. You can pull a defender to one side and then run to the other side. Some are even using the motion man for inside blocking. They snap the ball as he reaches the interior line. The motion man then cuts into the line to block for an inside run.

Offensive Shifts

F. Shifts are separate from motion aren't they? I mean, offensive players can shift anytime before the ball is snapped as long as they come to a complete stop prior to the snap.

C. That's not quite right. Once an interior lineman (center, offensive guard, or offensive tackle) assumes a 3-point stance, that is, puts his hand on the ground, he cannot shift. As you say, the other players can all shift at once as long as they are set for a full second before the snap.

F. Yes, I remember that now.

Do shifts really affect a defense that much?

C. Defensive players use formation recognition to help set themselves to counter the offense. Shifting around changes the formation on them. So to a certain extent you are trying to get them thinking about what you are doing and not what they plan to do.

F. Kind of distracting them to lessen their concentration?

C. Right.

Look, I'm going to have to run along. If you have other questions during the week, try to

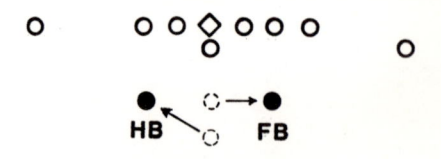

Offensive Shift
(from I to Pro Set)

F. catch me after practice or in the morning like this.

F. I will. Thanks for spending the time to go over the formations.

C. One of our defensive coaches stops here some days, and I think I see him coming in. I'll get him to go over some defensive formations with you. [To be continued].

DEFENSIVE FORMATIONS

Constraints

Unlike offensive formations, where 6 of the players are almost always in the same alignment, the positions of all 11 defensive players may change to some extent in the defensive formations employed by NFL teams. In addition to changes in positioning, different combinations of linemen, linebackers, cornerbacks, and safeties may be used on any play. Also unlike the offense, no rule requires a certain number of defensive players to be on the line of scrimmage at the snap. Finally, there's no requirement that any of the defensive men be stationary when the play begins.

Positioning of Players

While the entire offense is positioned at or close to the line of scrimmage, much of the defense is away from the line. The defenders must protect an area about 53 yards wide and from the line of scrimmage to the goal line in length.

So the defense balances its short stopping power with the ability to break up long passes and everything in between. The defense, after all, has to **react** to what the offense does. The defense men are placed so they can do this and stop all the likely plays in the shortest possible time. It's a compromise because they don't know for sure what those plays will be.

35

Deception vs. Execution

Just as the offense attempts to conceal its exact intentions from the defense on every play, the defense generally does the same. Specifically, the defense tries not to tip whether the pass coverage will be zone, man-to-man, or some combination, whether the linemen will come straight ahead or use stunts, whether the linebackers will blitz, and so on. This is important because all defenses have weak spots (often called "sweet spots"), and if the offense knows what to expect, they will be easy to exploit.

Concealing the defensive tactics to be used is thus an important aspect of defensive formations. However, execution after the snap remains the key. Defensive formations don't make great defensive teams.

Basic Formations

[After introducing Joe to the defensive coach, the offensive coach leaves. The defensive coach orders breakfast and Joe orders another cup of coffee. Then they begin discussing basic defensive formations. Below is a summary of their conversation.]

4-3 Defense

Introduced in the 1950s, the 4-3 was the standard defensive formation throughout most of the 1960s and 1970s. The recent trend has been away from this formation in favor of the 3-4. The 4-3 is still used by many teams, and discussing it first helps to highlight the modifications made to arrive at the newer 3-4 defense.

The 4-3 defense has 4 down linemen, 3 linebackers, 2 cornerbacks, and 2 safeties. A **down lineman** is a defensive player on the line of scrimmage in a 3-point stance (one hand on the ground) or a 4-point stance (both hands on the ground). The 4-3 defense is said to have a 7-man front. A **front** means the number of linemen and

When viewed from defense this is RIGHT side, so these are right DT & right DE

DE DT   DT DE

Defensive Linemen

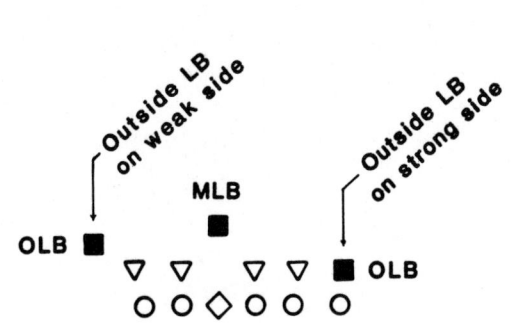

Outside LB on weak side   *Outside LB on strong side*

OLB   MLB   OLB

Linebackers

linebackers. The remainder of the players are in the secondary. So a defensive formation with a 7-man front means that there are 4 men in the secondary.

The two **defensive tackles** and two **defensive ends** make up the defensive line. In the standard form, each defensive tackle is lined up opposite an offensive guard, and each defensive end is lined up opposite an offensive tackle (usually toward the outside of the offensive tackle for a better angle). Note that the defensive tackles are not opposite the offensive tackles nor are the defensive ends opposite the tight ends. The defensive tackles are across from the guards and the defensive ends across from the tackles.

The **middle linebacker** lines up about 3 yards from the center. The **strong side linebacker** positions himself at the line of scrimmage across from or slightly to the outside of the tight end. He has to stop running plays to the outside of the offensive tackle and usually jams the tight end releasing to run a pass route. Therefore, he is up at the line. The **weak side linebacker** is near the line on the other side. He's about 1 or 2 yards outside and about 1 or 2 yards behind the defensive end on the weak side. His position may change depending on the pass/run likelihood.

Often the 4-3 looks more like a 6-1 when they line up. There are four down linemen (the defensive tackles and defensive ends) and the strong side linebacker on the line, with the weak side linebacker maybe 1 yard back. However, of these six defensive men only the linemen will be in 3- or 4-point stances. You will see the linebackers at either end of the line in 2-point stances (no hand on the ground). Operationally, the linebackers function as a backup to the line. Unless it is a blitz, they do not penetrate across the line and they drop off fast if a pass play develops. So, even with the strong side linebacker generally up at the line and the weak side linebacker close, the defense is called the 4-3 rather than a 6-1.

The **secondary** in a 4-3 defense is made up of two cornerbacks and two safeties. Their first responsibility is to defend against the pass, and initially they view each play accordingly. Only when they recognize a play to be a run do they concentrate on stopping the ball carrier.

The two <u>cornerbacks</u>, sometimes referred to as defensive halfbacks, are usually split wide to cover the flanker and split end. Each cornerback is about 3 to 9 yards deep depending on the situation and the individual style of play he uses. In a bump-and-run defense, where the cornerback chucks the wide receiver in an effort to hold him up or throw him off stride, the cornerback is right up at the line. In a prevent situation, the cornerback may be over 10 yards back, willing to give up a short pass to ensure against completion of a long one.

Cornerbacks

There are two safeties in a 4-3 defense. One is called the strong safety and the other the weak safety or free safety. The <u>strong safety</u> lines up about a yard outside the tight end and about 6 yards deep. The exact position may differ significantly depending on the defense called. The strong safety often covers the tight end in man-to-man pass coverage. The <u>free safety</u> (or weak safety) usually is positioned toward the weak side of the offensive alignment about 8 to 10 yards deep. His location can vary, and sometimes is more toward the middle or closer to the line. It depends on the game situation and the coverage to be used. The designation "free safety" arises from the fact that in many man-to-man pass coverages he has no assigned receiver to follow. Therefore, he is "free" to help out where needed.

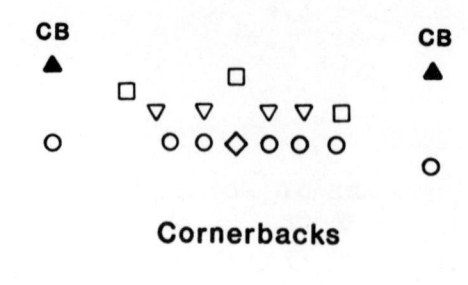

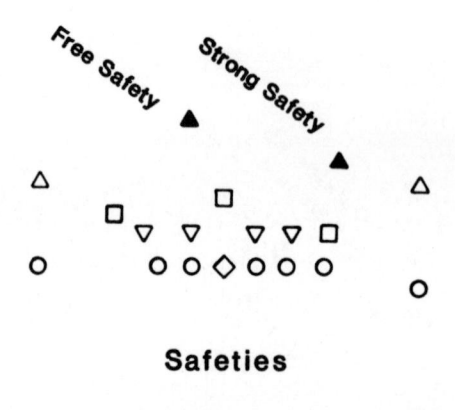

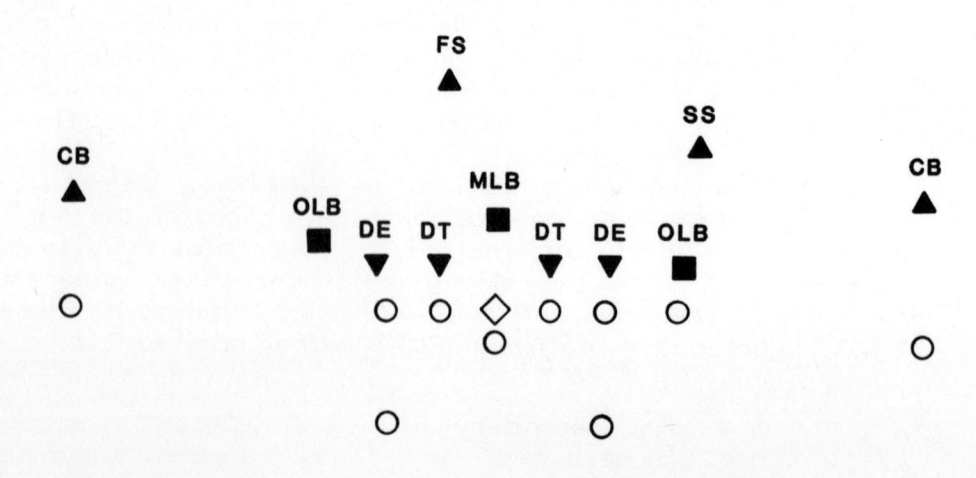

Safeties

4-3 Defense

The 4-3 is considered an **even defense** because there is no lineman opposite the center. It is the basic defense used by many teams because it provides a good combination for protecting against the run and the pass.

3-4 Defense

This formation rose to prominence in the 1970s and now is used by over half of the NFL teams. Instead of four defensive linemen, it has three. Both defensive tackles are removed and in their place one defensive man is substituted who is positioned directly across from the center. He is called the **nose tackle** (or nose guard or middle guard). The two defensive ends remain in about the same alignment as in a 4-3. The 3-4 is considered an **odd defense** because there is a lineman opposite the center.

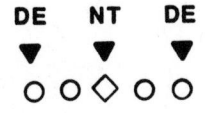

Loss of one defensive lineman is counterbalanced by the addition of one linebacker. So there are four linebackers — two **inside linebackers** who place themselves behind where the defensive tackles are in a 4-3 and two **outside linebackers** who are positioned about the same as the outside linebackers in a 4-3. Placement of the secondary (cornerbacks and safeties) is more or less the same as with the 4-3.

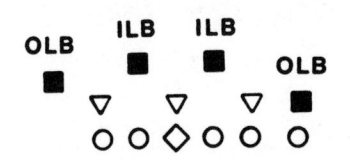

The three defensive linemen (nose tackle and two ends) are clearly outnumbered by the five offensive linemen (center, 2 guards, and 2 tackles). However, with four linebackers there is excellent pursuit to the ball carrier. The linemen attempt to neutralize the blockers and if they can't make the tackle, they must funnel the runner to a linebacker. Thus the job of the linemen is primarily sacrificial. If they carry it out, the linebackers can be very effective in stopping runs, especially to the outside.

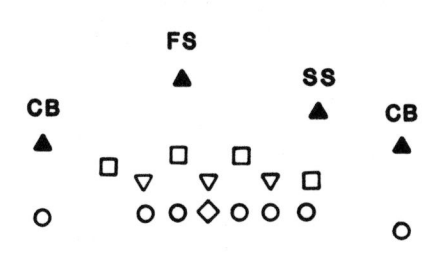

The intrinsic weakness of the 3-4 pertains to the pass rush. With only three down linemen, the rush is diminished from that of the 4-3. This puts a lot of pressure on the nose tackle position. The man who fills it must be strong enough to continually attract double-team blocks in order to free up the defensive ends. If the nose tackle can be handled by the center alone the guards can help the offensive tackles against the defensive ends and there won't be much of a pass rush at all.

Offensive linemen can now open their hands and extend their arms when pass blocking and thus are much more effective. Conversely, it is more difficult for the defensive linemen to overcome these blocks and pressure the passer. This has led some observers to favor the 3-4. They say it's better to have more linebackers and defensive backs defending downfield than linemen rushing the quarterback.

Nevertheless, a good pass rush is crucial to an effective pass defense. To aid with the rush, one of the four linebackers often blitzes, thereby simulating the effect of a 4-3. Transferring that role from linebacker to linebacker keeps the offense guessing. Moreover, many teams which use the 3-4 as their basic defense, go to four down linemen in passing situations to ensure a stronger rush.

The deciding factor as to whether a team will use the 4-3 or the 3-4 is often the number and talent of the linemen and linebackers on their roster. If the team's fourth linebacker is better than the fourth lineman, the coach will probably go with a 3-4.

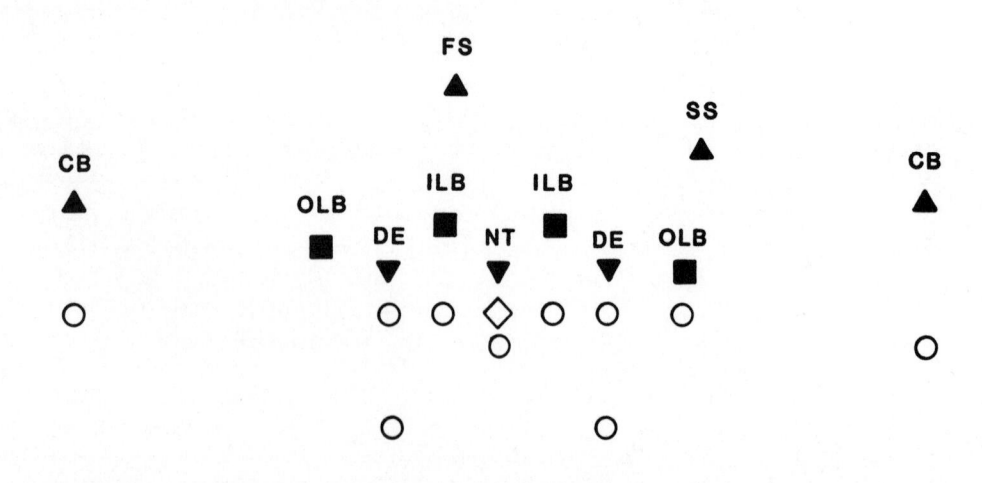

3-4 Defense

Variations of the 4-3 & 3-4

- Overshift

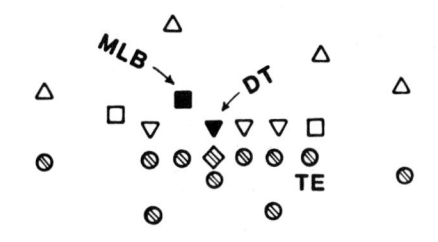

In an overshift, one or more defensive linemen shift <u>toward the strong side</u> of the offense. The shift makes sense if the defense expects the play to go to that side. It positions them to match the strength of the offense. In a 4-3 the result is generally an odd defensive alignment because there will usually be a defensive lineman opposite the center. The middle linebacker shifts in the opposite direction to cover the area exposed by the lineman who moved toward the strong side.

Overshifted 4-3

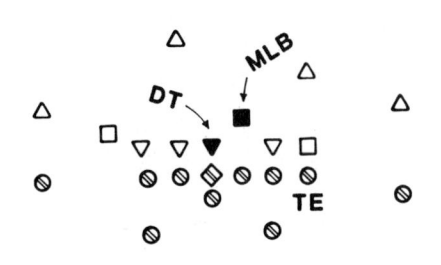

- Undershift

An undershift is similar to an over, except that the shift is <u>toward the weak side</u> of the offense. Now, the defense expects the play to develop to the weak side. In a 4-3 defense the middle linebacker again shifts in the opposite direction toward the uncovered area. Once more it generally results in an odd defensive alignment with a defensive tackle over the center.

Note that by blitzing an inside linebacker, either an overshift or an undershift can be simulated from a 3-4 defense.

Undershifted 4-3

- Gap Defense

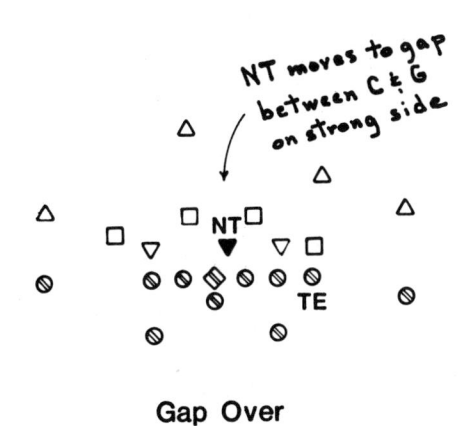

In this variation, one or more defensive linemen line up opposite a gap in the offensive line. This positions a defensive lineman to shoot the gap between two offensive linemen or to charge either left or right. The gap concept is used more extensively in goal-line or short-yardage situations.

This variation can be viewed as a modified over- or undershift. The closest linebacker may or may not shift away from this adjustment depending on the overall alignment and the defense's plan of execution.

Gap Over *(NT moves to gap between C & G on strong side)*

- Stack Defense

A stack defense places one or more of the linebackers behind defensive linemen. With respect

41

to each stack, the offense doesn't know from which direction the lineman or linebacker will come. The lineman can come straight ahead or charge left or right, and so can the linebacker, depending on which way his lineman goes.

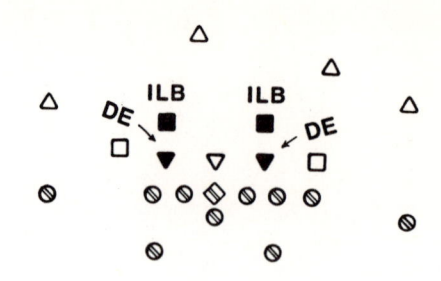

A stack aids in keeping blockers off the linebacker so he can read how the play is developing and head directly to the point of attack. A triple stack places each of three linebackers behind a different lineman. Double or single stacks are also used.

Double Stack

The Flex Defense

The flex is a specialized defense used by only a few NFL teams, principally the Dallas Cowboys who pioneered it. It is worth touching on because it illustrates a different approach to defense at the line of scrimmage.

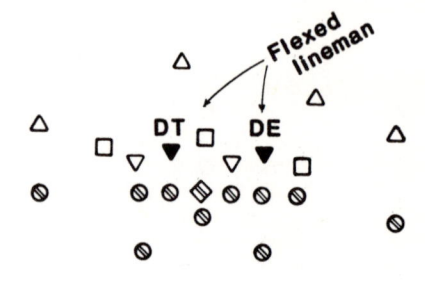

There are various forms of the flex. In two of its principal versions, the flex is similar to a 4-3 defense, except that a defensive end on one side and a defensive tackle on the other side line up about 1 yard off the line of scrimmage. When the strong side defensive end and weak side defensive tackle back off, it is a **flex strong defense**. When the weak side defensive end and strong side defensive tackle back off, it is a **flex weak defense**.

Flex Strong

The flex is a complicated defense and requires its players to protect areas in conjunction with how the play develops. It can be viewed as a kind of zone defense against the run. This is to be contrasted with other defenses where the players head for the ball carrier.

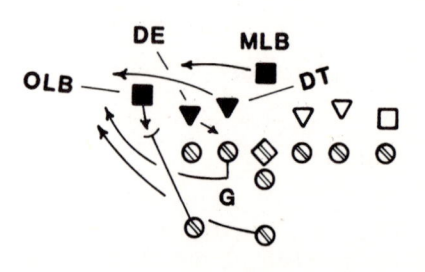

The flex involves a lot of switching assignments. For example, assume the weak side guard pulls to lead his running back outside. The weak side defensive tackle in a flex will go behind his adjacent defensive end and pursue to the outside trying to break up the play. The defensive end will not charge toward the ball carrier. Rather, he must slide over and protect the area vacated by the defensive tackle. The purpose of this is to protect against the running back cutting into the hole left

Flex vs. End Run

42

by that defensive tackle. The middle linebacker then has to shift and fill the hole left by the defensive end.

The flexed linemen are positioned to read the blocking as it develops, and have better pursuit angles. Another advantage is that only one or two teams use it. So their opponents don't see it much and are forced to make special preparations. All that shifting back and forth after the snap can be confusing to the offense.

Weaker against the pass because two rush men are off the line, the flex is used on probable running downs. It is designed to allow short yardage but cut off longer gains. The best way to attack the flex is to run straight at it.

Nickel Defense

The nickel defense is a situation defense and derives its name from the fact that 5 defensive backs (cornerbacks and safeties) are used. With a 5-man secondary, that means there must be a 6-man front. Thus, either 4 down linemen and 2 linebackers or 3 linemen and 3 linebackers can be employed.

The nickel was originally used only in obvious passing situations, like 3rd down and long yardage. Now that more teams are passing more often, the nickel is sometimes used on 2nd down and even in some 1st down situations. This makes camouflaging the defense more important. With the extra defensive back, players in the secondary can be moved around, making it difficult for the offense to discern their assignments.

The nickel is obviously weaker against a run. A 4-3 team generally takes the middle linebacker out, while a 3-4 team can pull one of its inside linebackers. If the remaining linebackers play outside, the formation is vulnerable to runs up the middle. If they play inside, the offense can sweep wide. This is relevant since the nickel is now being used in more than just must-pass situations.

Whether to have 3 or 4 linemen rushing the passer was touched on before. A nickel with a

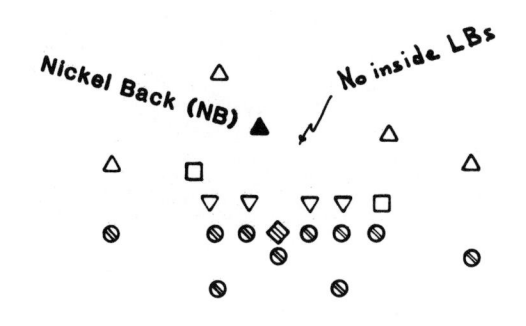

Nickel Defense

3-man line allows the use of 3 linebackers for better run support and to help against short passes. But in a passing situation the rush of only a 3-man line may counterbalance the use of 5 defensive backs. For this reason many 3-4 teams often use a 4-man line with their nickel defense.

A variation of the nickel is sometimes called the **dime defense** or the **double nickel**. It adds another defensive back for a total of 6. This is employed in prevent situations when long passes are likely. It is also becoming more prevalent against good passing teams when they line up with, say, 3 wide receivers and a tight end.

Goal Line Defense

One of the basic goal line defenses is the **6-2**. This short yardage defense involves a 6-man line, which may include one or two linebackers in 3-point stances. The linemen try to hit low to pile things up for no gain. The remaining 5 defensive players include 2 linebackers on the inside and 3 defensive backs on the outside. Because the line of scrimmage is so close to the end zone, there is no secondary, so to speak. Consequently, some refer to this defensive formation as a **6-5**.

The defensive tackles align in the gaps on either side of the center. They protect those gaps against a quarterback sneak and an inside run. The inside linebackers support the tackles and will try to stop any running back hurdling over the top. The defensive backs play close and can't let anyone get outside them. If any receiver splits wide, a cornerback generally plays him tight, favoring the inside to defend against a quick look-in pass.

In a goal-line situation the defense has to play the run first or the offense can make a yard or two every time. There is no room for error. If the ball carrier isn't hit straight up and knocked back, he can fall forward for a crucial gain. Concentration on the run clearly makes the defense susceptible to play action. A common error for a defensive back is to commit too soon to a fake run only to leave a receiver open for an easy pass.

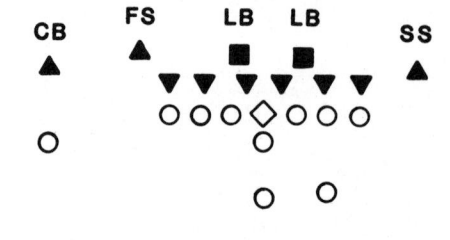

6-2 Defense

CHAPTER 4

PLAYS

This chapter deals with plays and how they are supposed to work. Both offensive and defensive plays are covered. The idea is to go over a few of the standard running and passing strategies in detail to see what the individual players are attempting to do. Plays don't always turn out like they are drawn up. There are 11 men on the other team trying to make sure of that. By looking at the whole scheme, it becomes apparent that 10 men can perform flawlessly and the play still won't work because the 11th man broke down. Moreover, all plays, both offensive and defensive, have their weaknesses. If the opposition guesses right, even a well-executed strategy can be beaten.

OFFENSIVE RUNNING PLAYS

[Joe arranged to meet with the defensive coordinator after that day's practice session and meetings were over. Despite his demanding approach, this coach is said to be well liked by his players. He's also sort of a football nut, in the sense that he'll spend hours talking football with anyone who will listen. They meet in a small empty classroom at the team's training facility.]

Off-Tackle Power Play

C. When I heard about you, I figured you'd call me. I know the sportswriters do when they're hard up for a story. I'm an easy mark.

F. As I mentioned over the phone, I'm hoping that we can discuss some plays and you can explain what each player does. As a defensive coordinator you must know a lot about how both offenses and defenses work.

C. Okay, let's start with a running play. Something off-tackle is about as basic as you can get. Let's say we run strong side and pull one guard to make it kind of a power play.

F. That means the ball carrier heads for the area just outside the strong side offensive tackle?

C. Correct. You said you went over formations with two coaches this morning. On the blackboard draw up the offense in a pro set, strong side right. And then show the defense in a standard 3-4.

....

F. (Finishing his diagram) How does that look?

C. It'll do. Now, who are you going to have as the ball carrier?

F. You know, I've never really watched which of the two running backs gets the ball on

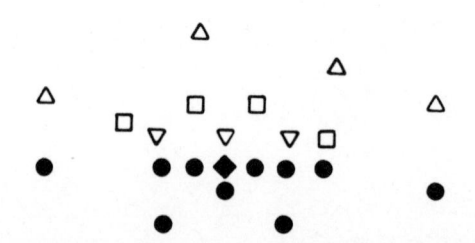

Pro Set vs. 3-4 Defense

different running plays. On an off-tackle play to the strong side I guess it would have to be the halfback. The fullback isn't positioned to take a handoff from the quarterback and hit off right tackle.

C. Okay, so you've figured out who the ball carrier is going to be.

F. This is getting pretty basic, isn't it?

C. (Starting to smile) At least you're trying, which is more than you can say for some people who criticize our plays and don't even know how they basically work. Now how are you going to block at the point of attack?

F. I'm not sure. I assume that the right offensive tackle blocks the defensive end across from him.

C. That's right, but to make sure we get some movement we double-team that left defensive end. On a double-team block there is normally a post man and a drive man. In this case, the offensive tackle is the post man. He meets the defensive end straight on and neutralizes his charge. Simultaneously the tight end hits him from the side and drives that defender back and to the inside (toward the center).

F. If the tight end blocks the defensive end, who blocks the outside linebacker on the strong side?

C. The fullback. He has to come up fast and kick out that linebacker.

F. Kick out?

C. **Kick out** is the term used for a block which drives a linebacker or defensive back out toward the sideline on an end run so the running back can cut in front and head upfield.

Now what does the onside guard do?

F. Onside?

C. **Onside** refers to the play side. In other words, the side to which the play is directed.

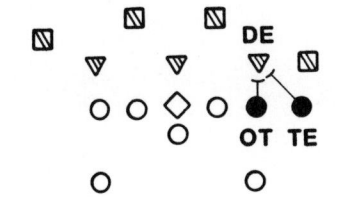

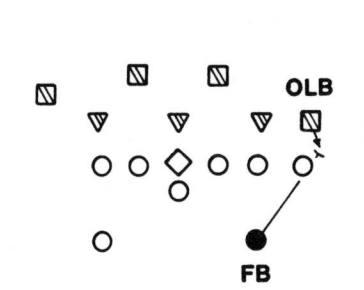

47

Offside refers to the side away from the play. These are also called the **front side** and **back side**, respectively. The onside guard here is the right guard.

F. Does he block the inside linebacker across from him? That linebacker is off the line and must be hard to block.

C. Yes, the onside guard blocks the left inside linebacker ("left" because when viewed from the defensive side he's on the left). If that linebacker is not blocked, he will scrape off behind the defensive end and fill the hole we've opened off-tackle. A linebacker **scrapes** when he loops right behind the tail of a defensive lineman. And a defender **fills** when he gets into a hole opened by the offense or an area vacated by other defenders.

That guard doesn't head straight out at the linebacker. Rather, he lead steps immediately to his right in order to get into the linebacker's scrape path and cut him off.

F. And the other guard pulls out from his position and heads down the line to the right to lead block for the halfback?

C. That's right. The offside guard pulls flat. He doesn't loop into the backfield but goes parallel down the line. He cuts behind the double-team block and turns upfield to block the first man he sees. The way I've drawn it assumes he seals off pursuit from the inside. And note that he has to sprint down the line to beat the halfback to the hole.

F. Does the center block the nose tackle?

C. Yes, and the offside tackle cuts off the right defensive end from pursuing. I might add, the center has a tough block. He is working against the nose tackle alone and can't allow him to penetrate. That could knock the pulling guard off course and he'd never make it to the hole.

F. What about the wide receivers?

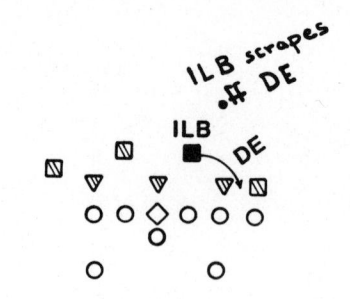

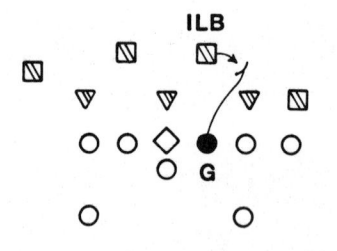

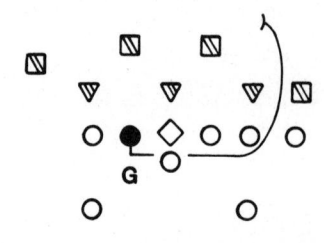

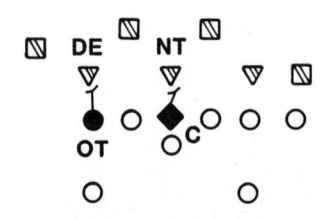

C. The flanker on the strong side has an important role. He comes off the line hard to drive back the corner covering him. At the same time he has to watch what the defense is doing. If the strong side safety has primary run support responsibility, he will come up to make the stop or turn the play inside to the middle. In that case, the flanker breaks off and blocks that safety, as I've shown.

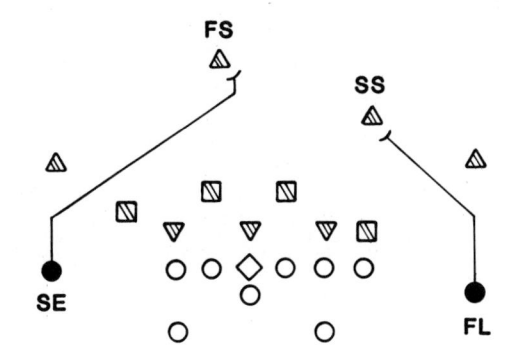

The split end heads toward the free safety and attempts to block out his pursuit.

F. And the halfback takes a handoff from the quarterback and heads for the off-tackle hole.

C. Yes. The quarterback makes the handoff as deep in the backfield as possible. The reason is to give the halfback a split second more to see how the blocks are developing and take the proper course. The initial objective is to hit directly off-tackle. But depending on how the blocking goes, the halfback may choose to go outside behind the block of the fullback on the linebacker.

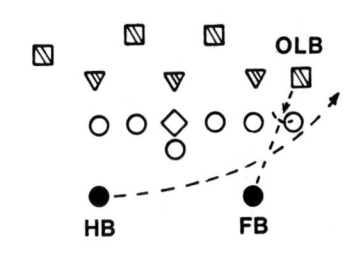

Let me illustrate by using dashed lines. Suppose the outside linebacker squeezes down inside as the tight end double-teams on the defensive end. The fullback probably won't be able to kick that linebacker out and instead will try to keep him from penetrating and pursuing outside. The halfback reads this and cuts outside instead of off-tackle. This is the "run to daylight" concept in action. The halfback doesn't have to go off-tackle, he goes to where the best hole is.

F. The halfback must have to make up his mind fast.

C. He sure does.

Let me point out one other modification that might be caused by how the defense reacts. Consider the double-team block. Suppose the defensive end charges inside, toward the onside guard. As the tight end lead steps he sees the defensive end going inside, so the tight end releases for the inside linebacker.

The right guard, who initially steps toward the end to cut off the linebacker, now double-teams the end with the onside tackle.

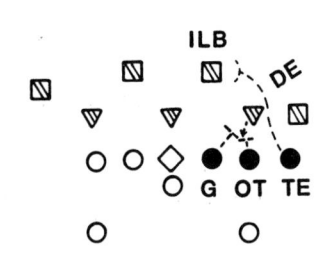

49

Alternate Blocking

Rt. G and TE coordinate blocking based on DE's charge

Off-Tackle Power Play

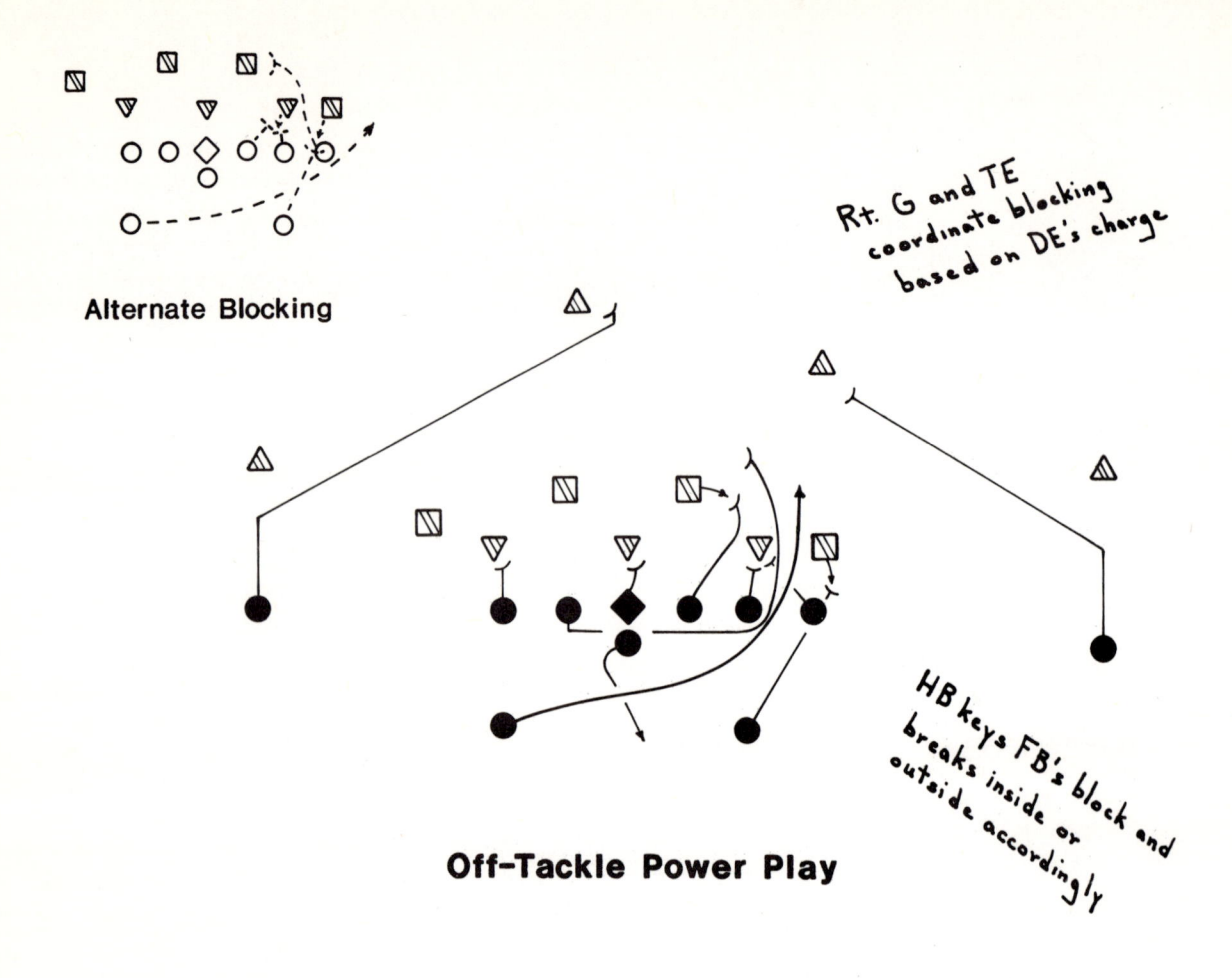

HB keys FB's block and breaks inside or outside accordingly

In essence, the inside charge of the defensive end has caused the tight end and the guard to switch assignments.

F. Does that mean that when you see a play diagrammed it just represents the original plan of execution? But actually several of the players could have alternative assignments depending on how the defense reacts?

C. That's exactly right.

Quick Trap

C. Now let's look at an inside running play, the quick trap. Are you familiar with what a trap block is?

F. I believe that involves an offensive lineman who lets one of the defensive linemen come

50

across the line, say, by vacating his normal position. At the same time another offensive lineman pulls from the other side of the center to block the defensive lineman as he comes across. If it works right, the pulling offensive lineman hits the defensive man from the side, which is a better angle than straight on.

C. And it works best against a hard-charging lineman who can be surprised by the maneuver and be blocked before he recovers.

The quick trap can work in a passing situation if one of the defensive tackles has been putting on a strong rush. It's also helpful if the linebacker is laying back some. Draw up another pro set, but this time put the strong side on the left. And use a 4-3 defense.

F. (After making his sketch) How's that?

C. Okay. Assume their right defensive tackle has been coming at us hard all day and we are going to try to trap him.

F. That means our left guard has to let him across.

C. And the left guard can do that by dropping back as if to pass block or maybe pull out to the left. In any event, the right guard will then pull out and trap that defensive tackle. Note that after the right guard pulls out, depth is not desired. He goes tight behind the center and angles toward the man to be trapped.

Now, who should handle the defensive tackle over the trapping (right) guard?

F. Probably the center.

C. Yes. The center has to take that tackle out, drive him back if possible. And the right offensive tackle cuts off the defensive end over him.

F. I assume the ball carrier is going behind the trap block. It seems like the halfback has the best angle to do that fast.

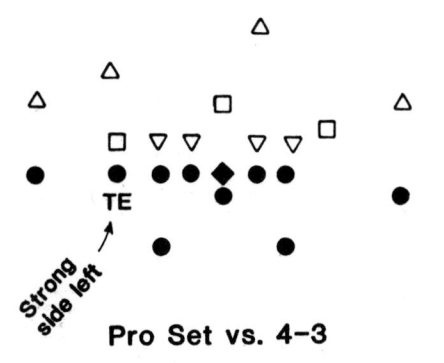

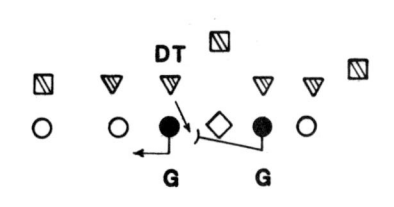

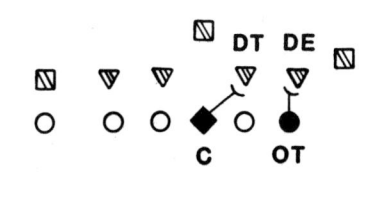

51

C. Correct. The halfback carries.

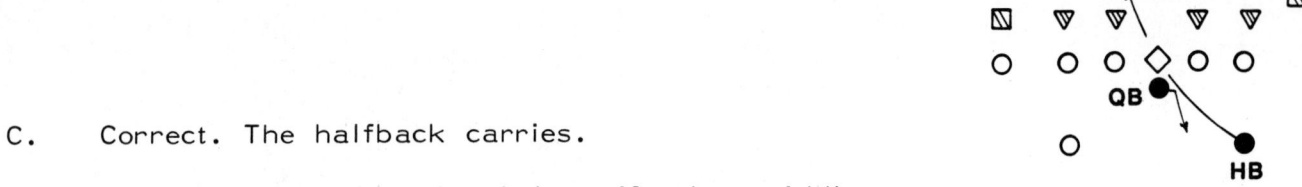

F. I can see why it helps if the middle linebacker is playing deeper than normal, or even toward one side. Who blocks him?

C. The left offensive tackle. He goes to the inside of the defensive end across from him and heads for the middle linebacker. We might try to influence the middle linebacker by sending the fullback to the right or left, trying to draw him out of position. The fullback could also be used against the right defensive end.

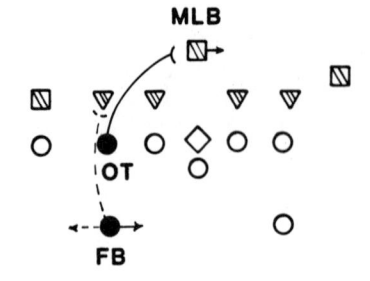

F. How about the tight end and wide receivers?

C. The tight end tries to get off the line quickly to block on the strong safety. The flanker works on the cornerback and the split end will head for the free safety.

The play goes fast. It's up to the center and the trapping guard to open the hole.

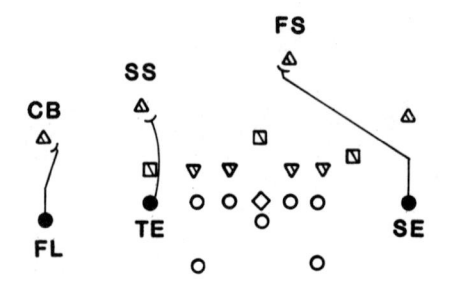

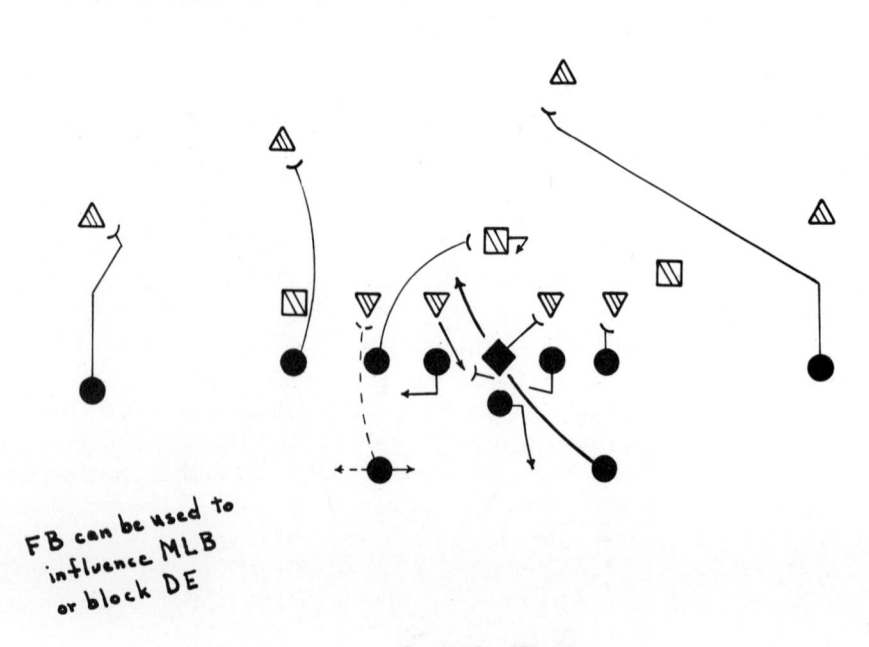

FB can be used to influence MLB or block DE

Quick Trap

Misdirection Play

C. As a final offensive running play, let's consider a misdirection out of the I formation.

Draw up another diagram. Make it an I formation, strong side left, and put the defense in a 3-4. The inside linebackers should be a little deep for this play.

Most teams are probably right-handed in the sense that the strong side is on the right side most of the time. I had you use a strong side left on the quick trap and we'll also use it on this play, so you'll keep in mind that the strong side varies.

F. (Drawing) Strong side left means the tight end is on the left side ... I formation puts both running backs behind the quarterback ... 3-4 means three down linemen with four linebackers and he wants the two inside linebackers a little deep ....

C. All right. Who do you think is going to carry on this one?

F. The tailback. The I formation positions him deep so he can read the line play and pick the best opening.

C. Correct. And his depth means he can start in one direction and cut back before reaching the line. The little extra time he takes in the backfield also helps to get the defense flowing in the wrong direction.

What we are going to do is fake a blast play to the weak side of the center. A **blast** is an inside run up the middle, with the upback lead blocking for the tailback. After starting in that direction, the upback will cut to the strong side, the left side here, and go for the best opening.

F. How do you set up the fake?

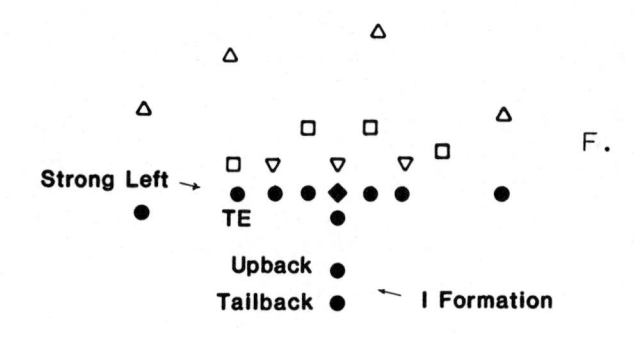

I Formation vs. 3-4

53

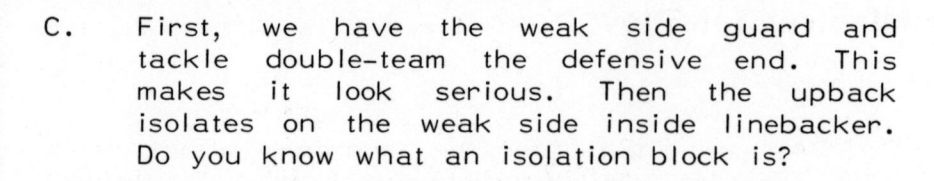

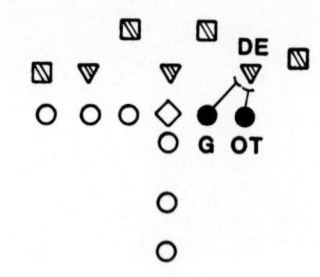

C. First, we have the weak side guard and tackle double-team the defensive end. This makes it look serious. Then the upback isolates on the weak side inside linebacker. Do you know what an isolation block is?

F. No.

C. An **isolation block** is aimed at a linebacker who plays well off the line to facilitate lateral pursuit. It is executed by a blocking back coming out to lead for the ball carrier. He takes the linebacker on one-against-one. In our case that's the upback on the weak side inside linebacker. The upback has to get out there hard and fast.

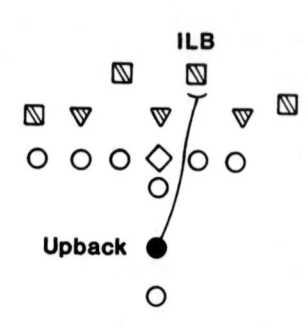

F. If the fake is to the weak side but the run is actually going to the strong side, which way is the nose tackle blocked? He's right in the middle.

C. Well, the center blocks the nose man. And we hope he takes the fake. The center fires straight out at the nose tackle. If the nose man reads the isolation and tries to penetrate weak side, the center yields, thus taking him out of the play. But the center must not allow strong side penetration.

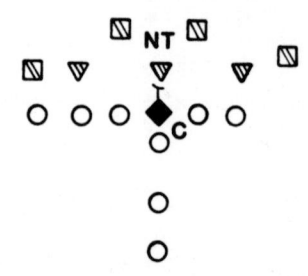

F. What's the blocking scheme on the strong side?

C. The strong side guard blocks out on the defensive end. And the strong side tackle pulls toward the weak side. By doing this we hope to get the inside linebacker thinking weak side. We also get leverage on the defensive end by having the guard blocking out.

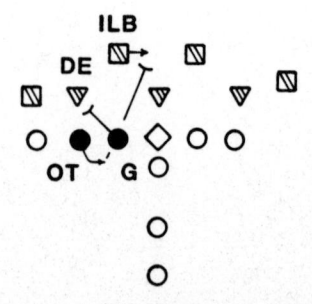

Now the pulling tackle has an important role. First, he gains a little depth. In other words, he angles back from the line and starts toward the weak side. By doing this he doesn't cover as much ground, which allows time for the defense to react to the fake. He then cuts sharply for the inside linebacker, who we hope has started toward that fake blast.

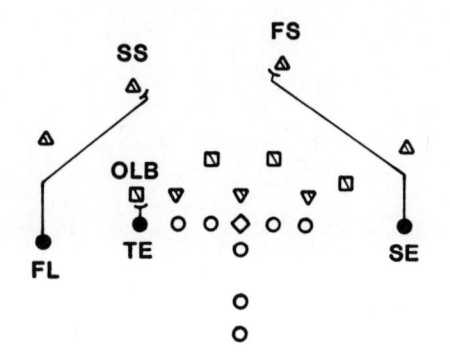

F. And the tight end blocks out the outside linebacker?

C. Yes. He has to cut off that linebacker's pursuit. If that backer plays off the block, he can stop the play short.

The flanker heads for the strong safety and the split end goes downfield to cut off the free safety.

F. How does the tailback execute the fake?

C. The quarterback opens up (pivots) toward the weak side. The upback breaks straight for his isolation block. The tailback follows the upback for two steps. This coupled with the line blocking makes it look like a blast. Then, the tailback cuts to the strong side. The quarterback continues his pivot and hands off as the tailback explodes for the hole behind the left guard's block. If you can get the defense flowing a step or two, there should be room to run. If not, the tailback gets what he can.

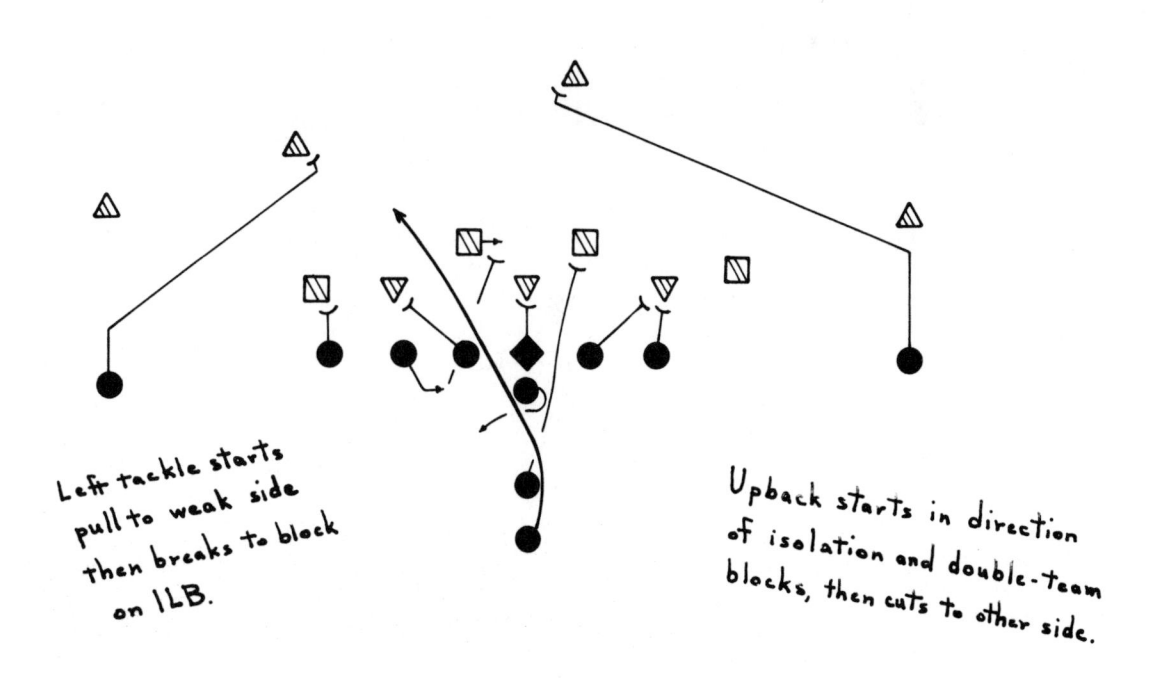

Left tackle starts pull to weak side then breaks to block on ILB.

Upback starts in direction of isolation and double-team blocks, then cuts to other side.

Misdirection Play

DEFENSIVE PLAYS

[Joe and the defensive coordinator next discuss defensive plays. They focus first on the defensive linemen and then on the linebackers and secondary. The following is a brief listing of the techniques covered.]

Slant

- Instead of charging straight ahead, one or more of the defensive linemen go on an angle to the left or right.

- Good for 3-4 defense where 3 defensive down linemen are outnumbered by 5 interior offensive linemen; coming at different angles adds an element of uncertainty to help offset the numerical superiority of the offense.

- The linebackers adjust to cover the area away from the slant.

    Note: The slant and the other defensive maneuvers that follow can be executed by either a 3-4 or a 4-3 defense. The accompanying diagrams use one or the other defense for purposes of illustration.

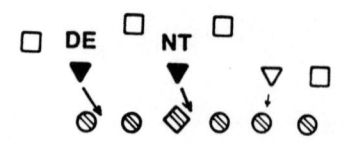

Pinch

- 2 or more defensive linemen angle toward the same spot in the offensive line.

- Good for stopping inside runs (if defense guesses right).

- Keeps blockers off linebacker, as it closes down a bubble area. A break in the defensive line is called a **bubble**. It is considered an area of weakness because the defender (linebacker) is off the line.

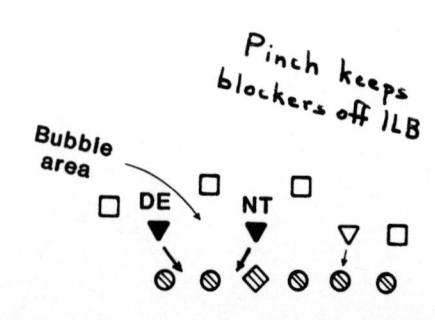

Inside Charge

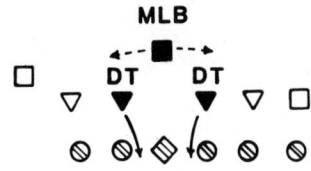

Inside Charge by DTs

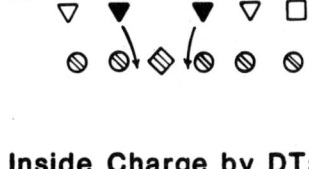

- Defensive tackles penetrate to inside of the offensive guards opposite them.

- Given the inside charge, the middle linebacker now is responsible for the area outside the defensive tackles.

- Middle linebacker reads and shifts to side where play is developing.

Outside Charge

Outside Charge by DTs

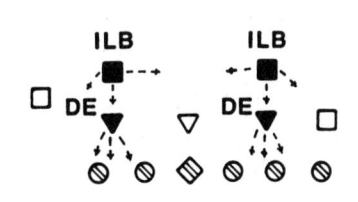

- Defensive tackles drive hard to outside of offensive guards.

- Middle linebacker now has inside responsibility between the offensive guards; can't let center or guard block him from that area.

Stack

Stack

- As discussed previously, a stack places a linebacker behind a lineman.

- Offense doesn't know whether lineman or linebacker will come right, left, or straight.

- Another purpose is to shield linebackers from blockers so they can head directly to the point of attack.

- If protecting a linebacker, the defensive lineman won't slant around the block of the offensive lineman.

- A **gap stack** has the lineman shift over and position himself opposite a gap in the offensive line. A linebacker then stacks behind him.

Key Defense

- In a key defense the linemen don't fire across with complete abandon.

- While driving hard, they watch for keys by the offense.

- Example: If defensive end sees offensive tackle block down (**block down** means a block in the direction opposite the flow of the play) on defensive tackle next to him, the defensive end reads trap; if offensive tackle hooks him (**hook** means to prevent the defender from pursuing to the outside), the defensive end expects an end run; if offensive tackle drops back to block, it indicates pass.

- Sometimes only one or two defensive linemen will key (with controlled charge) while the others fire across.

- Key defense is good against runs.

Defensive Line Keying

Blast (Charge)

- Here the defensive linemen try to blast across the line as they attempt to reach the passer.

- No holding back; defensive linemen are expected to read keys as they move.

- If it turns out to be a run, they adjust as best they can.

- Leaves defense vulnerable to draw play where quarterback fakes a pass and hands off.

- For this reason, combination key-blast is sometimes used, with one player lagging slightly to protect against runs.

Defensive Line Blasting

Linemen & Linebackers

- The linemen and linebackers work together in carrying out assignments, as do all the defensive 11.

- As discussed above, middle linebacker has outside responsibility when defensive tackles go inside and inside responsibility when defensive tackles charge outside.

- Similarly, if defensive end takes an inside rush, the outside linebacker has responsibility for the area outside the offensive tackle; if defensive end charges outside the offensive tackle, linebacker has inside responsibility.

- When a linebacker recognizes play to be a pass, he drops off into pass coverage while the linemen continue their rush; linebackers don't penetrate across line unless they are blitzing.

Containment of End Run

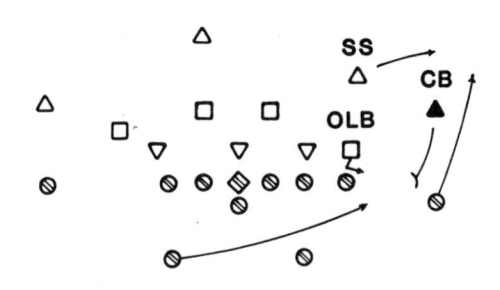

- Containment is an essential element of pursuit. The objective is to force the ball carrier who is headed outside back inside toward the pursuing defenders. If the ball carrier gets outside, he can go for big yardage since only one defender may be in a position to catch him.

- Three players normally work together on containment: the outside linebacker, the cornerback, and the safety.

- The outside linebacker first protects the off-tackle area. If the ball carrier goes farther outside, the linebacker pursues inside-out to meet him at the nearest possible point.

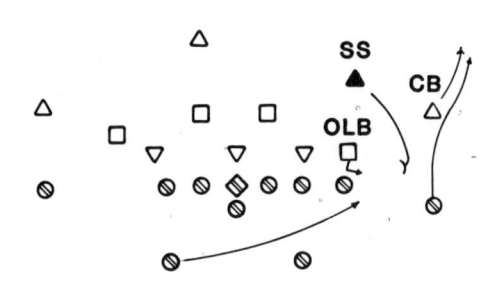

- The safety and the cornerback have complementary assignments. One will have primary pass responsibility and the other furnishes run support. Both respect the pass first, but the defensive back with primary run support must come up fast when a run shows. He takes an outside-in approach to ensure containment of the play. He can't let the ball carrier get outside.

- Whether the cornerback or the safety has primary run support can change from play to play. The assignments are determined independently for the strong side and the weak side.

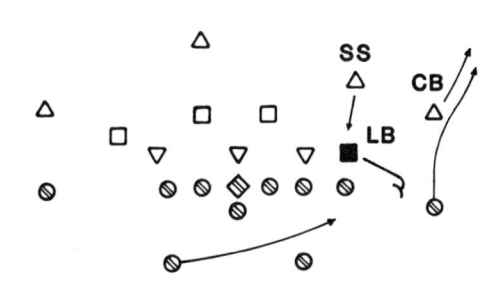

- The linebacker is sometimes the force man (rather than the safety or cornerback). In that case, the linebacker must move to stay outside the ball carrier and contain him. The defensive back (safety or cornerback) with primary run support now pursues inside-out to fill the area vacated by the linebacker.

CB Forces

SS Forces

LB Forces

59

Pursuit

- Pursuit is an important part of run defense; it isn't a mad dash to the ball carrier by the defense, but requires each player to take the proper route to minimize the probability of the runner breaking free.

- For purposes of pursuit the defense can be broken down into three basic groups: force unit, contain unit, and backup unit.

- The force unit is made up of the defensive linemen and the inside linebackers. They pursue directly to the ball. They move laterally down the line and once the ball crosses it, take the most direct angle to the runner. The force unit must be careful not to overpursue.

- The contain unit, discussed above, involves the outside linebacker, safety, and cornerback on each side. They keep the ball carrier from getting outside and pressure him back into the force unit.

- The backup unit is composed of the contain unit away from the run. Since the play is going to the other side, their job is to cover deep and protect against any cutback or reverse.

    - The outside linebacker protects against a reverse; he must hold his position until he is sure of no counter play.

    - The safety and cornerback rotate deep watching for any cutback; as potentially the last defenders to make the play, they must first get depth and then approach the ball carrier on an inside-out angle.

Note: The terminology can be confusing. The term "force" is used not only for the primary pursuit unit (force unit) but also to designate the defensive back in the containment unit who has primary run support. He is often called the **force man** since he comes up and "forces" the ball carrier inside.

Pursuit

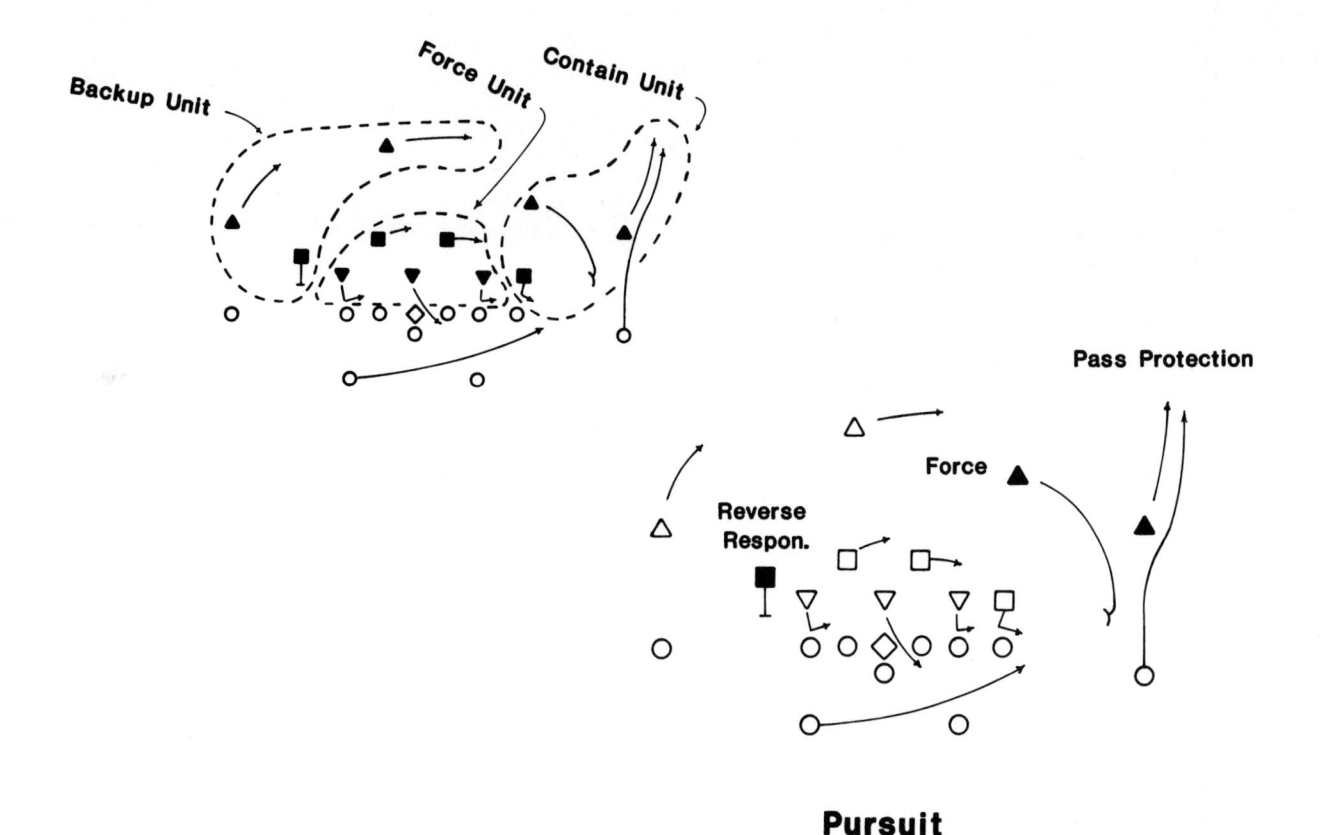

Stunts

- Stunts involve 2 or more linemen and/or linebackers who on a coordinated basis charge the line other than in a normal straight ahead manner.

- The slant and pinch maneuvers discussed above can be considered stunts.

- More visible are tactics sometimes called games, deals, or twists, where players effectively switch assignments.

- Generally only part of the defense (2 or 3 players) will stunt at one time.

- Stunts are used as a change-up or surprise tactic and are not employed continuously.

- Stunts are good against offenses that trap, cross block, and double-team a lot.
- But if the stunt sends a defense man in a direction away from the runner, the runner will probably find a hole.

- End-Tackle Stunt

- Defensive end charges across offensive tackle and penetrates inside the guard.
- Defensive tackle fakes guard and then loops behind defensive end to the outside.
- The idea is to get both offensive tackle and guard tied up with the defensive end to free up the defensive tackle.
- These stunts are easier to execute with a 4-man line; with a 3-man line the spacing of the defenders is generally too far apart (however, on passing situations a nose tackle will occasionally loop behind a defensive end).

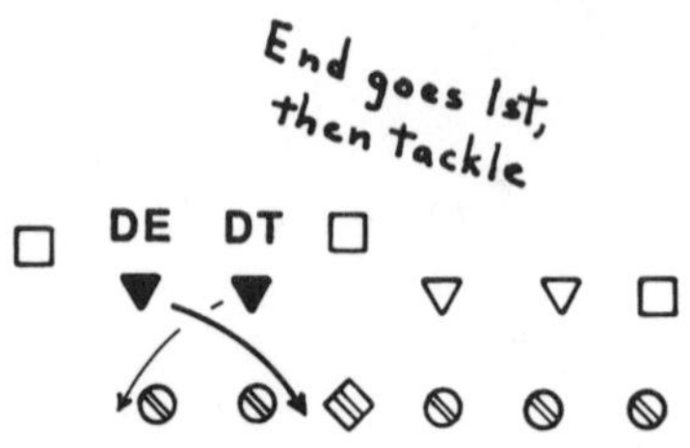

End-Tackle Stunt

- Tackle-End Stunt

- Same as end-tackle stunt, except defensive tackle goes first and tries to attract offensive tackle and guard in order to free defensive end looping to the inside.
- During these stunts the linebacker is alert in case of a breakdown; these stunts are generally good against passing, not running plays.

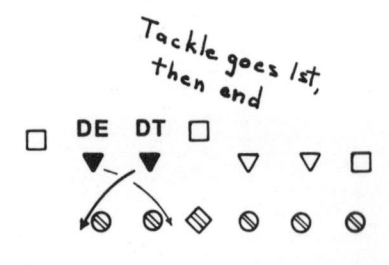

Tackle-End Stunt

- Tackle Stunt with Linebacker

- Here one defensive tackle drives across guard and center in order to penetrate inside the opposite guard.
- Other defensive tackle crosses behind the first defensive tackle toward the other side.
- Middle linebacker charges to the outside of one of the guards.
- Good for confusing the offensive linemen, but if they pick it up, middle area will be open for a run.

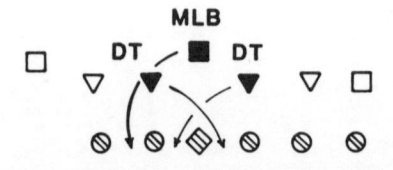

Tackle Stunt with Linebacker

Blitz

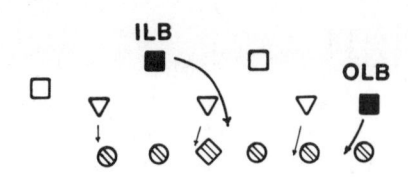

Weak Side ILB & Strong Side OLB Blitz

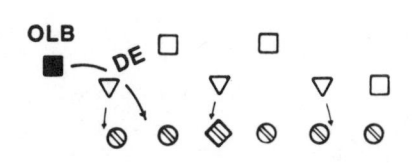

Weak Side OLB Blitz Inside

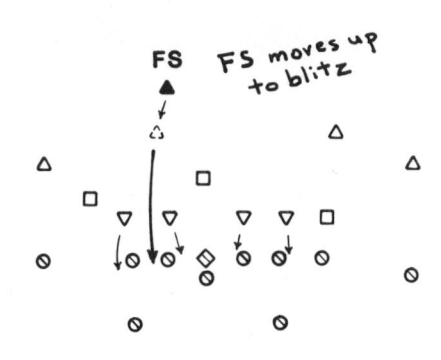

FS Blitz (FS moves up to blitz)

- A blitz involves having a linebacker or a safety charge across the line in an attempt to get to the passer.

- Also can be effective against a run <u>if</u> ball carrier is in the same area.

- One or more linebackers and/or a safety may blitz.

- Blitzing linebacker will coordinate his rush with one of the linemen.

- For example, the weak side linebacker may go <u>inside</u> the offensive tackle while the weak side defensive end goes <u>outside</u> the offensive tackle (defensive end now has contain responsibility for that outside area).

- One of the 4 linebackers in a 3-4 defense often blitzes in order to have a 4-man rush; blitz responsibility changes among the 4 linebackers to keep offense guessing.

- A blitzing player may attempt to maintain his normal position until ball is snapped in order to conceal the intent.

- This is hard for the free safety who is normally at least 6 yards behind the line; easier for the strong safety to disguise because he sometimes is up close to pick up the tight end.

- Conversely, some players fake a blitz before the snap and then fall back into normal coverage to confuse offense.

- Blitzing is more prevalent because of the increased emphasis on passing and the greater difficulty in mounting a rush given the more lenient blocking rules.

- Blitz must be used judiciously to retain an element of surprise; this is necessary to offset the weakened pass coverage which the defense is risking.

PASS PLAYS

The different components of pass plays are summarized below in the following order:

Pass blocking
Wide receiver pass routes
Tight end pass routes
Running back pass routes.

Potential pass patterns (the combined routes of all the receivers) are almost unlimited. This section closes with two examples.

Pass Blocking

- The Pocket

- On a straight dropback pass, the center and guards form front of the pocket (cup-shaped wall of blockers); the closer to the line of scrimmage they can stop the defense, the more room they give the quarterback to step up if pressured from the sides by the defensive ends.

- The offensive tackles form the sides of the protective wall; they can allow deeper penetration to the outside without hampering the quarterback, but not penetration to the inside.

- If quarterback rolls to one side or the other, the pocket must be set up accordingly.

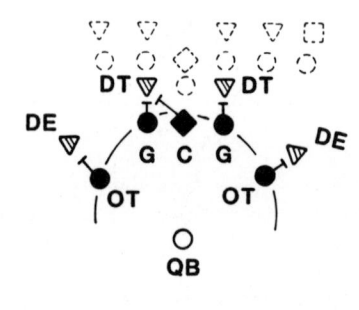

Passing Pocket

- Man Blocking

- Each lineman is responsible for a particular defender, usually the man over him (across from him) when the ball is snapped.

- If the defensive linemen stunt, each blocker follows his man as he slants across or loops behind.

- If assigned man doesn't come (e.g., a linebacker), the offensive lineman helps another specified blocker.

- Area Blocking

- Also called zone blocking. This method makes each lineman responsible for a particular area as opposed to a particular defender; he takes whoever comes.

- Proponents believe this scheme avoids the confusion and missed assignments that can result with man blocking when working against a stunting defense.

- If no defender shows, lineman looks for a teammate needing help; he checks inside first (the shortest route to the quarterback), then down the line.

- Play Action

- The nature of the blocking changes on play action; offense is faking a run before quarterback sets up to pass.

- Linemen must simulate run blocking or defensive secondary will read pass and can easily defend against it.

- So linemen must fire out and block aggressively instead of dropping back immediately.

- Presents problem for uncovered lineman; he can't go downfield on a pass play (linemen must make contact within one yard of the line of scrimmage when blocking for a pass); so, if he can't make contact as he lead steps, he turns and helps closest man toward the play side (with his fake block), then pivots back for pass protection.

- The back side linemen (side away from the fake run) cannot allow a defender through — this is the quarterback's blind side.

- Running Backs & Tight Ends

- The running backs and tight end can play an integral role in the pass-blocking scheme — they represent three additional potential blockers.

- For maximum protection, both backs are held in to block; tight end ordinarily releases on pass plays but occasionally blocks, especially against a blitz from the outside.

- Release of one or both running backs may be conditional on checking for blitzing linebackers first; if linebacker (or safety) comes, running back must pick him up; if no blitz, back releases into pass route or becomes flare control man (for quarterback to dump off short pass as last resort).

- Problem: Delay blitz — linebacker holds until back releases, then comes.

- If running back releases immediately, he may be the designated blitz control man; if blitz comes, he yells "blitz" and quarterback throws immediately to him.

- On play action, the running back who fakes run into the line picks up any blitzing linebacker in the area; otherwise, he gets into short pass route to give quarterback an additional option.

- Examples

Man Blocking vs. Even Defense

- Each lineman blocks man over him.
- Center is the uncovered lineman.
    - He blocks middle linebacker in whatever hole he comes.
    - If no middle linebacker blitz, center helps on side the running back released (there is a running back on the other side to help).

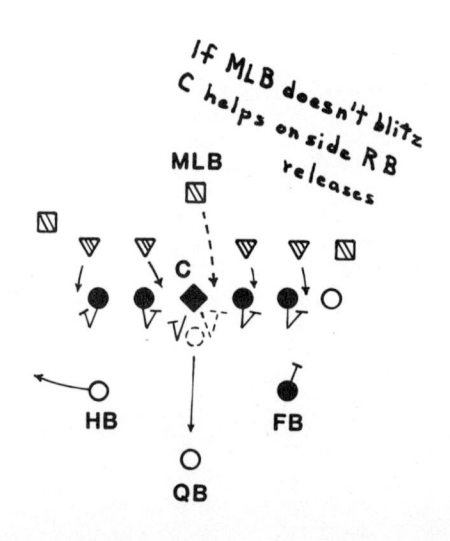

If MLB doesn't blitz C helps on side RB releases

Blocking vs. Even Defense

Man Blocking vs. Odd Defense

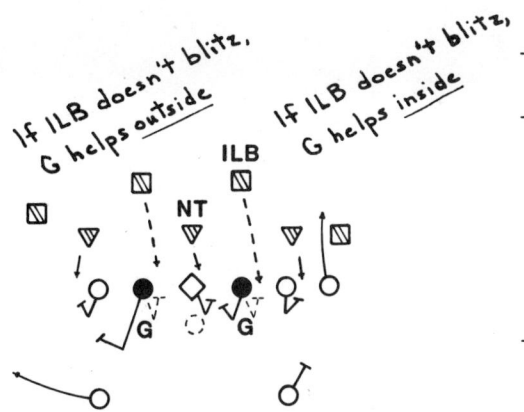

- Guards are now the uncovered linemen.

- Guard on side the running back <u>releases</u>:
    - Blocks the inside linebacker head up with (i.e., across from) him.
    - If no inside linebacker blitz, guard pulls to the outside to help (no running back to pick up outside linebacker).

- Guard on side the running back <u>holds</u>:
    - Blocks the inside linebacker head up with him.
    - If no inside linebacker blitz, he checks center's block against nose man and then tackle's block against defensive end (running back is there to pick up outside linebacker).

Blocking vs. Odd Defense

Blocking vs. Stunt

- To illustrate the potential problems caused by stunting and blitzing defenses, consider the situation where the strong side running back releases immediately.

- Assume the center blocks the nose man and the tackles block the defensive ends.

- Suppose the nose tackle drives hard into center-guard gap on weak side, such that he ties up both the center and the guard on the weak side.

- If both inside linebackers now blitz strong side, that guard is faced with blocking two men at once; and since running back on that side has released, there is no help behind — one of those linebackers will probably get through untouched.

- Adjustments to the blocking can be made to handle this type of situation, but it points out that the linemen must be prepared to deal with many different defensive attacks and be able to react quickly.

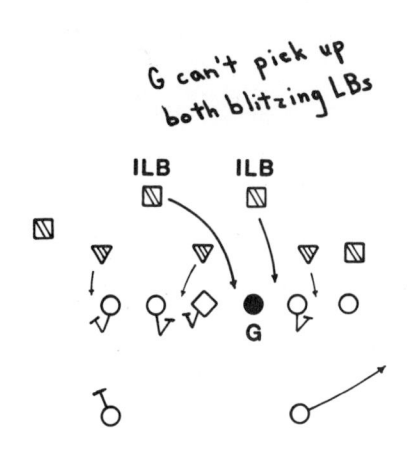

Blocking vs. Stunt

Wide Receiver Pass Routes

- Split out toward sideline, the wide receiver is positioned to get immediately into his route.

- Good wide receivers tend to either have great speed or exceptional moves; one or the other is a minimum requirement because wide receiver has to get open.

- Routes used should be those which exploit the receiver's abilities.

Slant or
Quick
Post — After 2-3 steps receiver cuts toward middle on angle; quarterback throws when receiver comes open; receiver is looking while angling in (also called "look in"); this can be tough on receiver — with number of defenders in middle area, he is likely to get hit hard while catching ball.

Hitch — After 3-4 steps, receiver stops and turns back toward quarterback for quick pass; quarterback throws as receiver stops and before he turns.

Short Out — Receiver starts 4-6 yards downfield and breaks outside at a 90-degree angle; precision pass for short yardage; interception a real problem because there may be no way to catch defender.

Square In
or Out — At 12-15 yards from line, receiver cuts inside or outside at a 90-degree angle; another precision pass; quarterback must anticipate and throw before runner makes break; like slant, square-in sends wide receiver toward middle where he is likely to get hit hard.

Curl or
Hook — Receiver drives 12-15 yards downfield, then curls in a step or two; quarterback must anticipate and throw before receiver turns.

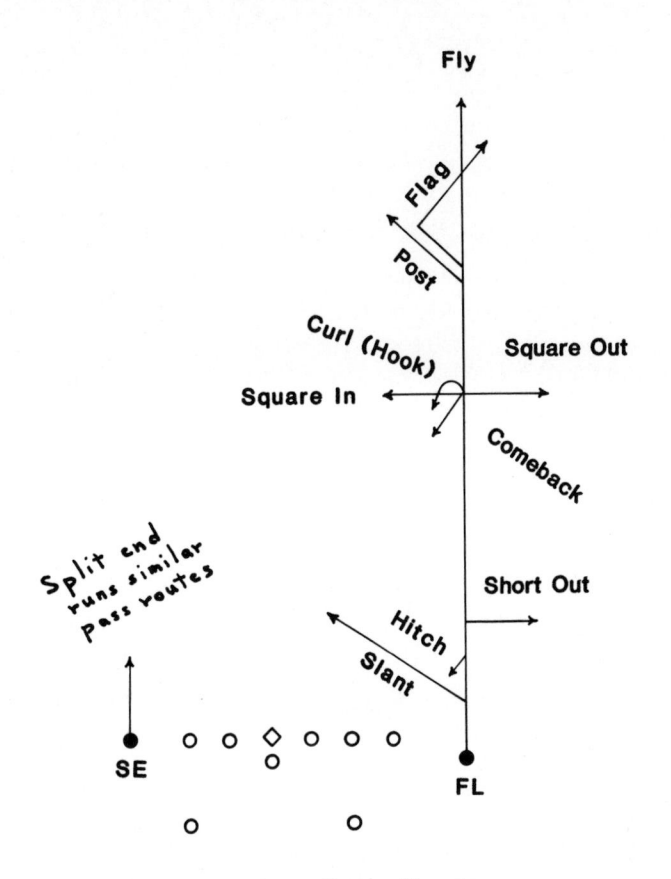

Wide Receiver Pass Routes

Comeback — Similar to curl but this time receiver comes back 2-3 yards toward quarterback; throw is made <u>after</u> receiver has made turn; accuracy is essential to completion.

Flag or
Corner — A deep route; receiver heads downfield and breaks toward corner of field; if receiver is close to sideline, he will generally slant in first to set up angle to head for corner.

Post — Usually a deep route; receiver runs downfield and breaks inside toward goal post.

Fly or
Go or
Streak — Receiver heads straight upfield; on this one receiver tries to simply outrun defender.

- Routes shown above are the basic forms of some of the more common ones.

- Often the actual path taken is a combination of different basic routes.

69

- In addition, to get open the wide receiver uses fakes, speed, changes of pace — whatever works for him.

- Examples include an out-and-up, zig-out, hitch-and-go, fast-glide-fly.

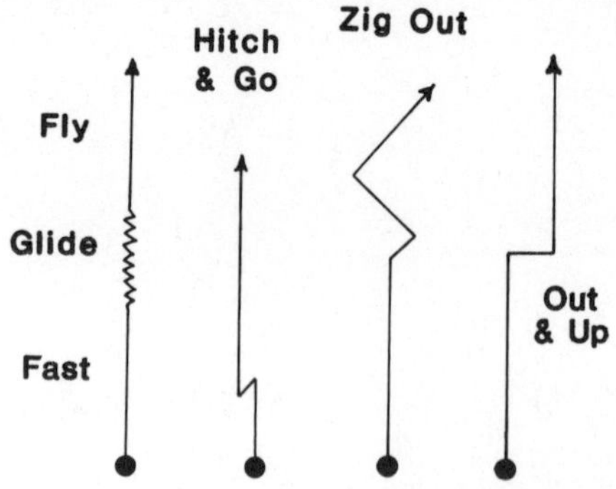

Tight End Pass Routes

- Tight end will usually be jammed at line by strong side linebacker to hold him up (this also gives strong safety time to pick up tight end if he releases); delay at line has to be taken into account regarding any pass route the tight end runs.

- Bigger, stronger tight end is more suited to passes in middle area than wide receiver.

- Speed is becoming a bigger factor as teams begin to rely more on tight end as a pass catcher, rather than mainly a blocker.

- Though fast tight end may go deep, most tight end routes are short to intermediate.

- Many of the routes for a tight end are similar to the corresponding routes of a wide receiver.

- Routes that differ are noted below.

Bench   – Tight end drives out for sideline (bench) area just cleared by flanker running a deeper route.

Delay   – Tight end check blocks (unsustained block) lineman or linebacker and then releases into short route.

Drag   – After starting downfield, tight end breaks to outside, angling slightly back toward line of scrimmage.

Look In – Similar to slant of wide receiver.

Crossing – This route brings tight end out and across middle of field.

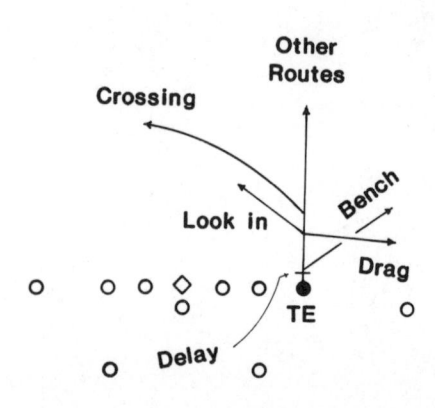

Combination Pass Routes

Tight End Pass Routes

Running Back Pass Routes

- Most are short routes which make for safe passes and rely on the back's running ability to make yardage after the catch.

- These routes are good for influencing the linebackers who normally cover the running backs man-to-man or who play the short zones in a zone defense.

- Short routes also set up the running back as a safety valve receiver to avoid a sack.

- If back releases immediately, he can run an intermediate route; against a zone defense these are often aimed at the area (seam) beyond the short zones and in front of the deep zones.

- Starting in the backfield it takes time for running back to get out into a route; normally they do not run deep.

- However, if offense can isolate a fast back on slower linebacker (man-to-man coverage) that back should be able to go deep for big yardage.

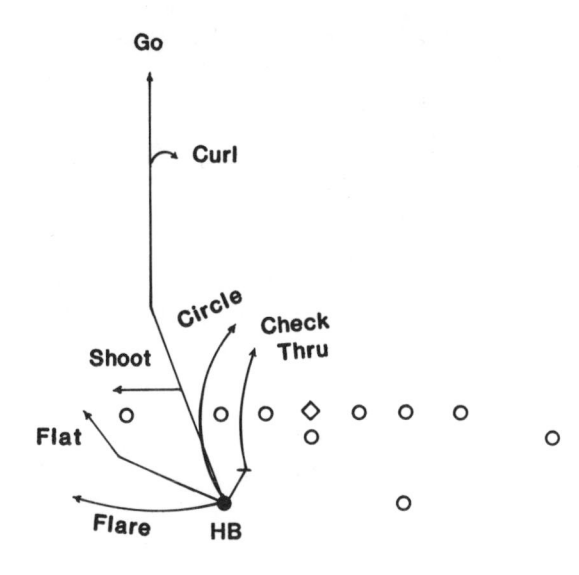

Running Back Pass Routes

Flare — Moves to the outside while curving back slightly.

Flat — Heads to flat, looking back for pass (flat is area just beyond the line of scrimmage and outside of where the wide receivers normally line up).

Shoot — Used with play action, running back starts toward linebacker as if to block, then cuts out parallel to line.

Circle — Circular route around or through a gap in the line; gets running back into middle area.

Check Thru — Running back check blocks (unsustained block) defense man, then releases through gap between tackle and guard.

Curl — Intermediate route; back goes downfield 12-15 yards and curls back toward quarterback in seam between zones.

Go — Running back goes fast and deep attempting to outrun defender; heads for open area downfield.

Pass Patterns

- Possible combinations of wide receiver, tight end, and running back pass routes are unlimited.

- Routes are combined so as to influence defenders and get at least one receiver free.

- **Timing patterns** are sometimes set up to help the quarterback find an open man; receivers make their breaks at varying distances so they get free (if at all) one after another; if first man is not open, quarterback checks second, then third.

- **Choice patterns** give receivers optional routes, depending on the defense they encounter; quarterback must read the defense and how the receiver will react — this takes practice and experience.

- 2 pass plays are illustrated, a square-out pattern and a curl pattern; additional plays are discussed in the following chapter.

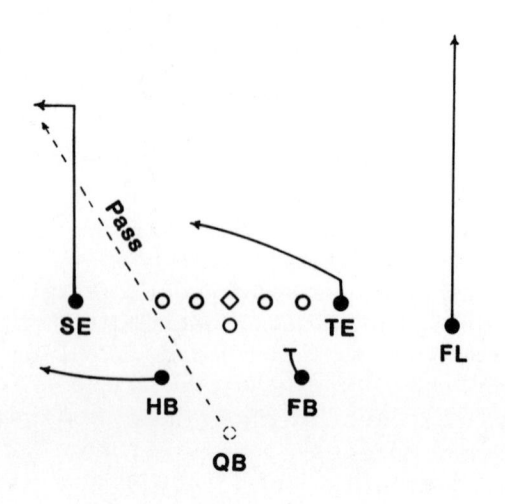

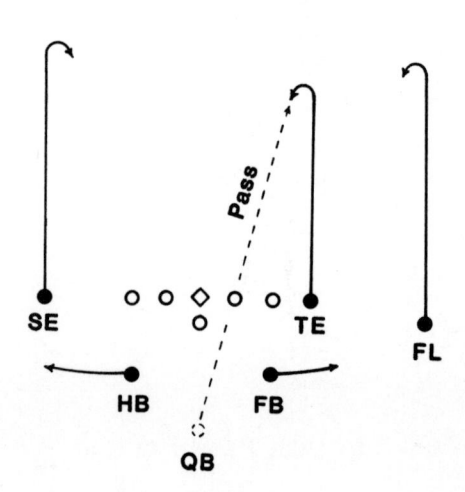

Square-Out Pattern

Curl Pattern

PASS DEFENSES

There are basically 3 types of pass defenses being used: man-to-man, zone, and combination defenses.

Man-to-
man
- stick with man; go wherever he goes
- don't let him fake you, outrun you
- short or deep he's yours
- watch man and when he goes for ball, you do too.

Zone
- defend an area, not a specific receiver
- ignore fakes, watch quarterback and receivers in area
- when quarterback throws, go where ball is headed and break up pass
- in deep zones, don't let receiver get behind you; keep dropping back.

Combina-
tion
- some defenders play zone, some play man-to-man.

In the late 1960s the trend in pass defense was away from man-to-man in favor of zone coverage. By the mid-1970s the evolution to multiple defenses and combination coverages had begun. With the advent of situation substitution, the trend in mixing up coverages continues. However, now that the one-chuck rule is in effect, there is increased emphasis on man-to-man coverage. Due to the free movement receivers have downfield, it is more difficult to defend using pure zones.

The defensive situation is aggravated by the more lenient pass-blocking rules. The result is the quarterback has additional time to find an open receiver. This coupled with the one-chuck rule has forced defenses into covering more receivers with two defenders. At the same time, blitzes are being used to mount a stronger pass rush against the now more effective pass blockers. Finally, complexity is an end in itself. The simpler the coverage, the easier it is for the quarterback and receivers to read and dissect. So defensive coaches try to make them as varied and complicated as possible.

The 3 basic coverages are summarized below. Five examples of man-to-man coverage, 6 examples of zone coverage, and 3 combination coverages are outlined. The examples are designed to illustrate the fundamental concepts involved. More complicated coverages essentially involve variations or combinations of those presented. For instance, although pure zones are not used consistently, many other coverages involve some zones or zone concepts.

Note: To keep the examples as simple as possible, most have been illustrated using a 4-3 defense. As previously noted, 3-4 defenses often blitz a linebacker or switch to a 4-man line in passing situations. Thus, the 3-4 is frequently somewhat similar to a 4-3 against the pass. Using mainly one basic defense also makes it easier to highlight variations between the different coverages.

Man-to-Man Coverages

Linebacker Short Zones

- Though it may seem a strange way to start, an understanding of some short zone terminology is important when dealing with man-to-man coverages.

- Linebackers are typically assigned to cover running backs in man-to-man coverage; but if a running back stays in to block or flows away (goes to other side), the linebacker drops back from the line of scrimmage to defend against short passes and give help underneath (in front) to those defenders covering receivers who may go deep.

- The exact terminology and locations for these zones vary from coach to coach. The diagram shows a simplified scheme.

- There is one hook and one curl zone on each side of the field with the flat area on the outside; thus there are 6 specific short zones spread across the field, all of approximately the same size.

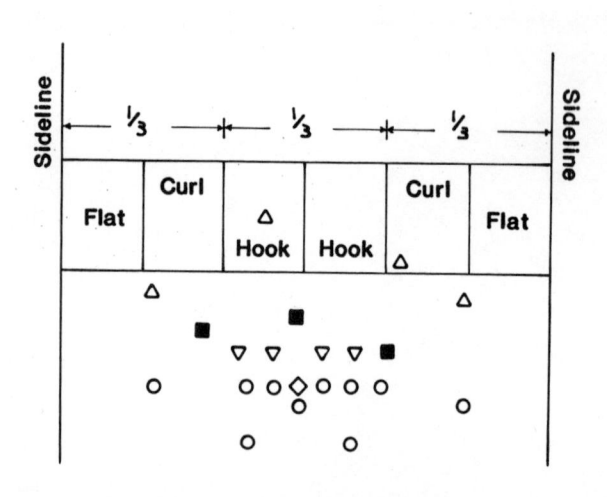

Linebacker Short Zones

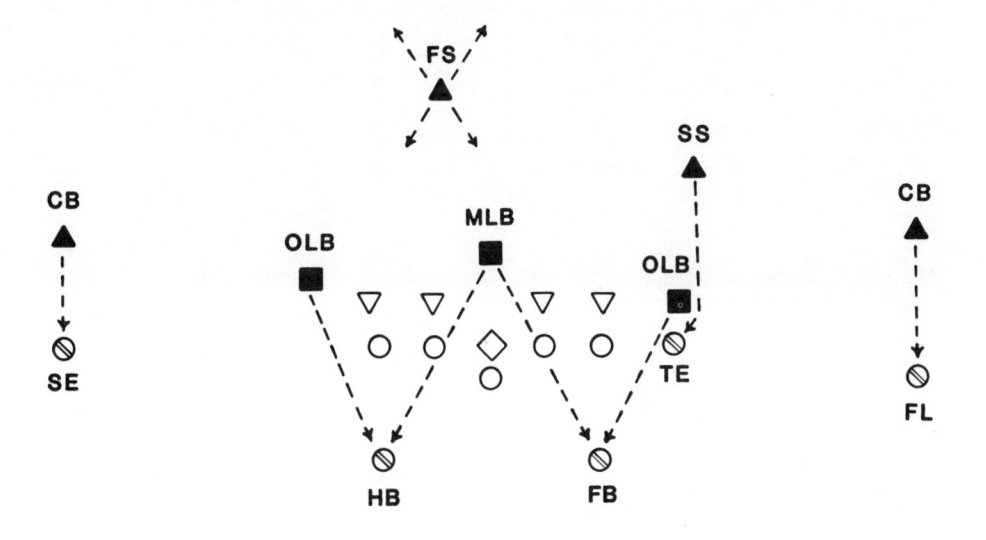

Free Safety Defense

(Man-to-Man Pass Coverage)

Free Safety Defense

- This is basic man-to-man coverage:

    Cornerbacks cover the split end and flanker.

    Strong safety covers tight end.

    Outside linebackers cover the running back who goes to their respective side.

    Middle linebacker covers running back checking thru line or second back out to one side.

    Free safety (weak safety) is free to help where needed.

- Strong side linebacker can't let tight end charge off line; quick inside release puts tight end in clear until strong safety can catch; so strong side linebacker must jam tight end.

- If running back stays in to block, respective outside linebacker drops back about 10 yards into the curl zone on his side to help cornerback and safety underneath (outside linebacker still responsible for running back on delay pattern).

- Middle linebacker, if not covering a running back, drops to one of the hook zones, depending on the pass pattern he sees.

- Cornerbacks and strong safety know they have help inside (free safety) if receiver runs post route, so they can be more aggressive in defending to the outside.

Double Coverage on Split End

- Same as above except free safety is no longer "free".

- He doubles with weak side cornerback on split end.

- All defenders know free safety isn't there to help.

- Cornerbacks and safeties can key running backs to determine if they have help underneath (if running back stays in to block, linebacker will drop back to short zone).

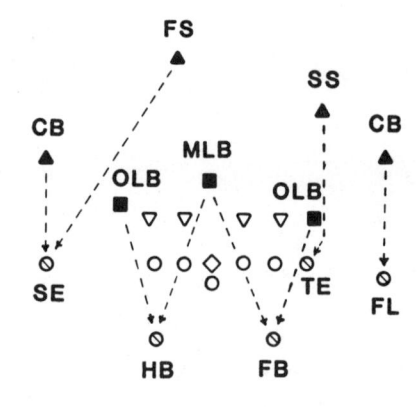

Double Coverage on SE

Double Coverage on Both Wide Receivers

- Same as above except now strong safety doubles with cornerback on flanker.

- Strong side linebacker must pick up tight end.

- Middle linebacker has strong back wherever he goes (middle linebacker and weak side linebacker may switch if weak back blocks and strong back flares to weak side).

- Strong side linebacker knows he has no help with tight end deep (he may switch with middle linebacker if tight end releases inside and crosses toward middle).

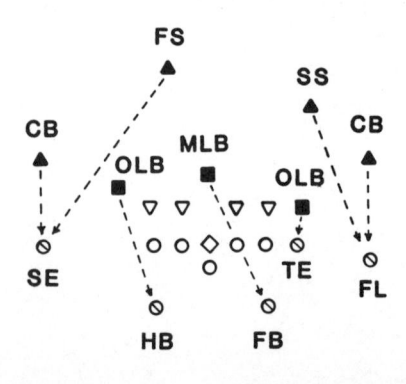

Double Coverage on WRs

76

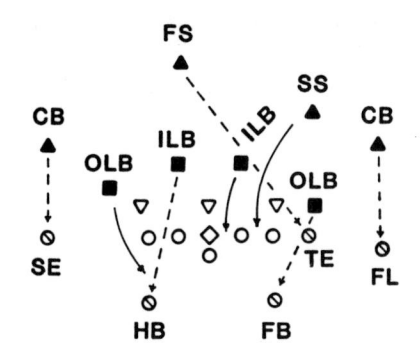

Heavy Blitz (3-4 Defense)

- A 3-4 defense can blitz 2 linebackers and 1 safety and still cover all the eligible receivers man-to-man.

- Free safety now picks up tight end (strong side linebacker has to hold him up at line to give free safety time to come up).

- Inside linebacker on weak side covers weak back. Strong side linebacker has strong back.

- All defenders know there's no help deep.

Heavy Blitz (3-4 Defense)

Nickel Defense

- Nickel defense uses 5 defensive backs; middle linebacker generally comes out for fifth defensive back.

- Nickel allows double coverage of 2 receivers even when offense goes to multiple receiver formation.

- Free safety and cornerback double on split end.

- Strong safety and cornerback double on flanker.

- Nickel back covers slotback man-to-man.

- Strong side linebacker takes tight end.

- Weak side linebacker (shown shifted inside) has single set back.

- Example shows only one possible coverage; with 5-man secondary many other combinations of assignments can be used, which makes reading defense difficult for offense.

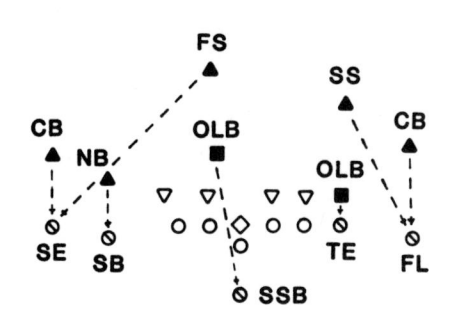

Nickel Defense (Man-to-Man vs. 3 WRs)

Zone Defenses

Strong Side Zone (4 Under, 3 Deep)

- This is a basic zone defense. Upon recognizing pass:

    Strong side cornerback covers short zone.

    Weak side cornerback, free safety, and strong safety all rotate toward strong side into 3-deep zone.

    Linebackers rotate away from strong side into 3 remaining short zones.

- Rotation favors coverage of receivers on strong side.

- The 4 underneath or short zones overlap the 6 basic short areas discussed previously; essentially, the middle linebacker and strong side linebacker are each covering the hook and curl zones on their sides, while the strong side cornerback and weak side linebacker cover the flats.

- Note that the strong side cornerback lines up almost in the strong side short zone as

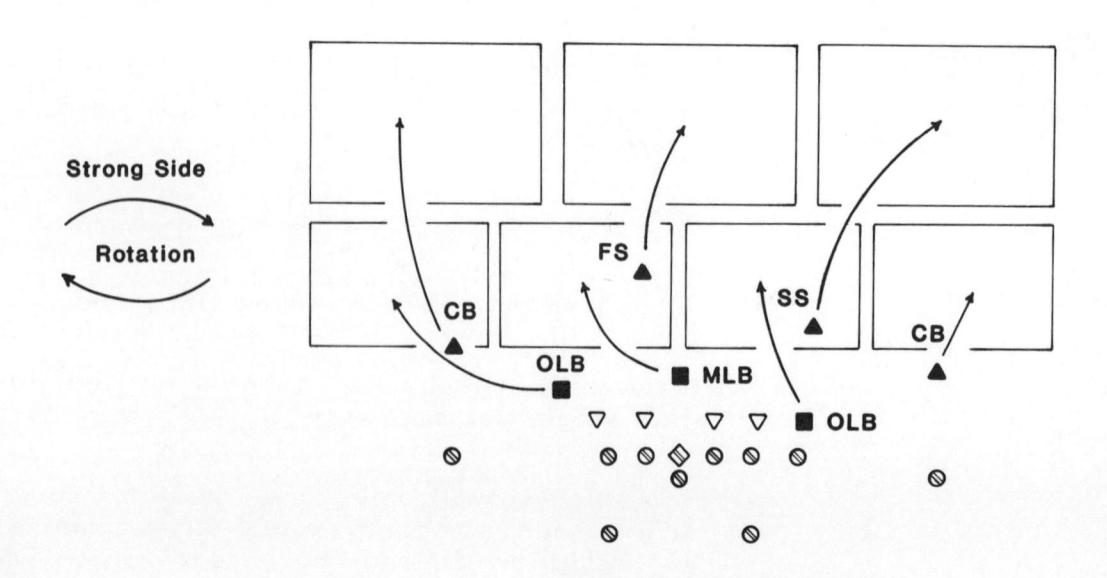

Strong Side Zone

compared with the distance the weak side linebacker has to cover to get into the weak side short zone.

- The strong side cornerback has containment responsibility. He is the force man on any end run that might develop to that side.

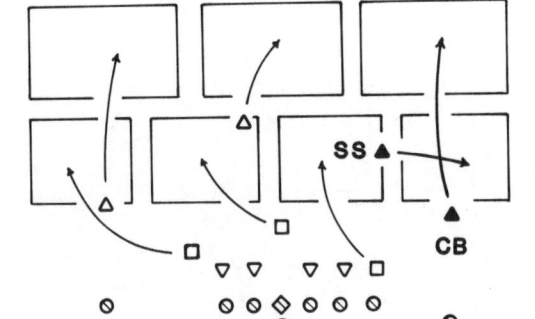

Strong Side Inverted Zone

- Same as above except strong safety and strong side cornerback switch.
- Strong safety takes <u>short</u> strong side zone.
- Cornerback takes <u>deep</u> strong side zone.
- Strong safety now has containment responsibility on that side.
- Sometimes called "strong safety X zone" because of crossing paths of strong safety and cornerback.

Strong Side Inverted Zone

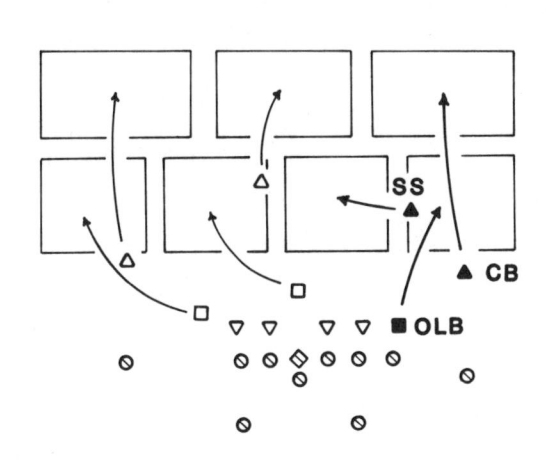

Strong Side Linebacker Zone

- Same as above except strong side linebacker now has strong side short zone.
- Linebacker still has to chuck tight end to prevent quick release.
- Strong safety takes inside short zone.
- Cornerback covers strong side deep zone.
- Strong side linebacker has force responsibility on outside.
- This zone coverage and the inverted zone above provide change-ups in the basic strong side rotating zone defense.
- It is important to make coverage difficult for quarterback and receivers to read; all pass coverages have strong spots and weak spots; moving them around prevents the offense from easily exploiting the defense.
- For example, this strong side linebacker zone defense is weak against short to intermediate

Strong Side Linebacker Zone

out routes by the flanker — the cornerback is retreating deep and the strong side linebacker has to get out to the flat; but this defense is strong against inside routes by the flanker and short routes by the tight end.

Weak Side Zone

- Rotation is now toward weak side; favors coverage of receivers on weak side.

- Weak side cornerback is very close to his weak side short zone as compared with distance strong side linebacker must cover to get into strong side short zone.

- Variations of the weak side rotating zone are similar to the inverted and linebacker variations of the strong side zone above.

Weak Side Zone

Double Zone (5 Under, 2 Deep)

- Cornerbacks take the 2 outer short zones.

- Linebackers cover the 3 inside short zones.

- Safeties are responsible for the 2 deep zones.

- Provides for double coverage of wide receivers (short and deep); this defense is sometimes called the double-double zone.

- With 5 short zones, the double sets up a picket line at about 10-15 yards deep to break up passes and stop runs to either side.

- Cornerbacks can come up to the line and chuck wide receivers to slow them down (cornerbacks know that the safeties will pick up deep).

- One weakness is the deep middle.

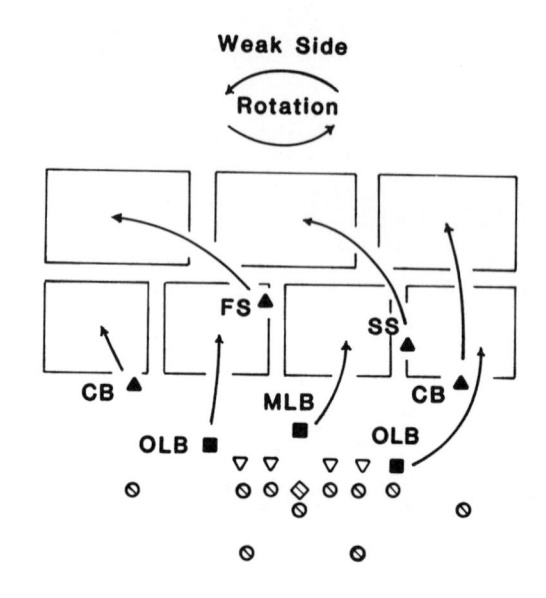

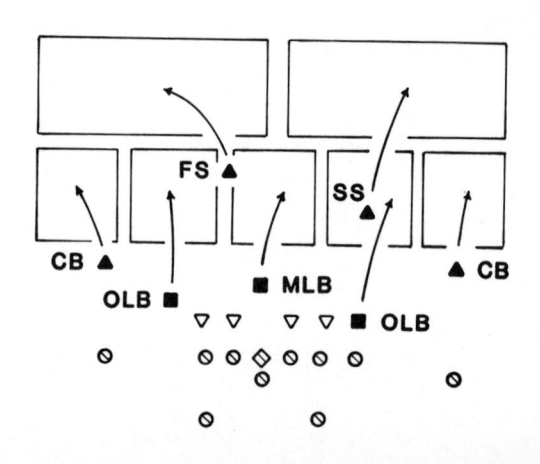

Double Zone

5-Under, 3-Deep Strong Side Zone (3-4 Defense)

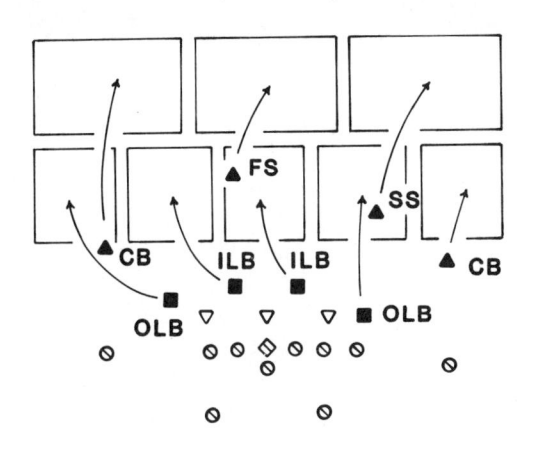

- This 8-man zone coverage is made possible by use of only 3 down linemen.

- Thus, this is one possible coverage out of a 3-4 defense.

- 8 zones provide a strong defense against passes short and long, as well as possible runs.

- But the trade-off is a reduced pass rush which can give the quarterback and receivers their most precious commodity against any pass defense — time.

5-3 Strong Side Zone

Combination Coverages

Man Under a 2-Deep Zone (Nickel Defense vs. 3 Wide Receivers)

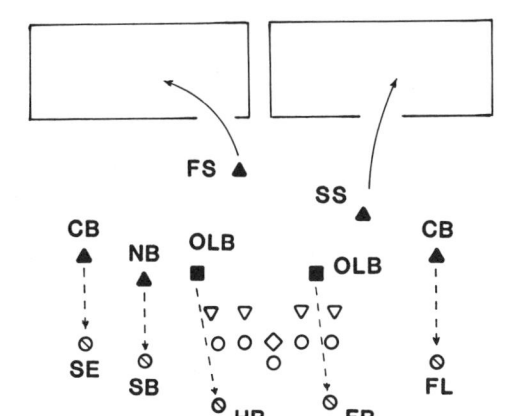

- This coverage is part zone and part man-to-man.

- Free safety and strong safety cover 2 deep zones.

- Cornerbacks cover split end and flanker man-to-man wherever they go.

- Nickel back does same versus the slotback.

- Right outside linebacker covers halfback if he releases; otherwise, linebacker drops to curl zone on his side.

- Left outside linebacker covers fullback if he releases; otherwise, linebacker drops to hook zone on his side.

Man Under a 2-Deep Zone (Nickel vs. 3 WRs)

81

Mombo Coverage
(Nickel Defense)

- Combination coverage of two defenders on one receiver is called a "combo"; this can be inside/outside or short/deep.

- "Mombo" refers to combination coverage in the middle (a combo in the middle is a mombo).

- In most combination coverages, the defenders' assignments are dependent upon what route the receiver runs.

- The example focuses on the tight end:

  - if the tight end breaks <u>outside</u>, the nickel back and strong safety cover him short/deep and the free safety plays a deep middle zone;

  - if the tight end goes <u>inside</u>, the nickel back and free safety cover him short/deep and the strong safety takes the deep middle area;

  - the cornerbacks cover the wide receivers and the linebackers take the running backs.

**Mombo Coverage
(Nickel Defense)**

Zone with Designated Chaser
(Nickel Defense)

- When the offense has a receiver who is particularly difficult to defend against, the defense may assign one player to cover him wherever he goes.

- The remaining defenders are used in zone coverage; this gives the man-to-man defender help over most of the field.

- In the example, the weak side cornerback is the chaser versus the split end, the remaining defenders go into a 4-under, 2-deep zone.

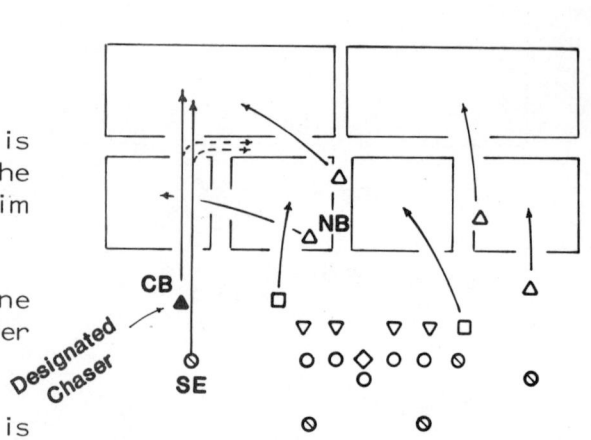

**Zone with Designated Chaser
(Nickel Defense)**

CHAPTER 5

PASSING ATTACKS

This short chapter supplements the preceding one as it relates to pass plays. The discussion considers both offensive and defensive passing strategies together. More specifically, it deals with some offensive maneuvers used to counter certain common pass defenses.

[Returning to the discussion between Joe and the defensive coordinator.]

Throw Away from Rotation

F. With all the possible patterns and defensive coverages, which pass plays are good against which defenses? For example, I realize that against man-to-man coverage the receivers have to work free from the man guarding them. But what are some ways of attacking the zone concepts used?

C. Well, why don't we look at a couple. Suppose I tell you that the defense will be in a normal strong side zone. What would be a good passing strategy?

F. Let's see. There are 2 receivers, the flanker and the tight end, to the strong side. Why not send them up the sideline in some kind of combination pattern?

C. Bad theory. In a strong side zone, look at where the defensive backs are heading.

F. Basically, toward the strong side, to cover the 3 deep zones and the short zone on the strong side.

C. And where are the linebackers heading?

F. They are all drifting toward the weak side. Some have farther to go to get into their zones.

C. Especially that weak side linebacker. Remember, I pointed that out before. He has to get out to his short zone fast. And he can't cheat by lining up wider before the snap to shorten the distance, because he'd tip the coverage.

If the free safety shades toward the strong side, there are 3 defensive backs and 1 linebacker on the strong side of the pass coverage but only 1 defensive back and 2 linebackers on the weak side.

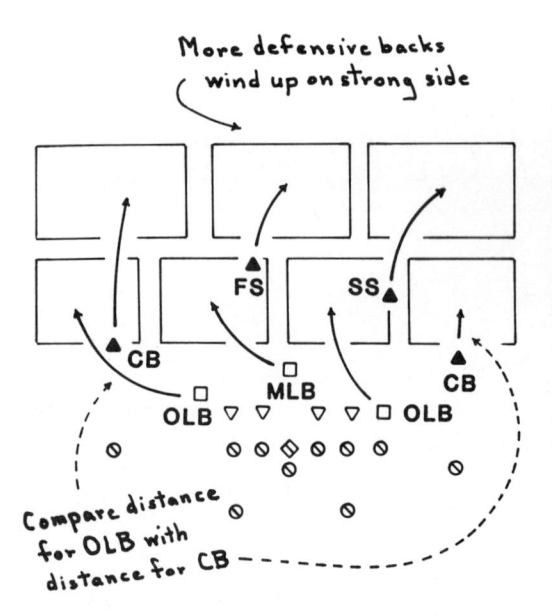

Strong Side Zone

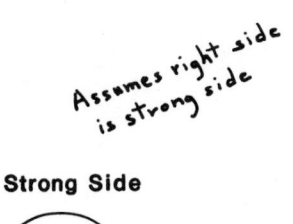

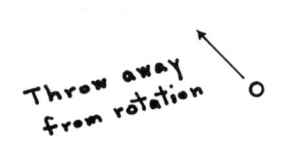

Strong Side Rotation

Assumes right side is strong side

Throw away from rotation

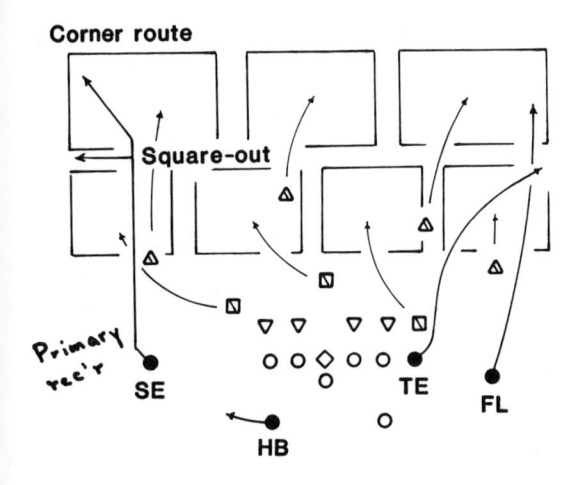

Alternate Weak Side Pass Routes

Corner route
Square-out
Primary rec'r
SE TE FL
HB

Seams Between Zones

Seams

F. And defensive backs are faster, better at pass coverage.

C. That's their specialty.

F. It sounds like the pass should be to the weak side.

C. That's rule No. 1. <u>Throw away from the direction of the rotation.</u> If it's a strong side zone, throw to the weak side. If it's a weak side zone, pass to the strong side.

By rule, I don't mean things have to be done that way. It's more of a generalization. The intrinsic weaknesses are away from the rotation.

F. How about a square-out against the weak side linebacker or a corner route against the retreating weak side cornerback?

C. They might work. However, going deep against a zone is very difficult. That's what they are designed to stop. But if you are going to try, probably the best place is the deep corner away from the rotation.

F. Do you ever throw toward the rotation?

C. Like I said, we're dealing with generalizations here. There are exceptions to everything. Teams like to do different things. For instance, if the flanker gets off the line without being bumped and the strong safety is a little slow in reaching that deep outside zone, the flanker may get open on a deep corner route.

Stretching Zones

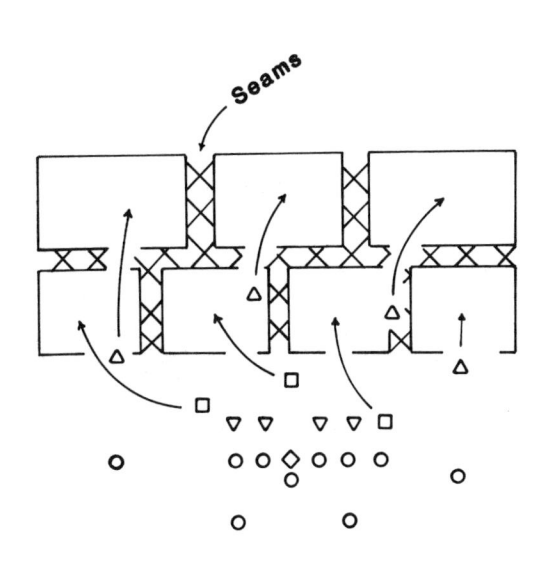

F. What about the "seams" we always hear about? Those are the areas between the zones of the different defenders aren't they?

C. Yeah, I drew the zones as nice little rectangles. They aren't always that neat or symmetrical. If one guy is faster than another, effectively his zone is larger than the other guy's. Depending on how the play develops, one defender may have to hold up longer before he drops, so his zone shrinks a little and the adjacent zone gets larger.

F. But basically against zone coverage you try to throw into the seams.

C. You do more than that. First, you try to enlarge them. This is done by stretching zones horizontally (from sideline to sideline) or vertically (from short to deep).

To stretch them horizontally you run receivers to the edges of the zones which are about the same distance downfield. The defenders are playing zone but they gravitate toward the man in their respective areas. As a result, the zones get pulled out of shape and at least some of the seams have to get bigger.

To stretch them vertically you do the same thing, except the pass pattern takes the receivers varying distances downfield. In other words, the receivers are spread out up and down, rather than across, the field.

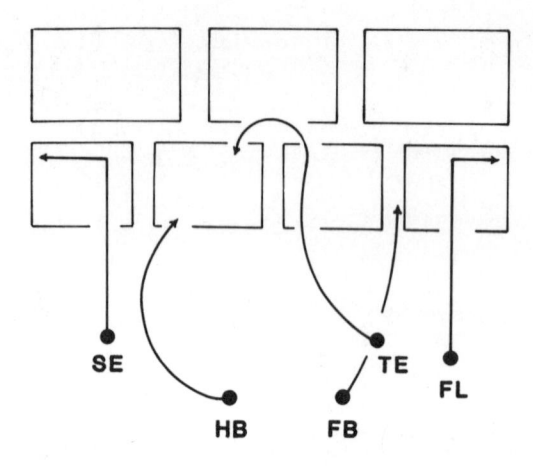

Stretching Zones Horizontally

Flooding Zones

C. Another way to attack zone coverage is to use a flood pattern.

F. I've heard of that. It sounds like sending several receivers into a particular zone to overwhelm the defender.

C. That's right. Assume the defense uses a weak side zone. So you want to throw away from it to the strong side. You could send the flanker on a fly pattern to drive the strong side cornerback deep. Then flood the strong side short zone by having the tight end run an out pattern to the back of the zone and the fullback swing out to the front of the zone.

The general rule from a defensive standpoint is that the defender plays the deepest receiver in his zone. That's in keeping with the theory of zone defense — to stop the long pass while possibly giving up some short completions.

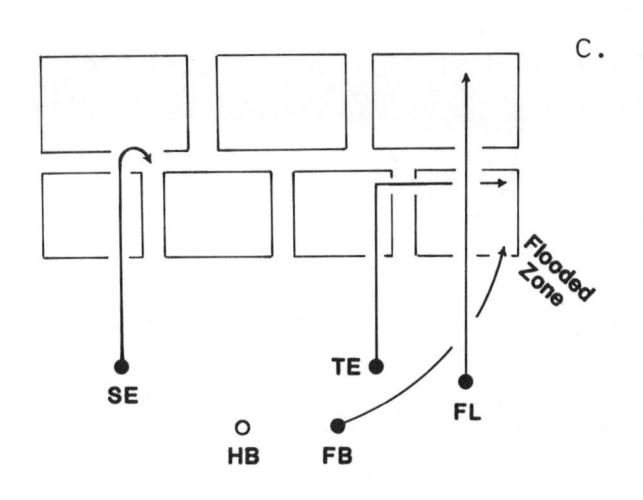

Flooding Zone

F. So the strong side linebacker will defend against the tight end.

C. Well, he's playing a short zone, not a deep one. In a short zone his assignment is to position himself to stop any pass in his area. Only when the ball is thrown does he go to the intended receiver.

That's the theory, but in practice the defender has to decide on a given play, based on how it's developing, when to abandon the zone and play a man. By flooding the zone, you're trying to force him to decide, or else play neutral, <u>away</u> from both.

The quarterback keys the strong side linebacker. If he goes toward the tight end, the quarterback throws to the fullback; if the linebacker favors the fullback, the pass goes to the tight end.

Using a Slot

C. You said you discussed formations with two of the other coaches. So what's a good formation to use against a zone coverage?

F. Hmm.... I'm drawing a blank. I must admit it takes a little time to digest some of this.

C. How about a slot formation?

F. Yeah, that's right — now it's coming back. I was told that a slot is good against a zone and to avoid double coverage. Based on what we've just discussed, I suppose a slot sets up a flood pattern rather well.

C. That's right. Or at least it sets up a good combination pattern. The split end will run an out and the slotback will run an in or vice versa. Or one may run a clearing route and the other will cut underneath (into the area cleared out).

On the other hand, a slotback sometimes gets double coverage inside/outside by the safeties. This can result in single man-to-man coverage on the split end and tight end (or flanker if three wide receivers are used).

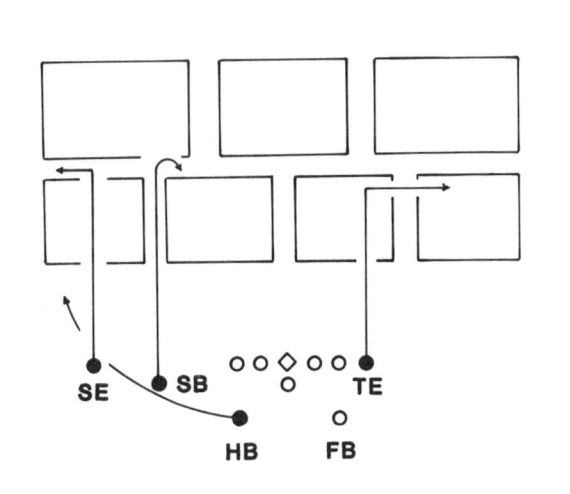

Slot vs. Zone Defense

A double slot formation is sometimes used against a man-to-man defense. Instead of 1 slotback there are 2. A cornerback might cover the inside slot man and a nickel back would take the outside slotback. If you leave the tight end in on the other side, the strong safety has to provide run support as well as respect the pass since he's the only one deep over there.

F. What about the 3 defensive backs on the split end and 2 slotbacks?

C. The strength of the double slot is that it sets up good combination patterns. Suppose you have the split end run a post, so he cuts toward the middle. Then you have the outside slot man run a flag, so his path will cross that of the split end. Finally, as these two are heading deep, the inside slotback cuts across both their paths. It's kind of like a busy street corner out there with everybody going different ways. If all 3 receivers run tight, disciplined routes, they make it very difficult for the defenders to stick close to their man. There's a good chance at least one receiver will come through with a step on the defender.

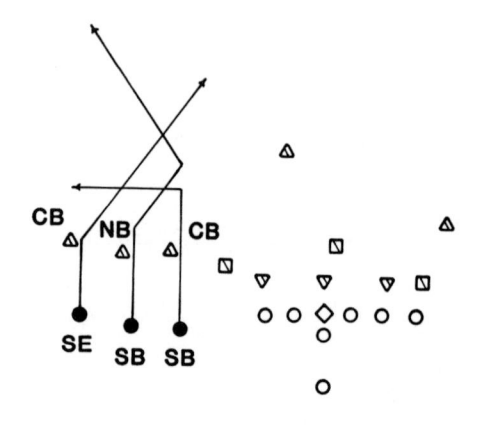

Double Slot

F. Is that a pick play?

C. A pick occurs when a receiver screens off a defender to take him out of the play. Downfield blocking is illegal on a pass play. So the officials will call pass interference if a receiver makes any contact that will knock a defender out of his effort to cover another receiver.

To work a "legal" pick play, the receivers have to avoid contacting the defenders. They must run precise routes and hope the defenders get in each other's way, become momentarily confused by the pattern, or are somehow impeded by the receivers crossing closely together.

A pick is a tough call for an official unless he's looking right at it. And the closer you run these tight combinations, the greater the risk of a penalty.

Controlling Linebackers

F. How do running plays affect a zone coverage?

C. That's an important aspect. The linebackers are really the key. If they drop off too fast to get into their zones, the defense against the run will really suffer. At the same time, what do you think the offense wants the linebackers to do on a pass play?

F. I'm not sure I follow.

C. Well, they want the linebackers to do the opposite. In other words, they don't want the linebackers to take their drops. They want to hold those linebackers up near the line as long as they can. So they use play action. Here's where good fake handoffs and fake runs into the line help. Just holding the backers momentarily may delay zone coverage enough to allow a receiver to get free.

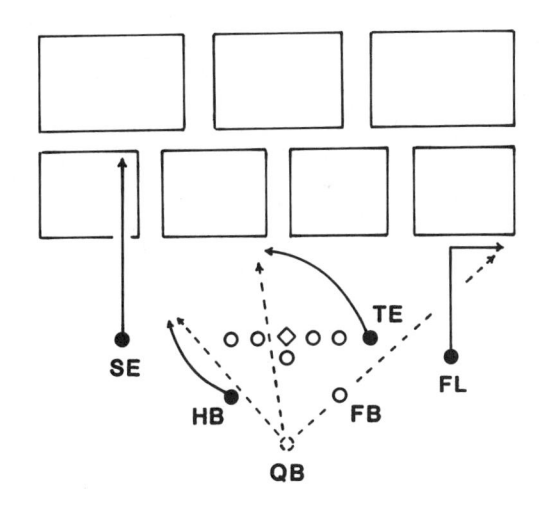

Throwing Underneath

F. What if you have trouble holding the linebackers in?

C. Then you may have to be patient and keep working to get someone open.

You take what they give you. If they are dropping off fast, you throw underneath the short zones and make them tackle your receiver. Linebackers drop about 12-15 yards for short zones, so there is room to pick up short yardage.

A good short passing attack does more than just cope with the zone. If you're successful, you will keep a drive going. Pretty soon they have to come up, and then openings start appearing downfield.

Throwing Underneath

Which Way to Rotate?

F. How does the defense determine which way to rotate?

C. It depends on the situation. Who are the best receivers and how are they lining up? What type of routes do they run? What down is it? How far do they have to go? What's the score? Is the wind at their backs?

Similar considerations are involved in whom to double cover in a man-to-man or combination defense. The direction of the rotation must take into account the run possibilities too. Rotation affects how run support is handled. If there's a strong possibility that they may run weak side, you may rotate that way to do a better job containing the run. And then too, you have to change up. You can't keep showing the same defense. The direction of rotation is one of the variables.

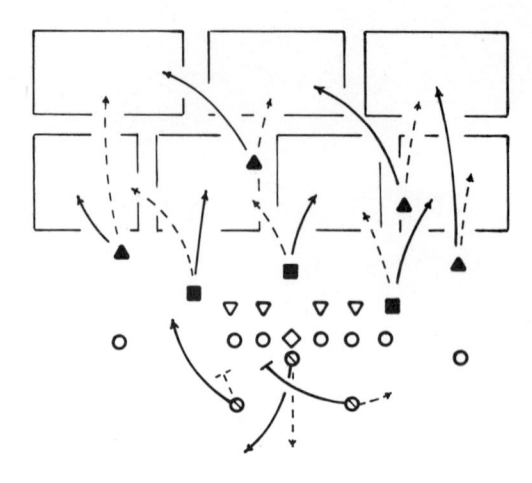

Having said all that, the direction of rotation can be keyed to certain action taken by the offense. For example:

- if quarterback drops back:
    rotate toward strong side
- if receiver goes in motion:
    rotate toward motion
- if quarterback rolls out:
    rotate toward roll
- if backfield flows to one side:
    rotate toward flow.

—— Play Action
---- Dropback

Direction of Rotation

Throw Away from Free Safety

F. We've talked a lot about attacking zone coverage. What about man-to-man?

C. Man-to-man basically involves match-ups. Try to get a mismatch in your favor — a possession type (man with good moves) versus someone inexperienced, fast versus slow, tall versus short, whatever. But there's more to it. There's double coverage, combos, mombos, and other things you still have to deal with.

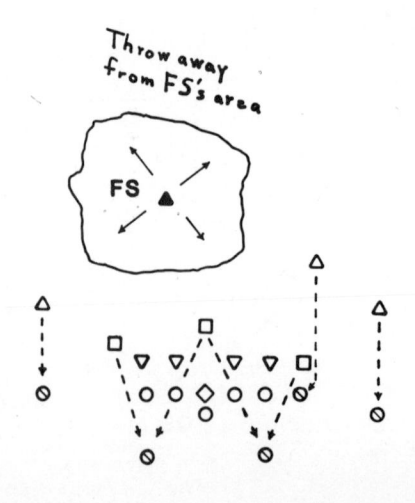

Throw away from FS's area

Passing vs. Man-to-Man

For instance, in basic man-to-man, the free safety is free. That means you want to throw to someone away from the free safety's area if you can, so there's only one defender involved and not two.

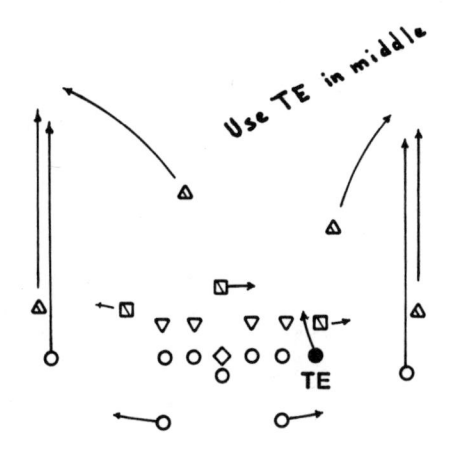

Tight End vs. Double Coverage

F. What about when the free safety is doubling with a cornerback on one of the receivers?

C. And suppose the strong safety is doubling with the other cornerback on someone else. That means each wide receiver is being covered by two defenders. If both receivers stay on the outside that leaves the middle relatively clear. That's why a fast tight end who can catch is such an asset. He'll be man-for-man against one of the linebackers, and have a good chance to get open. The running backs can help by running routes to control the other linebackers.

Attack Middle vs. Double Coverage of WRs

Offensive Line's Role

F. I think I'm reaching the saturation point. I'd like to let this sink in.

C. Sure. Anything sounds complicated when you start delving into it. Just try to grasp the main points, like what the individual offensive linemen try to do in the three running plays we started with, and how the linebackers and defensive backs work together on zone coverage. And things like how they use change-ups to make it hard for the offense to see what coverage the defense is using.

Once you understand most of the basic maneuvers and a few of the details, you'll start to get a feel for the whole thing. That's when football becomes interesting from a strategic standpoint.

Finally, note that we have talked at length about just a few aspects. For example, we haven't dealt with one of the most important factors in a passing attack — the offensive line. Give me a line that can consistently hold off a pass rush for about 4.0 seconds and I'll put an average pro quarterback in the Hall of Fame. Given time to throw, any defense can be beaten. Just start timing the protection a quarterback gets in any game. If it's much longer than 3.5 seconds, then the quarterback is going to do well. If it's much less than 3.0 seconds, then that quarterback is in real trouble regardless of who he is.

CHAPTER 6

THE PLAYERS

This chapter deals with the players, position by position. It covers some of the responsibilities, problems, and techniques of each. The length of treatment varies from position to position, and the items covered are representative, not all-inclusive. Most of the items concern general aspects, while others involve minor details. The intent is to give a few insights into the demands of the different positions and what individual players must cope with.

Your Thoughts

We'll start by letting you indicate what you think about the different positions. Below are two columns. You know the rules. Match each characteristic or quality listed in the second column with the position in the first column it is most closely associated with. Each characteristic in the second column can be used only once.

____	Offensive linemen	1. Confidence
____	Running backs	2. Form
____	Wide receivers	3. Split personality
____	Tight ends	4. Concentration
____	Quarterbacks	5. Aggression
____	Defensive linemen	6. Vision
____	Linebackers	7. Rhythm
____	Cornerbacks	8. Discipline
____	Safeties	9. Instinct
____	Kickers	10. Range
____	Punters	11. Reaction

Our (Suggested) Answers

Before we give you the answers, we know you may not agree with some of them. And several could apply to more than one position. Remember, the purpose of the chapter is to provide insights to better evaluate, appreciate, maybe tolerate, the players as you watch them.

Offensive linemen	–	Discipline (8)
Running backs	–	Instinct (9)
Wide receivers	–	Concentration (4)
Tight ends	–	Split personality (3)
Quarterbacks	–	Vision (6)
Defensive linemen	–	Aggression (5)
Linebackers	–	Reaction (11)
Cornerbacks	–	Confidence (1)
Safeties	–	Range (10)
Kickers	–	Rhythm (7)
Punters	–	Form (2)

Offensive Linemen

The Invisible Men

Picture yourself on the 6-yard line. It's the end of a long, hard, emotional game. You are the right guard. The packed stadium has just erupted. The tension of the last five minutes has been broken. The fans are wild. You and the right tackle have just opened a good hole for the star halfback to score the winning TD. Pandemonium reigns. Are they cheering for you? Of course not. They're cheering for the halfback — he did it.

Ninety percent of the fans don't even know which hole he went through. On TV they will make a nice comment about the blocking during the replay. Then they'll show four different angles of the halfback crossing the goal line and strutting his victory stuff. Welcome to the offensive line.

The offensive linemen get more attention than they used to. But not a lot. Before about 60,000 fans and national TV, they toil in relative obscurity. They recognize that fact. And the linemen don't seem to begrudge the quarterbacks, running backs, and receivers all the fanfare they get. It's something linemen live with.

They can't star individually. Their success is based on teamwork. Their job is to open a hole for the runner and protect the passer — truly team efforts. Just look at the published statistics. There aren't any for the offensive linemen. Nothing like passing percentage, yards gained, interceptions, tackles, field goals. The number of sacks allowed pertains to the offensive line, but it's based on their performance as a group.

Technique & Discipline

Technique is important. A well-executed play, a good gain, is premised on <u>every</u> lineman carrying out his responsibility; four out of five is not good enough. This requires perfect timing, coordinated blocking, leverage, angles — in short, overall precision as a unit. The offensive line's intrinsic advantage is two-fold: (1) they know where the play is going, and (2) when it will begin. Their attack must utilize this advantage.

Contrast this with the defense. They react. They rely on speed, power, and agility to counterattack. Defenders can use their hands — and they do — to grab, pull, push. The offense can't (are not supposed to) use their hands except to push off pass rushers. (That's why you can tell the offensive linemen from the defensive linemen by their uniforms — the offensive linemen have tight-fitting jerseys with short sleeves so there's less to grab.) Thus, in man-to-man confrontations the defender has the advantage. The offensive lineman must fight him off, turn him, block him within the rules. With all the pushing and shoving and heated emotions the offensive linemen must exercise control.

So discipline is one of the main attributes of this group. They must be methodical, precise, with good technique. Offensive linemen are expected to stay cool. Emotional highs work better on defense.

Hitters Too

At the same time the offensive line is no place for cautious play. To gain control of the line they

> **Just look at the published statistics. There aren't any for the offensive linemen.**

have to be quick, explosive, strong, and tough. It's imperative they come off the line hard and fast. In fact, some recent lists of the NFL's hardest hitters have included a few offensive linemen. That's right, offensive linemen. True, they don't tackle, and pass blocking is mainly a retreating affair. But when a running play is called they can even up the score for all the abuse they take on passing downs. The offensive line can strike out and really apply those blocks. They can deliver a blow with their forearms and shoulders, and even slide a helmet up under an opponent's chin.

Centers

The Snap

The first responsibility of the center is obviously the snap. The snap is taken for granted and probably should be. But when you stop and think about it, centering the ball is somewhat odd. There's the center in position, the ball in hand (some use both hands), legs spread (not too wide for mobility to start his charge), with the back of the quarterback's hands spread under the center's butt (pressing against the buttocks so the center knows where to hike). If this were a new sport, there probably would be some suggestions about starting play a different way.

In any case, the center is a blocker as well as the snapper. He must start his charge as he snaps. If you watch closely, you'll see his back bow and his body start moving forward while snapping the ball back. Moreover, he has to pop it right into the quarterback's hands with a slight turn so the laces are under the quarterback's fingers — same place every time. It is up to the quarterback to "ride" slightly with the center's movement until he has a firm grasp of the ball.

... the center controls the timing for the entire line. He can't anticipate the quarterback's call.

Note that the center controls the timing for the entire line. He can't anticipate the quarterback's call. The defense goes when the ball moves, whereas the offensive line goes on the call. So if the center is half a count early, the defensive line is already coming.

On pass plays, the center can't drop back immediately. Rather, he takes a short step forward to allow completion of the exchange and to enable the quarterback to start his drop first.

Line Calls & Blocking

The center gives most of the line calls. If the defensive alignment makes the planned blocking scheme difficult, he calls out adjustments. This could involve changing a particular block or switching assignments between two linemen. He has to do this loud enough for the entire line to hear him even though all are not affected, to avoid tipping the play. The job is a lot harder with the increased emphasis on stunts and blitzes. He has to stay calm when the defense starts jumping around before the snap and make the right adjustments so each defender is picked up.

After centering, what does he do? Against an even defense his usual responsibility is the middle linebacker who is 2 to 3 yards off the line. Given that distance and the middle linebacker's intent to stay clear of blockers (to allow pursuit), the center has to be quick. Mainly, he tries to get in the way, cutting the middle linebacker off however he can. If the block doesn't look good, that's not important.

The real challenge is against an odd defensive alignment. Now there is a big, tough nose tackle directly over him. This makes things much rougher on the center. He not only has to be quick, he has to be strong. This isn't a linebacker breathing in his face, it's a lineman hand-picked on the basis of his strength and toughness. So the center has to snap and boom — get into the block strong, with good balance. Otherwise, the nose man can jerk the center to one side and bull his way past, or just play off the block and go for the tackle. Because this is asking a bit much of the center, he often gets help from a guard in blocking the nose man.

Guards

Strength with Speed

The offensive guard executes the greatest variety of blocks. He zone blocks, cross blocks, fold blocks, pass blocks, pulls to trap, and pulls to lead plays around end. Because of his inside position a guard must have strength and size. And to pull outside and lead plays he needs some speed

> (The center) has to . . . make the right adjustments so each defender is picked up.

or he won't make it down the line and around the corner before the runner gets there.

Due to all the different techniques required of the guard, his stance is important. Mention stance and people start to yawn. But on the front line, a good stance is what positions the man for that initial blast that determines who controls the line. In addition, the guard may go forward, back, to one side, pull flat (along the line) or deep (start back at 45 degrees), and he can't tip the play. So he needs great mobility to come out of that stance and move quickly.

Pulling

When a guard pulls he mentally shifts his weight before the snap. On the count he has to get out of the stance fast. The lead step is with the foot toward the pull. To help him turn out, he jerks his lead arm back and parallel to the ground. Then it's get the head around and stay low as he starts down the line.

On a short trap, the guard goes slightly into the line, right on the tail of the center. On a long trap he needs more depth so he angles back away from the line. He has to do this because the lineman he's trapping is farther away and has more time to penetrate and/or react to the trap. On a sweep, the back guard should be at least a yard behind the line after he pulls out so he won't get caught up in the front side blocking.

Assignments

Versus a 4-3 defense, the guard works against a strong, quick defensive tackle. Versus a 3-4 defense he goes out and blocks a linebacker or angle blocks on the nose tackle or defensive end. When blocking a linebacker it's more important to drive him back than to try to get position and turn him one way or the other. But he still has to be quick off the line or that linebacker will be gone.

On pass blocking, the guards form the front of the pocket. They can retreat 3 to 4 yards, but they have to stop the rush there. Any farther and the quarterback, who sets at 7 to 9 yards back, won't be able to step up if pressure on the outside from the defensive ends gets too great. In addition,

When blocking a linebacker it's more important to drive him back than to ... get position and turn him ....

the deeper the guards drop, the harder it is for the quarterback to see around them. The guards usually get help from the center (if uncovered) with their pass blocking.

A guard is often right in the middle of a defensive line stunt. He has to see what's happening and react right away. The same for a blitz. The shortest route to the passer is through his area. He has to pick up the right man right away.

Offensive Tackles

Slower But Taller

Compared with a guard, an offensive tackle stays at his home position more. His run blocking is less complicated — mainly straight ahead or on an angle. Thus speed is less of a requirement than size and strength. For example, he has the key block in the off-tackle play. He has to move that defensive end. At the same time, very few linemen in the NFL can dominate their opponents. They have to learn how to play the angles and use the right techniques. Height is also an asset for an offensive tackle. The defensive ends they oppose are usually tall and like to grab and jerk a lot. A tall offensive tackle is harder for an end to unbalance since the tackle has more leverage to resist the pulling.

Pass Blocking

On pass blocking the tackles form the sides of the passing pocket. Here's where they need some agility to go along with their size. Being on the outside the defensive end has more room to operate in than a defensive tackle. Consequently, the end can use more moves on the blocker. The offensive tackle has to be agile enough to outmaneuver the end. He should honor all inside fakes and ignore all outside ones. The tackle respects the inside moves more because they are aimed at the direct route to the passer. On these he has to get his head in front and drive the defender down the line of scrimmage (toward the center). On an outside move the tackle can wait for the defensive end to commit to the outside and then use a momentum block to ride the end wide of the quarterback.

> (The tackle) should honor all inside fakes and ignore all outside ones.

Pass Blocking

Pass blocking is among the most difficult techniques in football. Essentially, the goal is to hold off the pass rush for about 3.5 seconds. Not long if it weren't for the size and ferocity of the charging opponents.

The offensive lineman has to keep his man out but without aggressive force. He can't fire out at his opponent. That's because defenders don't try to run over offensive linemen. If you watch, you'll see that pass rushers use power and finesse to get <u>by</u> the offensive linemen. If a defensive lineman catches a blocker just slightly off balance, he'll grab, pull that blocker to one side, and charge into the backfield. So pass blockers don't attack, they let the defenders come to them.

The defensive linemen can come straight ahead, to the inside, or to the outside. Blocking the latter two approaches was mentioned in the offensive tackle section. The straight rush is the most difficult to handle because there is no angle. The offensive lineman battles in retreat. He will drop back a step or two, set, and absorb the charge by striking at the defender's numbers with his fists and forehead (front of helmet). Then he rips upward into the chin area with his helmet and fists, finally pushing off while pumping his legs for balance and moving his arms to keep free of the defender's grasp. Foot speed is important. Overextension is the cardinal sin. Keep the butt sunk and legs coiled. Don't drop the head.

He steps back again, sets, absorbs the charge, and hopes to keep this up for 3.5 seconds. At least that's the theory. Now that pass blockers can open their hands and extend their arms, they push more. And pass rushers don't just ram, ram, ram straight ahead. They maneuver. Straight, then inside or outside, and back again. That's why balance is so important. One of the common criticisms of rookie linemen is they leave their feet too soon. Why do they go down? They've been outmaneuvered.

Blocking

Run Blocking

Just brief comments on some of the different kinds of blocks employed. A few have been mentioned previously. In case you've never thrown a block, the elements of the shoulder block are summarized.

Shoulder Block (Basic Block)

Approach — Normally 1 or 2 short steps to get momentum and be in position.

— If the defensive man is right over the offensive lineman, that lineman may have to lunge out; just come right out of his stance without moving his legs (the alternative is a short step back and then a step forward).

— On the step before impact, cock the striking shoulder back.

Contact — Explode into defender. Don't block at him, block thru him.

— Hit the <u>middle</u> of the man with the forehead (this is to make sure the defender doesn't evade the block); just as contact is being made, slide the head to the side and let the shoulder do the work.

- The hit is actually with the shoulder, upper arm, forearm, and fist (arm is bent at elbow with fist in front of chest).
- Impact has to be strong enough to stop the opponent's charge; blocker drives upward and thru, creating a lifting action to help stand his man up.
- Note: Introduction of the face mask greatly improved blocking by allowing blockers to keep their heads up and so avoid missing defenders.

Follow Thru
- Don't stop. Defender will recover and react. Stick and stay (hit and stay with him).
- The blocker uses short driving steps to maintain the block and move the defender as needed.
- The shoulder block is good against a defender holding his ground since he has little momentum. It is not so good against a defender charging in or moving laterally and hand fighting to string out the play.

Scramble Block (Crab, Cutoff)

This one is easy to spot — the blocker is on his hands and knees. Basically, the blocker tries to get his head, shoulder, and arm past the defender as he contacts the defender's legs with his thigh. Then he goes on all fours and crablike pushes himself sideways into the defender. This block is good for when the ball carrier is going to the other side. It ties up the man, keeps him away from the play.

Cut Block

With this block the offensive player cuts a defender's legs out from under him with his shoulder. It is often used by a smaller blocker against a big defensive lineman.

Hook Block

The hook block is executed on a defender to prevent outside pursuit on an end run. The offensive lineman may turn sideways and hit with his outside shoulder. Or he may swing into a reverse block with his feet behind the defender and head facing back toward the backfield.

Kick Out

This involves driving a cornerback or linebacker out toward the sideline on an end run so the running back can cut behind and upfield. (Example: The pulling guard kicks out the force man on a sweep.)

Double-Team

A double-team employs two blockers against one defender, usually right at the point of attack. One blocker is the post man and the other is the drive man. The post man neutralizes the defender's charge and the drive man turns him to one side.

Cross Block

Two adjacent linemen switch blocking assignments against the two defensive linemen directly over them. The man outside goes first and blocks down on the inside defender. The other offensive lineman takes a slight drop step and then drives right behind his teammate and out on the other defender. This block can sometimes provide better angles and confuse the defenders' keys.

Fold Block

Similar to a cross block, the fold block is used against a lineman and a linebacker — that is, one of the defenders is off the line. The man blocking the lineman goes first. The other offensive lineman then slides laterally (folds) behind him to head for the linebacker. Because the linebacker is off the line, the fold block takes longer than a cross block.

Influence Block

This consists of blocking action intended to mislead the defense. The classic example actually involves no block at all: a guard pulls to the outside as if to lead a sweep. The intent is that the defensive tackle or linebacker will also break to the outside and then the running back cuts into the vacant hole.

Running Backs

Instinct

Running backs do what they do mainly by instinct. No one coaches great runners on how to make great runs. The runners can't anticipate how a play is going to develop, where all the defenders will be. When they get the ball, they just run with it. Some can't even explain everything they did. Parts are simply a blur in the memory.

Minimum Requirements

When you start listing the necessary qualities, and there are many, a <u>quick start</u> is one. Two steps are about all the good ones need to get up to speed. It's essential not only for getting off the mark and into a hole, but after cutting, twisting, or slowing. Bursts of speed are more important than being able to outrun everybody once the back gets going. Still, pure speed is a nice optional accessory. It's the stuff breakaways are made of.

The ability to see what's happening and decide on the best hole is another requisite. The time frame for this is instantaneous, and it's done on a dead run. The back has to survey an area, find the openings, check the angles his blockers have, judge the best route, and go for it right then. No second thoughts. The good backs do this and are right consistently.

Strength is a requirement. Strong not only in the sense of being a powerful runner, but also in terms of durability. That is, being able to absorb the physical pounding a running back receives. Playing running back isn't a passive thing — run with the ball and go down when they tackle you. The good backs dish out a lot of punishment. When cornered they explode into would-be tacklers, or shove a stiff arm to the face. That way the defender is less likely to get a good shot, and more likely to share in the suffering. And there is a lot of suffering. Every time a back carries the ball, he's hit — usually by several players, usually all bigger.

Toughness and determination are intangibles that can't be measured. But these qualities are apparent to coaches and fans alike. Those who possess them slam into the line. They don't go down when they should. They strain for that extra yard. They don't fumble. They make something out of nothing. When a back like that walks off the field, you don't say he's relying on his physical skills.

> **Bursts of speed are more important than being able to outrun everybody once the back gets going.**

Stance & Start

A running back in a 3-point stance places only his fingertips on the ground. He can't put too much weight on the down hand. He has to move out fast in different directions, not just forward. And the stance should be essentially the same regardless of the play to avoid tipping off the defense.

The running back goes on the quarterback's call. If the quarterback uses a rhythmic cadence, the running back can anticipate the call and start an instant before. But a rhythmic count also makes it easier for the defense to guess. So the quarterback will probably use a nonrhythmic one, and the running back has to concentrate. If the play is on two (hut, hut), the back goes on the second "h", not the second "t".

Handoff

To receive the handoff, the running back makes a pocket with his arms and hands. It's up to the quarterback to put the ball in as the running back heads toward the line. The runner doesn't look at the handoff, he has to watch the line, so he works by touch.

There are several ways of taking the handoff. The standard procedure has the running back put the arm closest to the quarterback up and across his chest with the palm down. The other arm is across his belt with the palm up. Holding up the arm closest to the quarterback allows the quarterback to place the ball at the running back's midsection. When the running back "closes down" the pocket, one arm is over and one arm is under the ball. So he can tuck the ball in his outside arm, the arm away from where the tackler will be coming. That way the impact of the tackle won't be on the arm with the ball.

Approaching the Line

Some running backs approach the line full blast. The hole is picked by their third step. Others slow ever so slightly as they read and then blow through the line.

With option blocking, the back is free to choose the hole. That is, the play will have a designated hole or point of attack. But if that hole is not open, or others develop, the running back is free to run where he chooses — run to daylight. Since option blocking allows the blocker to take the defensive man the way the defender wants to go, where the best hole will be is unpredictable.

The runner doesn't look at the handoff, he has to watch the line . . . .

For most plays it's a matter of getting to the hole before it closes. However, on some the running back can get to the line too soon, before the blocking forms. On others, like an end run, the back needs to see how the block on the outside man is going, in order to decide whether he should run outside or cut inside.

Beyond the Line

Running plays are designed to break the line of scrimmage. Beyond the line the running back is pretty much on his own. It comes down to how well the runner can elude the pursuit. If he can get past the first wave, then pure speed is a big help. And he has to carry the ball with the correct hand — away from pressure.

One noteworthy exception is when he has blockers out in front. He must know how to use them and when to break away from them. This is really a combined action, because the blocker should know how the running back reacts to different situations and what his tendencies are. Nevertheless, even good backs and linemen occasionally get themselves entangled.

> **Running plays are designed to break the line of scrimmage. Beyond (that) the running back is pretty much on his own.**

Blocking

Blocking is an important role of the running back. Still, if a great runner is not a good blocker, he'll play anyway. The need for backs to block really depends on the offensive makeup of the team. A strong running team needs a good run blocker. The second running back is very important to the success of his running mate.

Two common running back blocks are the **fill** and **bob** blocks. On a fill, a back fills the gap left by a lineman who pulls, blocks down (blocks to the inside), or otherwise leaves the man across from him uncovered. On a bob, a back blocks on a linebacker or defensive end with an inside-out approach.

A strong passing team needs at least one good pass-blocking back. This is especially true if they throw long a lot. That requires additional time to get the pass off. When executing pass blocks, backs often go for the legs to cut the defender. The on-rushing linemen and linebackers they face are too big for them to block otherwise. But they need change-ups too. If they do the same thing all the time, defenders will anticipate their blocking moves and overcome them.

Blocking is a skill. You don't just give a good running back an assignment and assume that since he's a good athlete he'll get the job done. First, he has to know how to block, and then he has to know whom to block. But perhaps most important, he has to <u>want</u> to block. Blocking is a lot less glamorous than running for a touchdown. Unlike many running back qualities, blocking can be learned, but it takes dedication.

Faking

Good fakes are important for play action passes and runs based on deception. Faking is easier for superior backs because more defenders are keying on them. Speed seems to be the main ingredient, assuming a decent fake handoff and carry. It also must occur at the proper time. No one will pay attention to a play action fake if the offense is behind by two touchdowns and time is running out. The defense knows they have to pass.

The best result of a fake run is to be tackled. That takes the defender right out of the play. At a minimum, the object is to momentarily freeze the defense or just have them take a step toward the faking back. This will buy time for the passer and receivers or get the defense flowing away from the real runner.

Receiving

Once an optional accessory, the ability to catch passes is fast becoming standard equipment for running backs. With the emergence of the passing game, the running backs have to fit in. They are eligible receivers and if a back can't catch, people find out fast. The defense chalks off one potential receiver and coverage is made a lot easier. That's why some of the game's best runners

... if a back can't catch, ... the defense chalks off one potential receiver ....

107

are frequently pulled in passing situations. That's also why a good runner who can catch is so important — he's a dual threat on every play.

How long the present trend will continue is uncertain. Unless the rules are changed it could be for some time. In any event, scouts are looking for dual purpose backs more than they have in the past. And there is more effort being expended at integrating the backs into passing strategy.

Running backs are generally given short pass routes. One type of pass they don't like is the flare where the quarterback lobs it over as his last alternative. It can be a difficult pass, often thrown behind the runner or such that he has to stop and reach for it. The problem is the whole thing unfolds in front of a linebacker who can take a good shot while the running back is in that vulnerable position. The running back knows he must make yardage after such a catch and has to be thinking about the defender. The evidence is the number of dropped balls on this kind of pass.

Risk of Injury

For all their glory, the running backs pay a price. As a group, they are injured more than any other position. A study of player injuries was commissioned by the NFL Players Association and the owners' Management Council. The study analyzed player injuries in 1978 and 1979. Almost 21% of the injuries that required surgery involved running backs. Linebackers were the next highest group at about 13%. By contrast, offensive centers, guards, and tackles accounted for 2%, 8%, and 4% of the serious injuries, respectively. So running backs may receive a lot more attention than the offensive linemen, but the risk of a career-ending injury is also a lot greater.

Almost 21% of the injuries that required surgery involved running backs.

Wide Receivers

Possession Types & Burners

Good wide receivers come in two basic styles. First are the possession types. These are the receivers with the good moves. They can fake and cut and somehow get open even when double covered. These receivers work on the defender every play, setting him up, seeing how he reacts. They don't slough off even when the ball isn't going to them. When the ball is thrown to them, they catch it. They come through in the clutch. Accordingly, these receivers play a tremendous role in the flow and outcome of the game.

The other style is the burner. These wide receivers have great speed. They have the ability to outrun the defense. And that requires all but the fastest defenders to play off of them. They can go deep and score. They are the home-run hitters of football. Just their presence makes the defense deep-conscious and helps to open up the short passes and running game.

Possession types drive the defense crazy. Burners strike terror into their hearts. Together they can pull a defense apart. But individually a defense can smother any one receiver. A team needs two or three good ones with complementary skills. Each receiver runs a pass route. Together the routes form the pass pattern. And together they can stretch the defense and prevent the pressure from becoming too great on any one man. Thus, getting open is to a certain extent dependent upon the skill of the other receivers involved in the pass pattern.

Reading Defenses

Just as quarterbacks read defenses so do wide receivers. The objective is to get free, and the tactics vary with the type of coverage. Against man-to-man defense, the receiver attempts to shake the defender by faking, cutting, or outrunning. Against zone coverage, speed and moves are less of an advantage. A zone defense is set up to defeat speed by just backing up. And defenders ignore fakes and simply guard their areas. So the receiver's strategy shifts to looking for the open spots, the seams between the zones.

Determining whether the coverage is man-to-man or zone is just the first step. If it's man-to-man, the receiver has to know whether it will be single coverage, double coverage, or some kind of combo. Is the defender favoring the inside or the outside? If the receiver goes deep will another defender help, and who would it be? Against zone coverage, is it rotating toward or away? How many short and how many deep zones? Who will cover which ones?

The wide receiver doesn't just run a specific route precisely the way it was drawn up. He does if he can, but the defense he encounters could make the route as originally planned pretty ineffective. So depending on the offensive scheme, he often makes adjustments based on the defense he is faced with. Along this line, keep in mind that the wide receiver playing split end will deal with a different situation than the receiver at the flanker position, or than a slotback for that matter. Being on the same side as the tight end, the flanker may have a harder time getting open on intermediate routes because there are more defenders around.

> ... the wide receiver playing split end will deal with a different situation than the (one at) flanker ....

Turning the Defender

Up at the line, the wide receiver is split out wide. So the receiver looks at the ball as well as listens to the snap count. He has no excuse for jumping offside. But when he's in motion he can't do this. That's one reason some receivers don't like to go in motion. Their initial concern about turning downfield before the ball is snapped upsets their natural release from the line.

As the receiver starts downfield, the cornerback generally goes into a backpedal. This allows the cornerback to move to either side quickly along with the receiver as he makes his cut. The receiver, on the other hand, wants to get that cornerback to turn to one side or the other. To do this the receiver tries to force him downfield faster than he can backpedal.

In addition, the recevier wants to break the defender's cushion. That is, the cornerback tries to stay at least 3 yards beyond the receiver as they head downfield in order to maintain a reaction interval. So it's a lot easier to put a move on the defender if the receiver can close that gap.

Ideally, the wide receiver gets the defender turned in the direction the receiver doesn't intend to take. If he wants to go outside, he may just run downfield to the defender's inside, forcing him to turn in that direction. Or the receiver may fake a cut to the inside by making a move in that direction. In any case, he wants to get the defender to turn to the wrong side, and once he does, the receiver breaks the other way.

Timing Those Moves

At a certain time, the receiver is supposed to make his break or reach a designated area.

Most pass plays are based on timing between the passer and the receiver. At a certain time, the receiver is supposed to make his break or reach a designated area. For instance, it could be 3 seconds on a square-out pattern. The receiver may count "1000-1, 1000-2, 1000-3" and then break at 90 degrees toward the sideline. The quarterback checks the receiver and throws at, say, 2.7 seconds. The receiver hasn't even turned yet, but the quarterback knows he is about to and throws where he is headed.

Timing is critical in throwing the pass too. The time it takes for the ball to go from the quarterback to the receiver is the interval the receiver has to get to where the ball will come down. The quarterback mentally calculates this as he cocks his arm. That's one reason why receivers and quarterbacks have to practice so much together.

Running Under Control

The number of routes a wide receiver can run are countless. But all are really combinations of about 8 or 9 basic routes. (The slant, hitch, out, in, curl, post, corner, and fly are pretty much the basic routes.)

To make cuts and fakes and be able to catch balls requires a lot of body control. Wide receivers run fast, but only as fast as they can _and_ still be under control. They have to be able to drive the defender off, force him downfield, and then fake or cut almost without breaking stride.

Wide receivers are expected to stay on their feet. That may be obvious, but there's more to it than may be apparent. On a timing pass the quarterback throws just before the receiver makes his break. So what happens if the receiver cuts a little too sharply and falls just after the quarterback releases? The ball is everything but gift-wrapped for the cornerback who is covering the receiver. It may look like the quarterback threw an interception, but the guilty party is the wide receiver. The receiver can't afford to fall down on the job.

Running under control is one method for doing this. Once the final move is made, then the wide receiver can go all out if necessary, using that last burst he has been saving. This is to be contrasted with a fly pattern, where the receiver attempts to simply outrun the defense. In that case he may go all out until he has a step on the defense and then come under control to make the catch.

Watch the good receivers as they go downfield. They don't look like they are running hard. Their arms aren't pumping furiously; heads aren't bobbing; they don't reach out until the ball is almost there. All that arm action would make it

So what happens if the receiver cuts ... and falls just after the quarterback releases?

harder to cut or fake, that head bobbing would interfere with watching the ball in flight, and running with arms extended would slow one down. Most wide receivers go very smoothly. They run from the waist down.

Concentration Is Key

Concentration is really the key. Concentration on what the defense is doing as the receiver releases. Concentration on beating the appropriate defender. Concentration on running the route correctly. Concentration on breaking at the right time. Concentration on the ball in flight. Concentration on catching the ball. This explains how the same receiver can make a spectacular diving catch on one play and drop one thrown right at him on the next. Taking a catch for granted means no concentration.

If concentration is the key, intimidation is how the defense tries to break it.

If concentration is the key, intimidation is how the defense tries to break it. When a new receiver comes up, they test him right away — knock him around, play him tough, really punish him when he goes for the ball. If the defense can throw his concentration off even a little, that goes a long way toward rendering him ineffective. And if a receiver acquires a reputation that he can be intimidated, every team will give him a rough time.

Adjusting to Ball, Looking It In & Hanging On

A lot of passes are somewhat off the mark. This is to be expected given the operating conditions the quarterback works under. The good receivers can adjust to the ball. It takes a lot of agility to reach back and catch one that is underthrown or go down and scoop one up before it hits the turf. And it requires some strength to go up and take one away from a defender who is in better position to catch the ball.

A good receiver will "look" the ball into his hands. To do this for a ball thrown at the numbers, the receiver's head must pop down toward his chest. Otherwise, his line of vision will be a good 6 to 8 feet away from him and away from the ball. It's not clear how well the human eye can track a thrown object coming at high speed once it reaches close range. But coaches have receivers practice snapping their heads down on these passes. Watch for that in the replays when the ball should have been caught.

To complete a reception, the receiver has to put the ball away. Sometimes it's impossible. If the receiver is stretched out just getting his hands on the ball and the defensive back times his hit perfectly, there's not much the receiver can do. But usually there is time, and there is never an excuse for starting to run without the ball tucked away. Receivers are taught to put it away on every practice ball they catch — even when just throwing the ball around. It has to be an immediate and automatic reaction.

Tight Ends

Lineman & Receiver

The tight end position requires a "split personality". He has to be both lineman and receiver. This necessitates someone big and strong to block defensive linemen as well as fast and sure-handed to catch passes.

In his role as blocker, he determines the strong side of the line. If the tight end is not a good blocker, the team really has no strong side. He must be able to handle defensive ends and linebackers to make the strong side running go. With respect to other running plays, the tight end is positioned to block downfield on inside carries to either side. He can get there quickly with a reasonable angle. So the tight end is an important element in the running game.

As a receiver the tight end is an important element in the overall pass pattern. He is the receiver in the middle. If he's a passing threat, the defense has to protect that area, and since he can line up and go to either side it complicates the coverage. If he has good speed, he poses a deep threat and the defense must provide for contingent help downfield. Inside the 20, when the offense starts running out of open space, he's especially valuable. With his size, he presents a good target as things get crowded.

If the tight end is not a good pass catcher, strike the above. The defense is no longer faced with a multiple choice. They'll double the wide receivers, put a linebacker on the tight end and not worry about him. Pass coverage is a lot easier, pass completions a lot harder. Just ask the wide receivers. They know how much a good tight end can help stretch the defense.

Style of Play

In the past, many teams haven't relied heavily on the tight end as a receiver. He caught occasional passes, but mainly acted as a decoy. The assignments given the tight end, like all positions, depend on the abilities of the particular player involved. But because of the dichotomy between blocking and receiving, the link between ability and play selection is especially apparent in the tight end's case.

The emphasis has been on blocking. Blocking was the minimum requirement, and if the tight end was also a good receiver that was a big plus. Against the original zone coverages, tight ends were able to get free and catch passes. Thus their pass receiving became more prominent. But the sophisticated combination coverages which followed plugged a lot of holes and made things difficult for the tight ends as well.

With the trend toward increased passing, there is renewed interest in getting more receptions from the tight end. A few teams are lining them up in unconventional places and using them more like wide receivers. However, the majority still view blocking as the tight end's prime responsibility. Reasons? He has a key block on off-tackle and end

... the link between ability and play selection is especially apparent in the tight end's case.

runs. He plays an important role in getting production out of a good running back. The running game is still crucial to winning consistently and to having a good passing attack.

So it seems that most NFL coaches don't want to give up blocking for better receiving, at least not yet. What they want is a better athlete at tight end — one who can truly carry out both functions. That's a big order. A few teams have been lucky. They have such individuals and the results are dramatic. Most teams are still looking.

One thing is certain. The strategists are tinkering with the position. This includes use of an extra tight end in a wingback alignment, two tight ends as wide receivers near the goal line, and other deployments that would have been considered exotic not too long ago. So who knows what the future may bring.

Blocking

The tight end usually blocks on the linebacker across from him, down blocks on the defensive end, or maybe releases for an inside linebacker or defensive back. Blocks against the defensive end are often double-team blocks with the offensive tackle. Even when the tight end down blocks alone on a bigger defensive end, he has some advantages. The angle is good, and he knows where the play is going. But he has to get into the block right away before the end reads it. Holding the block can be the most demanding aspect. For example, if both guards pull to go around his side, he has to stop penetration until they both get past.

Holding the block can be the most demanding aspect.

Hooking the linebacker on a sweep is probably the toughest block for most tight ends. He has to cut off the linebacker's pursuit to the outside while at the same time not allowing the linebacker to penetrate inside. On this one the tight end may split out a little wider so if he can't hook that linebacker (stop outside pursuit), the running back will be able to cut inside them.

Releasing from Line

The tight end's release from the line of scrimmage is critical to his effectiveness as a pass

117

receiver. If he is held up for, say, 2 counts, he can't run far (remember the quarterback has only about 3.5 seconds to get the ball off), and he isn't going to be much of a passing threat. The linebacker across from him will be attempting to do just that — delay his release.

As an eligible receiver, one sustained block within the first 5 yards is all each defender is allowed on the tight end. So the linebacker will jam him as hard as he can to hold him up at the line, or at least knock him off stride. On man-to-man coverage, the tight end is often covered by the strong safety, or he could be covered inside/outside with a free safety/strong safety combo, or he might be taken by just an inside linebacker, man-to-man. In any event, if the linebacker over him doesn't have to follow the tight end out, he can concentrate on simply holding him up.

Positioning & Technique

So how does the tight end get a quick release? A combination of technique and positioning. Generally, he tries to line up so he can release either way, inside or outside. Lining up too close to his offensive tackle forces him to go outside. If he tried to go inside, he would be squeezed between the defensive end and the linebacker. Splitting wider gives more room to maneuver and facilitates release. But spreading too far reduces the ability to block down and can tip off the play. In addition, if the split is wide, it is easier for the linebacker to blitz into the resulting gap.

The release techniques are relatively straightforward. It's really a matter of execution and variation to keep the linebacker off balance. To release inside, the tight end takes a short step with his inside foot, drives his outside foot beyond the linebacker, and pulls himself past. He has to explode off the line and fight to stay on course since the linebacker will try to collapse the gap. An outside release is similar, except now he lead steps with his outside foot, thrusts his inside arm past the linebacker, and pulls to the outside.

Using a slam technique, the tight end fires straight out at the linebacker, meets force with force, and then slides off downfield. If that linebacker starts holding, the tight end can try to

The release techniques are relatively straightforward. It's really a matter of execution and variation . . . .

prevent it by use of the swim tactic. He throws his arm over the linebacker's pads and pulls himself by, something like a swimming stroke. Lastly, he can use some deception. Step and head fake in one direction and then take off in the other.

Being able to use these different methods gives the tight end several options. Watching how the linebacker positions himself (is one foot in? is he favoring one side?) may make a certain technique more appropriate. The object underlying all of this is not to blow the linebacker back, just get <u>by</u> him as fast as possible.

Size

Catching balls in the middle is a hazardous occupation. This is because there are a lot of defenders around and they can converge at good hitting angles. Compare this with a deep pass to a wide receiver where the receiver and defender are both going in the same direction. The defender goes for the ball also, and they both sort of fall down together. Or contrast it with an out route where the defender shoves the receiver out of bounds (again they are going in the same direction). But in the middle, the receiver can be going for the ball one way while the defender is timing his hit from the opposite direction. The collisions can really be brutal.

For this reason, wide receivers are not routinely sent on crossing patterns through the middle. They aren't built to withstand the pounding. Tight ends are. They're bigger and stronger. And the tight end is even expected to pick up some yardage after catching the ball. The good ones can knock tacklers off and bull their way downfield, unlike wide receivers who generally go down when they are hit.

Reading & Adjusting

Once off the line, he has to read what the defense is doing. Is it man-to-man, zone, some combination? Who is picking him up, what kind of zones are they, where are the open spots? The tight end runs routes in the middle where there are a lot of defenders. So the designated path may be clogged up and he has to adjust.

> *... in the middle ...*
> *the collisions*
> *can really be brutal.*

At the same time, he has to take into account if and how the wide receivers are going to adjust. Since his route is planned in concert with the other pass routes, he has to keep in mind his assignment in the overall pattern. He may be the sole inside receiver, but often his role is to help free up a wide receiver.

As an example, let's look at what the tight end considers when he runs a typical crossing route. He uses an inside release and heads for the other side of the field. If it's play action, the linebackers will hold while reading the fake run and the tight end should be able to clear them and get about 12 to 15 yards downfield. If the play is run as a straight dropback pass, the linebackers will drop immediately and the tight end must decide whether to run under or beyond them. This will depend on the depth of their drop.

He will read the inside linebackers immediately. If either blitzes, he goes for that linebacker's area and looks for the ball right away. If the defense plays the tight end man-to-man, he watches who is picking him up — the strong safety, the free safety, a linebacker? The key against man-to-man is to get across the field fast, shield the defender off, and try to get a step on him. If the linebackers on the weak side go into zone coverage, the tight end works downfield past the curl zone trying for the seam between the short and deep coverages.

Catching the Ball

A tight end usually runs shorter routes and as a result catches passes at short range. Thus, he must be especially sure-handed. On a pass that is thrown hard, his hands have to ride with the ball a little. On a soft throw, they just clamp on it.

One school of thought says that good receivers catch the ball mainly with their finger tips, rather than their palms. The fingers slow down the ball; the palms act only as a backstop — there's no give or control with the palms. And on really hard throws, they should bring the ball into their bodies rather than catch with the body. Given the velocity of the pass, it is easy for the ball to hit the receiver's chest or shoulder pad and bounce right out if he hasn't slowed it down with his hands first.

... on really hard throws, they should bring the ball into their bodies rather than catch with the body.

Quarterbacks

Height Is Important

Mention the physical attributes of a good quarterback and you'll generally hear about a good throwing arm, a quick release, mobility, and peripheral vision. Height is not one of the attributes normally focused on. But quarterbacks themselves mention it as a big asset. In fact, many wish they had an extra inch or two. The reason is simple. Given the size of onrushing defensive linemen, a quarterback standing in the pocket can't see some of the areas downfield. Passing against four big rush men with their hands up has been likened to throwing out of the bottom of a barrel.

Fans often complain about their quarterback not spotting an open receiver on some crucial plays. Sometimes it's not a case of overlooking that particular receiver. Rather, when the quarterback looked that way he simply couldn't see past the line.

On the other hand, several outstanding quarterbacks have not been particularly tall. And even a 6'3" quarterback can't see past a 6'8" defensive lineman with his hands up. Besides, it's the job of the offensive line to create passing lanes for the quarterback to see and pass through.

That's all very true. The point is, passing in the NFL basically comes down to where to throw. (If a quarterback doesn't have good mechanics, he wouldn't be on a pro team in the first place.) Given the size of offensive and defensive linemen and the way they get jostled around, a clear line of vision is no certainty. Being tall is a definite plus.

> *... a clear line of vision is no certainty. Being tall is a definite plus.*

No matter what size the quarterback is, he has to know exactly where the receivers are headed. Quarterbacks under a heavy rush have to look through the gaps, and some passes are thrown partly based on seeing and partly based on knowing where the receiver should be. Such passes are usually aimed downfield toward the sidelines, not the middle. There are too many defenders in the middle to throw a risky pass in that area.

Poise & Confidence

A lot is said about the intangibles associated with quarterbacking. Like it or not, the position automatically makes him the natural leader of the offense. What he does with that role is up to him. Two important traits are poise and confidence.

More than any other player, the quarterback has to retain his poise throughout — when the game becomes emotional, after a bad break, after a good break, and especially during a crucial down when time is running out. If he becomes rattled, goes through highs and lows, loses his poise, it's apparent to everyone. It will affect his teammates as well as his responsibilities. After all, he is supposed to be the steady guiding force out there.

Confidence in himself is more or less the flip side of poise. The good ones all have it. The fans can see it. It's obvious when those quarterbacks load up and fire away. Their actions are positive. Close game after close game they are always in it to the end. In an emotional game like football this affects the whole team. When they believe their quarterback can come up with a big play, watch out!

On the other hand, the quarterbacks without confidence are fairly obvious too. They are tentative. You can almost sense the indecision back there in the pocket. If a quarterback doesn't have confidence in himself, he can't expect his teammates to have it either. These quarterbacks don't last too long.

Looking & Seeing

Quarterbacks are, in general, excellent athletes. But they are not superhuman. With few exceptions, their peripheral vision is not much greater than anyone else's. What they do have is the ability to actually see what is going on in an area without focusing narrowly on one man. They can shift rapidly from section to section and have it mentally register.

With few exceptions, their peripheral vision is not much greater than anyone else's.

Although there is no scientific proof, it would seem that this is somehow tied in with poise and confidence. Those attributes allow them to concentrate on actually seeing what is going on. In the heat of battle it's easy to look and really not see. A quarterback has to do a lot of "seeing" very fast. This is basically what reading defenses involves. A quarterback has to check two or three areas, process the information in his mind, decide on one receiver, and then get the pass off, on target.

Pivots

Let's switch for a moment from the general attributes of a quarterback to one of his less glamorous duties. In case you've avoided watching handoffs in favor of the real action, there are several different pivots a quarterback uses throughout a game. The type of pivot employed on a particular play depends on which running back will carry the ball, his angle of approach toward the line, whether there will be a fake, how fast the exchange should take place, and other similar considerations. If you do watch the quarterback make a few pivots, you'll get a better idea how running plays start and the different ways a back approaches the line. Three of the basic pivots are the open, the inside, and the reverse pivots.

> **The type of pivot employed ... depends on which running back will carry ... his angle of approach ... how fast the exchange should take place, and other similar considerations.**

Open Pivot

- After taking the ball from the center, the quarterback opens up (turns) in the direction of the running back who will carry.

- He steps parallel to the line and hands the ball off.

- The open pivot is used for quick hitting and dive plays where the back takes the hand off and hits straight into the line.

Inside Pivot

- Here the running back will generally cut behind the quarterback, take the ball, and hit the other side of the line.

- The quarterback again opens up toward the running back who will carry, but continues to pivot until his back is turned toward the line of scrimmage.

- As the running back cuts behind, the quarterback makes the exchange.

Reverse Pivot

- This time the quarterback opens up away from the ball carrier and continues to turn until the appropriate point for the exchange.

- A reverse pivot is used on off-tackle runs and play-action pass plays.

- This takes a fraction of a second longer, but it is more deceptive because the ball is hidden from the defense as the quarterback turns.

In each case, the quarterback and runner have to get to the right spot simultaneously. When the quarterback pivots too shallow or deep, he seriously cuts down on the running back's angle of approach, or worse, causes a bad exchange or busted play. In all the pivots, the quarterback keeps his elbows in to make it harder for the defense to see the ball.

Reading Defenses

Most fans know that one of the main jobs of the quarterback is to read the defense on a pass play. He has to determine who is covering whom, how they will rush, where they are strongest, where they are vulnerable. So what does the quarterback do?

Let's take an example. Suppose it's 2nd down and short yardage. A pass play has been called. Up at the line the quarterback takes his pre-snap look. He observes the defensive linemen and linebackers to determine whether the blocking called will pick up all the apparent rushers. He then checks the defensive secondary for their relative positions and searches for any indication of the likely pass coverage.

In one system ... a detailed set of keys (directs the quarterback) from one receiver to another ....

This is all pretty standard. But what the quarterback does after the snap depends on the offensive philosophy of the team in question. That is, how the plays are designed and executed. In one system the quarterback is given a detailed set of keys to read which directs him from one receiver to another, depending on the actions of specific defenders. In another system, the quarterback reads the overall defense and is on his own to find the open man, or at least the one where the defense is weakest. In yet another system, the quarterback's actions could be governed by a combination of the preceding two.

125

Detailed Read System

A detailed system might work as follows:

At the snap, the quarterback checks the strong safety —

(1) If the strong safety heads for the right flat, that indicates inverted zone coverage.

He then checks the strong side cornerback; if he is dropping fast, that confirms the inverted zone — **throw** to flanker as he breaks to the sideline.

(2) If the strong safety heads for the deep right corner, that suggests either zone coverage or doubling on the flanker.

Quarterback looks to see if free safety is dropping to deep middle, which would indicate a 3-deep zone.

If free safety is headed that way, quarterback reads weak side inside linebacker:

(a) If linebacker heads for left flat or stays close to line of scrimmage — **throw** to split end curling in the seam between the short and deep zones.

(b) If linebacker is taking a rather deep drop — **throw** to the tight end coming underneath.

(3) If the strong safety comes up to cover the tight end, that implies man-to-man coverage.

Quarterback checks the strong side linebacker and **throws** to the fullback flaring out if open.

(4) The halfback is the safety valve if all else fails.

Though it sounds rather time-consuming when all the steps are listed (there could actually be more), the quarterback will only go through that group which the strong safety's reaction directs him to. So the process can be completed quickly. The point is, it is very detailed and mechanical.

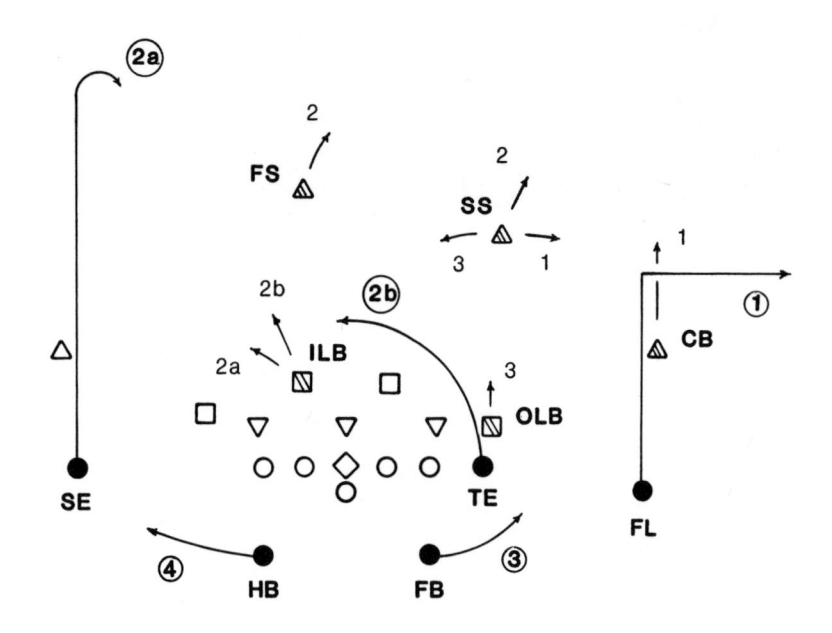

Detailed Key System for Quarterback Read

Free Read System

A free read system has the quarterback read the overall defense and look for the weakest area. From his study of the game films, he knows the opponent's defensive tendencies as well as the strengths and weaknesses of the individual players. So by checking the movement of a few defenders, he pretty much knows the overall scheme.

The quarterback may read the safeties first to get an idea of the deep coverage. For instance, if they split deep, it's a double zone. If the strong safety comes up for the tight end and the free safety goes to the deep middle, it's man-to-man.

Next, the quarterback might look at an inside linebacker for coverage underneath. Has he taken a deep drop (playing zone) or is he picking up the

127

back circling out? Based on this, the quarterback has a good idea which receiver has the best chance of single coverage or of getting to an open area. At this point he can start zeroing in on whether that man is open or not.

The procedures utilized in the second method obviously vary. Depending on the game situation, what he sees in his pre-snap look, or how the defense has been playing, the quarterback may be concentrating on (without looking directly at) one receiver right from the start. Whereas the first approach is very disciplined — you see this, you do that — the second approach gives the quarterback a lot more freedom, as well as a lot more responsibility. He has to be intelligent and experienced to carry it off.

Read Defense First

Note that so far we have talked about the quarterback checking the defense. He has to do that first. He knows where the receivers are heading and may not specifically look at them until the last second. The objective is to narrow down the possibilities. The sooner he determines which receivers the defense has taken away, the quicker he can check on the one or two receivers who should be open. For instance, if the quarterback sees the defense going into a double zone, that means essentially double coverage on the wide receivers. He may just eliminate them and concentrate on the halfback and tight end in the middle. So without looking at any receivers he's pared the choice down to two.

Why Reading Is So Difficult

There are two reasons why reading the defense is so difficult. First, the defense knows what the quarterback is looking for. So they do their best to disguise the coverage as long as possible. Take the free safety as a "for instance". Unless his area is immediately threatened by a receiver, the free safety won't start toward his assigned location right on the snap. He'll delay for a second so the quarterback can't immediately tell what he's going to do.

> **The sooner he determines which receivers the defense has taken away, the quicker he can check on the one or two ... who should be open.**

The second reason reading is so difficult is the time constraint. A good offensive line can hold the defensive rush off for about 3.5 seconds. The exchange between the center and the quarterback takes approximately 0.2 second. And the quarterback needs about 1.7 seconds to drop 7 yards and set up. This leaves about 1.6 seconds maximum at the set position to choose a receiver and physically throw the ball. Actually most passes are thrown within 3.0 seconds, which allows the quarterback to get the ball off without defenders hanging all over him. This means the quarterback has to know which receiver he is going to throw to in less than 2.5 seconds. With a quick release (the ability to throw without having to wind up) this can be stretched a couple of tenths, but on average the quarterback has a very short interval to read the defense and choose a receiver.

That is why the quarterback must start reading at the snap. As he's dropping back, he's looking downfield and selecting a receiver. By the time he sets up, the choice should be about made.

The Shotgun & Play Action

The shotgun is designed to give more time by having the quarterback stand about 5 yards back to receive the snap. It takes about 0.4 to 0.5 second for the center to snap the ball and the quarterback to catch it. Then he backpedals about 5 yards and sets. From the instant he catches the ball, the quarterback has full view of the defense. This is opposed to the 1.7 seconds during a normal dropback when the quarterback can't see the side of the field to his back. On the other hand, some critics of the shotgun point out that the initial reaction of the defense is critical to the quarterback's read and this formation forces him to spend the first 0.4 to 0.5 second just looking at the ball. This is contrasted with a normal snap during which the quarterback has about 0.2 second to catch a glimpse of the defenders' first movements.

Along these lines, a play action pass is significantly different from a dropback pass. On play action, the offense fakes a run and then passes. Thus, after the snap the first thing the quarterback does is turn his back to the defense

... a play action pass is significantly different ... the quarterback (turns) his back to the defense ....

and fake a handoff. Obviously he can't read a thing about the defense while he is doing that. And it can be a big mistake to rush the fake because it will be poorly executed, thus unconvincing, and thus won't fool anybody. Not only that, the quarterback will have wasted the time spent faking that would normally be devoted to looking down the field.

If the fake works, play action can be very effective. Still, this type of pass relies more on predetermined receivers simply because the quarterback has less time to read. In addition, by the time he does set up everybody is already moving around, which makes it even more difficult.

Defensive Linemen

Aggressive Play Required

Of all the different positions, the defensive lineman may best fit the football sterotype — big, powerful, punishing. The offense sets up a precision play. The defensive line attempts to destroy it. Jam it up, hit, push, shove — even more, punish them.

Emotion plays a big role for the defensive line. Given the free-wheeling style of defensive linemen (compared with the precise assignments carried out by offensive linemen), venting emotions can lead to better results. Intimidation is another factor. The defensive linemen try to unsettle the offensive linemen, running backs, and especially the quarterback. In fact, if a defensive lineman himself is on the receiving end of a good hard lick, he'll do his absolute best to show it didn't hurt — even if it's killing him. Any show of weakness is not in keeping with the intimidator role.

In short, the physical requirements are demanding, and aggressive play has to be their style.

Technique Too

Aggressive, emotional play doesn't mean the absence of technique. The defensive line doesn't crash the line of scrimmage in a wild frenzy. Remember, at the start, the offense has the advantage. They know where the play is headed and when it will commence. So the offense should get the jump. And the offensive linemen themselves are big people. Therefore, if they can start first and establish control, there's a good chance the play is going to work.

The defensive linemen have to react. This makes quickness imperative. To come off the line, a defense man can watch the ball (when it moves, he moves) or watch the man across the line (when he moves, the defender moves) or some combination of these methods. The point is to attack before the offense can get control. But keep in mind, the object is to stop the ball carrier or get to the passer, not defeat the opposing lineman.

When defensive linemen discuss their jobs, technique, not power, is the main topic. One reason is that good offensive linemen are using techniques against them. Moves are very important and individualistic. What works for some defensive linemen doesn't work as well for others. One may have a vicious forearm blow to attack a blocker with; another, tremendous upper body strength to throw a blocker away; a third, great quickness enabling him to fake one way and go another. One technique, however, is not enough. A defensive lineman has to be able to mix it up, keep his opponents guessing and off balance.

Scouting Opponent

Scouting the man opposite him is standard procedure for the defensive lineman. On the line it comes down to a man-to-man confrontation. And most

> *... the object is to stop the ball carrier or get to the passer, not defeat the opposing lineman.*

relish the challenge — otherwise they won't last week in and week out. They read scouting reports and watch the films. Many spend hours at night looking at every detail of the opponent's play. They focus on strengths and weaknesses, looking for new moves by old foes and assessing how their own repertoire matches up. Mentally, each defensive lineman prepares his own individual game plan.

Reading vs. Charging

A team's defensive philosophy figures greatly into the lineman's style of play. Two basic philosophies of defensive line play are reading and charging. With the reading approach, the linemen determine what the offense is doing and then react to it. Essentially, they play the run first. With the charging approach, the linemen blast across the line as fast as possible and read as they charge. They play the pass first.

The difference is not quite as great as it may seem. When the reading approach is employed, it's actually hit, read, and react. That is, they hit out hard for one step and then read if the play is not clear. It's this hesitation which makes the difference.

One possibility is to have part of the line charging and part reading. Although this tactic offers some advantages, it presents some problems. On a running play, the offense can take advantage of the charging linemen to create a hole. On a pass play, they can double-team the charging linemen since the others aren't creating as much pressure.

Another overall philosophy is to have the whole line reading to shut off the run. Then, when they put the offense in a passing situation, they switch to the charging approach. In both cases, all the linemen are acting in unison.

Personnel is another factor in the style of play. If one defensive lineman is strong against runs, traps, and screens while the man next to him is a good rusher, the two complement each other. The rusher may be allowed to free-lance more, given the steady performer beside him.

Personnel is (a) factor . . . . The rusher may be allowed to free-lance more, given the steady performer beside him.

Stunts & Blitzes

Use of stunts and blitzes has a direct bearing on individual play. Isolated stunts are helpful as change-ups for the defensive linemen. They force adjustments in the blocking patterns and keep the offense guessing. Blitzes provide for additional penetration across the line of scrimmage. Both stunts and blitzes require careful coordination between the linemen and linebackers involved.

Strong defensive teams used to minimize these techniques, especially blitzes. They were employed more by a team which had some weak points on defense and was willing to risk a big play by the offense to cover for these deficiencies. Because of the rule changes, offensive linemen have more leeway in their pass blocking techniques and are more effective. As a result, defenses are now incorporating more stunts and blitzes along with multiple coverages to mount a strong pass rush against the better blocking they are facing.

Defensive Tackles

Nose Tackle

The 3-4 defense has two defensive ends and one nose tackle (sometimes called the nose guard or middle guard). These three defensive linemen are clearly outnumbered by the five offensive linemen. So they can't afford a free-wheeling style of play. As previously discussed, the idea behind the 3-4 is to have the linemen neutralize the blockers so the four linebackers can tackle the runner or cover the receivers. The man at the center of all this is the nose tackle.

The nose tackle has a particularly difficult role. He acts as a sort of human bulldozer. Right in the middle of the line, he has to occupy at least two offensive linemen. The purpose of the 3-man line is to allow for an extra linebacker. So the nose tackle is in essence sacrificing himself to a double-team in order to free up another player. Thus, if the center can handle him alone the 3-4 is dead.

... the nose tackle is ... sacrificing himself to a double-team ... to free up another player.

Located in the heart of the legal clipping zone, the nose tackle is subject to continuous abuse. He is hit from the front, side, and back. For his attack he has few options: hit straight ahead, left, right, or occasionally stunt with a defensive end. Nose tackles tend to be somewhat short and squat for defensive linemen. The shorter stature helps the nose tackle get under the center's block and at the same time aids him in keeping blockers off his legs. He must be extremely strong to hold his ground and not get turned. This is made more difficult because he has to play tight to the line in order to keep the linebackers free.

Psychologically the double-teaming can be discouraging. If he does a good job, he probably won't get many sacks or much recognition. He'll be lost in the middle as he pounds it out with half the offensive line.

Defensive Tackles

... defensive tackles in a 4-3 have more freedom than the nose tackle ....

The 4-3 defense has two defensive tackles who are positioned across from the offensive guards. With four players, the defensive line is more evenly matched with the offensive line. As a result, the defensive tackles in a 4-3 have more freedom than the nose tackle, but they have only three, not four, linebackers supporting them. Consequently, the linemen in the 4-3 are more responsible for making the play themselves than the linemen in the 3-4.

Defensive tackles must have the strength to handle inside plays directed right at them and the size to withstand the angle blocks they are subjected to. It is especially important that the tackles be able to shed blockers and get to the ball. They must be agile and quick. They must also have some speed. Given their location in the middle, the defensive tackles are expected to pursue to either side.

Defending Against Runs

A defensive tackle must keep blockers off his legs. You play defense by staying on your feet. Working in a small area, this is directly related to the ability to throw off blockers before they reach the legs. The tackle drives into the blocker, stays square with him, grabs the blocker, and fights to gain control so he can release either inside or outside to the ball. He must use his hands and legs together to do this and to come off the block fast.

"Fight the pressure" is a standard instruction to defensive linemen. It means that if the blocker is pressuring the defender toward the outside, then the runner is going to cut inside behind the block. On the other hand, if the blocker is pressuring the defender toward the inside, then the runner is going to cut outside behind the block. So the defensive lineman knows by the way the blocker is attempting to move him where the play is directed. To stop it, he has to fight through the block, or fight through the pressure. If he tries to go around the blocker, he will lose too much time and the runner will be gone.

What if the defensive lineman encounters no resistance? Then he's either being set up for a trap or the play is going away from his position. Or maybe he is being influenced.

> *"Fight the pressure" is a standard instruction to defensive linemen.*

- If the defensive tackle is being set up for a trap and he recognizes it fast enough, he will try to get across the line, turn, and lower his shoulder into the trapping guard; then it's a case of trying to drive through that guard or at least jamming up the hole that the trapper is attempting to open.

- If the play is going away from the defensive tackle, he will locate the ball and pursue.

- If the guard pulls to the outside, it could be an influence block (sucker play) trying to get the defensive tackle to vacate his position for a delayed run through it.

- In any event, the tackle can't commit without reading. Otherwise he can take himself right out of the play.

Defending Against Passes

A 4-man line is commonly used to rush the passer. The role of the two defensive tackles is to collapse the front of the pocket. The aim is to force the quarterback, particularly an immobile one, back and out to the side where the defensive end can close in on him.

In rushing the passer a defensive tackle can overpower, slip by, or pull by the blocker. Overpowering rarely works and is reserved for a change of pace. The latter two techniques are used to get by the blocker after contact has been made. The first step, however, is to start on the snap. The tackle's inside position helps since he can easily see the ball out of the corner of his eye. Then the object is to avoid the blocker rather than tying up with him. Contact is made with the forearms and hands, not the shoulders and chest, as he works for leverage.

In a 4-man line each lineman is responsible for a rushing lane. The lane for a defensive tackle is from the center to the offensive tackle on his side. He can't allow himself to get blocked out of the lane, nor can he leave it to make an apparent sack. All too often a shifty quarterback eludes the lineman and heads down the vacant lane for a 1st down or big gain.

Tackles encounter different styles of pass blockers and must adjust accordingly. First are the pop-and-recoil types. They set quickly and give the defensive tackle a good pop, retreat, and do it again. Against these, the tackle tries to force the blocker to move so he can't gather himself to hit with a lot of power. Next are the deep setters or riders. They drop well off the line usually toward the inside and then attempt to ride the rusher past the quarterback. Defensive tackles should get to this type as fast as possible with a power rush. Then there are the cutters. This group, which includes a lot of running backs on pass blocking duty, tries to cut the defensive lineman's legs when he gets up close. The tackle has to read this and use his hands and feet to push the blocker down and away as he slides by. Finally, there are the aggressive ones. They strike out at the rusher and work to gain control rather than just give ground. Now that offensive linemen have freer use of their hands they can be more aggressive. Against them the defensive tackle looks for any overextension where he can gain leverage for a grab-and-jerk technique or dip his shoulder and go past.

> ... the object is to avoid the blocker rather than tying up with him.

What complicates the pass rush for the inside linemen is their run responsibility. When the offense runs a draw play they fake a pass to get the linemen into their pass rush. Then they send a ball carrier into the middle of the line right past the charging linemen. Thus, the tackles must constantly be aware of this possibility as they start their rush.

Defensive Ends

Working on the Outside

Positioned on the outside, the defensive ends have a lot of area to protect. The defensive tackles play in a smaller space and are better able to make up for a mistake. At defensive end, with open space out to the sideline, mistakes are more costly.

Defensive ends are big, tall, powerful, and mobile. The 3-4 versus 4-3 philosophies have already been discussed. There is more pressure on 3-4 defensive ends to soak up the blocking and rely on the linebackers to make the play. In the 4-3 the defensive ends have tackles at their flank and are given more latitude in containing and attacking the play. Regardless of the formation, mobility is required to deal with outside runs and for effective pass rushing. Good power is necessary to stand up to off-tackle plays and handle blockers the size of the offensive linemen they face.

> **There is more pressure on 3-4 defensive ends to soak up the blocking and rely on the linebackers to make the play.**

Defending Against Runs

Before the snap it is harder for the defensive end to see the ball out of the corner of his eye than for a defensive tackle. As a result, the first movement he goes on may be the down hand and head of the man directly across the line. Once off the mark, defensive ends must use their hands a lot to control the blocker and maintain position. For instance, when they hand fight their man to string out an end run. The rules give a defensive lineman almost unlimited use of his hands and he better utilize this advantage if he hopes to stay in the league.

> **Generally, the defensive end won't be able to split (a double-team block) unless he can spot it coming.**

The defensive end is often the object of a double-team, a trap, or an option block. The double-team is difficult to beat. Generally, the defensive end won't be able to split it unless he can spot it coming. In most cases the best he can do is hold his ground and not be blown back, enlarging the hole.

Against a trap, the defensive end has a little more time to react and turn into the trapper than the defensive tackle does in a similar play. That is because the defensive end is farther down the line (thus making the guard versus defensive end a "long trap" and the guard versus defensive tackle a "quick trap"). Lack of resistance is the first sign of a possible trap. When allowed to penetrate, the end should look inside and try to constrict the hole.

When utilizing an option block, the blocker takes the defender whichever way (inside or outside) the defender wants to go, and then the runner cuts behind the resulting block. Defensive philosophy enters into this. If the defensive line uses the charging approach, they are clearly vulnerable to the run. They must adjust as the play develops. Moreover, if the defender is very aggressive and very quick, it will be difficult for him to overcome an option block. In essence, he's charging right into it.

To defeat an option block, the defender has to square up the blocker and fight him off such that he retains control over his area of responsibility. The defender can't let himself be led to one side or the other by the blocker. It's a combination of reacting to how the play is developing and not taking himself out of it. If the defensive lineman can just jam up the middle of his area, that may be sufficient. It leaves little daylight on either side for the running back to hit.

Defending Against Passes

A defensive end has a big area to operate in, especially to the outside. He can make a wide turn when he goes to the outside. This helps because it allows the defensive end more flexibility in his rushing tactics. The basic rush strategy has the defensive ends pressuring the quarterback from the sides. This forces him forward in the pocket toward the defensive tackles.

Usually, the defensive end will take an outside charge. Once he gets the offensive tackle moving back, the end tries to shove him off and cut in front toward the middle and the quarterback. The offensive tackle, however, will be struggling to ride that defensive end out and behind the quarterback. If he can do it, the defensive end is probably out of the play. Once the end is ridden beyond the pocket he has to turn back and by that time the quarterback will have released the ball.

The defensive end has a major containment role on the pass rush. In a passing situation, if the quarterback gets outside the defensive end there's no one to hold him in. The linebackers are covering receivers man-to-man or are back off the line protecting the short zones. Thus, if the quarterback gets outside, the linebacker may be forced to decide: either stay in his pass coverage (allowing the quarterback to run) or come up to stop him (and maybe leave a receiver open).

Finally, play action passes, where the offense initially fakes a run, can be difficult for the defensive line. How difficult depends on how good the fake is. If the defensive lineman is positioned to see that no handoff is taking place, then he may be able to mount a pass rush without hesitation. But for others on the line, their view may be obscured, forcing them to hesitate and respect that handoff movement. This is particularly true when the defensive philosophy dictates that they play the run first. The problem arises from the hesitation. If the lineman slows, it's difficult to then start a hard rush and reach the passer in less than 3.5 seconds. First, the lineman has lost his momentum, and second, he's lost too much time.

> **The defensive end has a major containment role on the pass rush.**

Holding

The Rules

The rules state that, aside from the ball carrier, the offensive players cannot use their hands. The major exception is for pass blocking. A pass blocker can use his hands to push off a defender. But even then they are to be inside his elbows. Grasping or encircling an opponent is not allowed.

Nevertheless, defensive linemen expect to be held by the offense. They expect to be grasped, encircled, and even tackled on some plays. How can this be when the rules prohibit it? Quite simply because the rules regarding offensive holding are not rigidly enforced.

Incidental Holds

Incidental holds away from the action will not be called. For instance, if a minor hold occurs on one side of the line and the play goes to the other side, no whistle will result. If the hold occurs when the blocker is in front of the defender, it probably won't be called either. And we're talking here about when the holds are seen by the officials.

If an offensive lineman can get away without an official spotting him, the hold may be more than incidental. For example, one reason defenders don't choose to just run over a blocker is holding. When they collide, the blocker can grab the defender's jersey and pull him down as the blocker falls back. (It should be noted that not all linemen hold and not all holding is intentional.)

Holding Is Called

This does not mean that holding isn't called. It is. But the violation has to be seen and usually directly affect the outcome of the play. Otherwise, it has to be flagrant — something really obvious like a takedown.

Taking the Risk

In addition, sometimes it makes sense to risk a holding penalty. Let's say a team's main offensive weapon is it's quarterback, who has considerable passing ability. Let's also assume that the quarterback has recently returned from surgery. Under these circumstances, consider an offensive lineman who has let a defender get around him with a clear shot at the quarterback. If he doesn't reach out and grab that defender, he risks a quarterback sack — loss of 8 to 9 yards and, much worse, a potential injury. If he does hold, he may get called for it — loss of 10 yards but no loss of down. What would you do?

The Result

Defensive linemen seem resigned to the fact that they will be held. Particularly the great ones. They are often involved in overmatches with lesser-talented opponents. (Sometimes even with holding it's not much of a contest.) But as the holding gets more flagrant, it becomes more maddening. That's when the defensive linemen start complaining to the officials.

In summary, holding is really a judgment call where the officials are given substantial discretion. Due to the nature of line play and the rules under which offensive linemen must operate, some incidental and unintentional holding is inevitable. If the officials called all the holding that technically occurs, a game would degenerate into a series of penalties.

Linebackers

Physical Characteristics

The role of the linebacker is to back up the down linemen and assist the secondary with pass coverage. Therefore, they must be big enough to handle opposing offensive linemen and agile enough to cover receivers in the short zones. A linebacker has to move well. He needs first-step quickness, good lateral movement, and speed to chase down a ball carrier. He must also be good at changing directions fast. At the same time, the classic linebacker is one tough player, who thrives on contact. He's powerful enough to shed blockers and makes hard, sure tackles.

An inside linebacker or middle linebacker is usually more powerful, while an outside linebacker tends to be quicker, faster, and a better pass defender. That doesn't mean the linebackers in the middle are plodders. They can't be. They have to cover the entire field in the sense that they must be ready to pursue to either side on any play.

Linebacker assignments in the 3-4 are a little more straightforward than in the 4-3. The 3-4 linebackers can be more aggressive and, due to the way that formation works, they can play a more dominant role — they make a lot of tackles. The role of the linebacker in the 4-3, particularly the middle linebacker, is more complex. With only three backers instead of four, mistakes are more costly. They must be especially careful in order to avoid overpursuit.

> **The 3-4 linebackers can be more aggressive and ... can play a more dominant role ....**

Ability to React

Beyond the physical characteristics, linebackers need the ability to react almost instantaneously. Whereas the defensive linemen generally hit and then read, linebackers read and then react. The level of this ability to recognize what the offense is doing, determine the proper counterattack, and physically react is crucial to the linebacker's performance.

A linebacker can be an excellent athlete and a sure-handed tackler, but still be a dismal failure at the position. The reason is an inability to react. On the snap, he's not sure where to go; he hesitates too long. Or worse, he starts in the wrong direction a step or two. By then he's in trouble. And even though he's quick, it's too late. He's already out of the play. In effect, his delayed response neutralizes or even offsets his physical talents.

Good linebackers always seem to be involved in the action. Sometimes it's a little hard to believe that a linebacker got into position to make the tackle he did. It comes back to the ability to react immediately and correctly. Positioned close to the line, if he doesn't react right away, he'll be blocked out of the play by a big lineman or a receiver will get open behind him. Fast running backs and receivers can reach his area of defense in 2 seconds, which doesn't allow any margin for error.

Studying Opponent

This recognition and reaction process borders on instinct for the outstanding linebackers. They tend to have a nose for the ball. But a good deal of this is attributable to anticipation based on study and experience. By studying the scouting report and analyzing game films, a linebacker learns the opponent's formations and what plays they run out of each. He also looks for tendencies associated with field position, down and distance, or other game conditions.

With this background, play recognition is faster. In addition, linebackers read keys as the offense lines up and the play commences. But there's always an element of the unknown, and those who can diagnose a play and react fastest are the ones that last.

> *... those who can diagnose a play and react fastest are the ones that last.*

Reading Keys

Keys refer to the actions of opposing players that indicate the type and direction of the play. Offensive players key defensive players and vice versa. Consider the strong side linebacker. The tight end is his main key. If the tight end blocks down on the defensive end, the linebacker reads run and squeezes down the offensive tackle-tight end gap to protect the off-tackle area. If the tight-end attempts to hook the linebacker (turn him inside), the linebacker reads an end run and fights off the block to contain the ball carrier. If the tight end starts to release, the linebacker reads pass and tries to hold him up at the line.

That's how keys work. Except it's not that easy. The offense knows the defensive players are keying on them, and therefore they will do their best to send off false signals. For example, assume the tight end blocks out on the linebacker as the quarterback starts to hand off to the halfback. The linebacker reads the tight end's block as run and plays accordingly. However, it could be just the start of a play action pass with the tight end running a delay route. That is, the tight end comes off the block after a count or two and heads out for a reception.

Multiple Keys

So defense men have to key more than one player. Essentially what they are looking for is corroboration that the initial key is correct. While it is relatively easy for the offense to give one false key, it's difficult for them to coordinate two or three keys such that all disguise the play. Using one key, a linebacker is not going to be effective. Using two keys, he will improve. With three or four keys he should be good — able to recognize what is coming quickly and correctly.

So the strong side linebacker uses the tight end as his first key. The nearest running back may be the second key. And the near guard his third key.

Checking three players in, say, 1 second after the ball is snapped isn't always feasible. For some rookies, it's probably not possible. But it isn't a case of looking from one player to the next to the next. A linebacker will look through the tight end to the fullback and then maybe catch a glimpse of the guard at the snap. So it's not a case of concentrating or focusing, but merely catching sight of movement by the bodies most critical to the particular defender. Remember, before the snap he has already considered the game situation, the down and distance, the offensive formation, and the opponent's tendencies. Hence, he should have a pretty good idea about what to expect.

Another reason for multiple keys is that one or two keys may be inconclusive rather than misleading. For instance, assume the tight end blocks out on the linebacker and the fullback heads toward that linebacker and his defensive end. This indicates that a run is coming to his side, but it does not necessarily show which hole will be the point of attack. The action of the near guard down blocking, pulling, whatever, should provide additional information as to where the ball carrier is going to hit.

> ... it's difficult for (the offense) to coordinate two or three keys such that all disguise the play.

Inside Linebackers & Middle Linebacker

The inside linebacker in a 3-4 defense plays opposite an uncovered guard (actually he may be a little to the outside of the guard in order to maintain outside leverage on the gap). He's off the line at least enough to pursue laterally with freedom. Given his position, he is subject to attack by the interior line on every play. To give an idea of how an inside linebacker plays, consider the following example: Assume that an isolation play is directed at the inside linebacker. This has the fullback bursting out of the backfield to lead block for the ball carrier by driving the linebacker back.

Starting at the snap, the linebacker will see the guard blocking down on the nose tackle. Reading on the run, the linebacker will lead step with his inside foot. Noting the guard's action, he then brings his outside forearm and leg forward in case the offensive tackle is going to angle block on him. At the same time, he is catching sight of the lead back to see if an isolation block is coming. The instant he reads an isolation block, he steps up with his inside foot and takes on the blocker with his inside shoulder. He uses his inside shoulder in order to jam the blocker to the inside. And he wants to take on the blocker as close to the line as he can to stuff the hole with no daylight for the ball carrier.

No wasted motion. In setting up for his move, the linebacker has gone from guard to offensive tackle to fullback. Then he explodes into the blocker, using the proper angle.

In a passing situation, the guard will show pass by dropping back from the line to block. Assuming the linebacker isn't blitzing, he keys the quarterback for the direction of the throw. Depending on the coverage, he checks for a wide receiver cutting inside or a back releasing and goes to the curl or hook zone as appropriate.

(The inside linebackers) should not cross the center too fast . . . .

The inside linebackers, and even more so the middle linebacker in a 4-3, can't afford to overpursue. They must keep an inside-out angle on the ball carrier. They should not cross the center too fast or they'll risk being victimized by a misdirection or counter play.

Outside Linebackers

The inside linebackers and the middle linebacker are expected to make a lot of tackles. The outside linebacker is not expected to make the tackle on some plays that come into his area. The reason for this is tied in with his containment role. It is his job to contain the ball carrier and force him inside toward the pursuit. If the ball carrier does get outside, then the outside linebacker has to force him as deep as possible to buy time for the defensive back with run support responsibility to get outside.

On a sweep with pulling guards, about the best the outside linebacker can do is penetrate to cause the ball carrier to dip deeper before turning. He will also attempt to jam up one or both of the guards. If he accomplishes this, he may look bad, but he sets the stage for the pursuit to make the tackle.

If the cornerback or safety has primary contain responsibility and the outside linebacker can't make the tackle, he tries to strip away blockers. This enables the contain man and pursuing defenders to make the stop. If the ball carrier gets by with blocking in front, those blockers may take out the contain man, thus opening up the sideline to the runner. Then it's a case of whether anyone can catch him.

Outside linebackers are generally better pass defenders than the backers on the inside. This shows up in passing situations where the middle linebacker or an inside linebacker is replaced by an extra defensive back. The outside linebacker often winds up in man-to-man coverage on a running back, a tight end, or even a slotback. In man-to-man coverage it makes a big difference whether the linebacker has help deep. If there is help, the linebacker can play a more reckless coverage and attempt to take away short passes by defending in front of the receiver. With no help deep, the linebacker can't let the man get behind him and must play a more conservative, looser coverage.

> **(The) outside linebacker is _not_ expected to make the tackle on some plays that come into his area.**

Cornerbacks

Defensive Secondary

The defensive secondary is the last line of defense. Composed of the cornerbacks and safeties, the secondary's main responsibility is: they can't let the ball get behind them. Thus, they play the pass first and the run second. Only when he is sure the play is not a pass will a defensive back come up to stop a run. The efforts of the secondary are directed at preventing the big play, sometimes at the expense of giving up shorter gains.

Pressure, Pressure

The cornerbacks are constantly under pressure. Their mistakes can be the most costly on the team. Their mistakes are also the most apparent. When they are beaten on a long pass, it's a touchdown. When it happens, everyone is watching. Replay after replay will show just how the cornerback failed. And it could happen on any down. Every time they line up, they know this could be it.

Speed, Speed

Although quickness and speed are always mentioned as necessities for the other positions, outstanding speed is an absolute minimum requirement for the cornerback. The faster the better. Cornerbacks have to cover the fastest men in the game, as well as those with the best moves. There is no substitute for speed.

Use of zone coverage and a lot of experience can help a cornerback who has lost a step on his former self. But there is a high minimum limit below which most cornerbacks will be too vulnerable to the fleet wide receivers. Despite what some people may think, the veteran corners who continue year after year haven't lost much of their original speed — maybe a tenth in the 40 at most. Like any other position, there are exceptions, but not many at cornerback.

Balance, Confidence, Short Memory

Being fast will not make a player a good cornerback. Speed is only the minimum requirement. Good reactions and good balance are important. Covering wide receivers is rarely a straight-line affair. The receiver will fake, cut, change speeds, and make his break. One slip, one slight loss of balance, leaves that receiver wide open. 6 points!

For this reason, a cornerback needs a lot of confidence in himself. He has to go after his man without hesitation and without fear of being beaten. He should be somewhat of a gambler. While he can't play with reckless abandon — the stakes are too high — he should figure the odds, know when they are in his favor, and be willing to take a chance.

Finally, the cornerback needs a short memory. Or at least selective amnesia. Sooner or later he is going to be beaten, and it may happen in a crucial game. Whenever it occurs, he has to be able to forget. Given the continual pressure, play after play, the cornerback who can't forget his mistakes

> *Speed is only the minimum requirement. ... Covering wide receivers is rarely a straight-line affair.*

starts to tighten and lose a little confidence. Once he thinks he can't cover, he's on his way out. So if a cornerback doesn't seem morose after being burned once or twice, he is just displaying one trait of the good ones.

Backpedalling

Running backwards is an important skill for a cornerback. Normally, he will set up about 3 to 9 yards from the line of scrimmage. As the wide receiver starts downfield, the cornerback backpedals to keep that receiver in front of him. The corner will not commit himself by turning one way or the other until he knows for sure where the receiver is headed. Backpedalling allows him to keep the receiver and offensive backfield in view, as well as enabling him to go either left or right quickly.

Cornerbacks practice running backwards, and coaches time them at it. Given his initial position off the line, if a corner can drop at least 15 yards backpedalling, he can cover most of the short and intermediate pass routes before turning. Against a fast receiver he'll have to turn and run at some point, but the farther he can go backing up, the more options he has for his defense.

To give an idea of how carefully techniques are broken down, here are a few comments about backpedalling. First, the knees should be bent from the start. Analysis of films shows that if a cornerback stands straight before the snap, his first reaction is to bend his knees. The backpedal itself consists of reaching back and pulling the weight of the body over the feet — elementary, but focusing on the objective helps. The movement is done on the balls of the feet and they should just clear the ground as he steps back. Raising them high takes time and is wasted motion. Don't backpedal at full speed. Take a little off. At full speed the corner has to come under control before he can react to a receiver's cut; at 90% speed, reacting is easier and faster. Finally, keep the upper body slightly forward for balance and to facilitate a forward move if the play turns into a run.

Some cornerbacks prefer a slide step to backpedalling in certain situations. Whichever method is used, it illustrates the need for fast movements other than straight-line running.

Cornerbacks practice running backwards, and coaches time them at it.

Taking Something Away

Good receivers can make sharp cuts (sharp, not rounded) almost without slowing down. Moreover, receivers know where they are going and cornerbacks don't. As a result, cornerbacks don't like to let receivers get head up on them (where the receiver is directly in front of the retreating cornerback). The reason is it gives the receiver too many alternatives.

So if a particular receiver has a good outside move, the cornerback may stay to the outside of the receiver. He plays him tough to that side, recognizing that he is giving something away to the inside. But he's also taking something away. If the receiver wants to go outside, he will have a much harder time.

In addition, the cornerback may have help to the inside. And knowing where help lies, in itself, is important. When a cornerback gambles, he should know somebody is back there in case he misses.

... knowing where help lies, in itself, is important.

Don't Get Turned

The cornerback may switch during the game, playing to the outside on some downs and to the inside on others. As mentioned in the section on receivers, the corner can't let the receiver get him turned in the wrong direction. Otherwise, that cornerback is in big trouble.

Playing to one side can help in this regard. For the receiver to get the defender turned in the wrong direction and then break free, he usually needs two cuts. But with the cornerback committed to one side, that first move may have to be so pronounced that the second cut brings the receiver right into the defender.

Maintaining cushion is important. If the cornerback can't keep some reaction interval between himself and the receiver, the corner is forced to run with him hip-to-hip. That makes it easy for the receiver to cut away and get open (or much worse, get past for a long ball). On the other hand, too much cushion makes it easy for the receiver to curl in or comeback for a pass in front. So the corner has to play each receiver just right.

Watch the Belt Buckle?

On man-to-man coverage, the standard rule for a defender is to watch his receiver's belt buckle. The receiver can fake you with his hands, shoulders, arms, or feet, but his body is where that buckle is — or so goes the rule. Cornerbacks, it seems, watch whatever works for them best. But they do play the man first and go for the ball only when the receiver does.

Cornerbacks study receivers. They watch their movements in films and analyze their tendencies. They look for things like whether a particular receiver chops his steps just before he cuts. And then they write it down in their books. That's right, a good cornerback keeps a book on the receivers he faces. Knowing what a receiver is likely to do when he moves a certain way or runs a particular route is a big help in anticipating the play. And anticipation is what interceptions are based on.

Leaping Ability

An attribute which is not often discussed is leaping ability. Even when the defender sticks with the receiver, if the receiver outjumps him, it's a completion. In addition, cornerbacks are often shorter than the men they cover. And the receiver usually has better position. So the defender not only has to jump higher, he has to reach farther.

Move Men Wear Them Out

Working against receivers with great moves can be more of a problem than those with great speed. Especially if they are the type that work on the defender every play. (Some receivers slack off if they are not a primary target.) A move man who just won't quit can really tire out a corner. This is partially attributable to the pressure on the cornerback. The receiver knows when he's a decoy, but the cornerback doesn't. He's on edge every play, every cut, until the ball is in the air.

Relief with Zones

Zone coverage does take some of the pressure off. The cornerback's technique changes to just

They look for things like whether a ... receiver chops his steps just before he cuts.

dropping back. He tries to keep the receiver far enough in front so that he can see through the receiver to the quarterback. Unless it's an obvious running play, the corner covering a deep zone can start dropping right away. The cornerback covering a short zone can drop too. Or he may play tight initially, knowing that once the receiver leaves his area he's someone else's problem.

More Demanding Than Ever

Playing cornerback today is more difficult than in the past. It used to be that defenders could knock receivers around all they wanted until the ball was in the air. This meant that receivers had to look out for defenders and try to stay on course as they ran their routes. Over a period of time such contact has been curtailed to the point where now it's one chuck per defender within the first 5 yards, period. From then on the receivers have clear sailing. They can go all out and just concentrate on getting downfield and open. Thus, cornerbacks who could play with less speed and more aggression under the old rules are outmoded. Now, teams are drafting backs who can run with receivers all over the field.

The emphasis on passing and use of special defenses have put the cornerback more in demand. Two good starters are no longer enough. With the nickel coverages and other multiple-back defenses a team needs three or four good corners.

Complex coverages are also giving rise to some false accusations. Because they are complex, assignments are sometimes blown. If a linebacker or safety is guilty, it may not be apparent. Yet it can make a cornerback look like a total incompetent. Suppose the cornerback has underneath coverage with help deep. The cornerback plays the receiver tough against a short pass, but as the receiver runs past, the corner sees that the man assigned to pick him up isn't there. All the corner can do is start chasing and, boy, does he look bad. If the receiver catches one for a TD, it appears to be all that cornerback's fault. So before you boo, you better know what defense was called. Each year a lot of innocent players are hung by the fans.

> ... cornerbacks who could play with less speed and more aggression under the old rules are outmoded.

Safeties

Range

The safeties back up the middle and provide help to the cornerbacks when possible. As their name implies, they are the safety valves of the defense. But they also have specific coverage responsibilities. To carry out their assignments they need great range. With that ability they can provide deep pass coverage, shut down runs up the middle, give outside help to the corners, come up to force end runs, and occasionally blitz the quarterback. They cover a lot of ground. When a runner gets past the linebackers or a long pass is completed, it's usually up to the safeties whether the play is going for a score.

Speed-Reader

Safeties need speed, but not quite as much as cornerbacks. The safeties can be and generally are a little slower. In fact, some safeties are converted cornerbacks who just weren't fast enough. However, these days they need better marks in the speed category to play 2-deep zones and other types of pass coverage currently being used. In the age of throwball the emphasis is away from the bruising hitter and toward the safety who is a good cover guy.

Along with speed, a safety needs the ability to read offenses rapidly. Whereas a cornerback is generally glued to one receiver, the safety's responsibility is often dependent on what action the offense takes. He must know the assignments of his teammates and how well they can carry them out. Then it's up to him to analyze the situation quickly in order to take the correct course of action. Is it pass or run? Where is the ball headed? Who needs help? Should he gamble or play it safe?

> ... *the safety's responsibility is often dependent on what action the offense takes.*

Sure Tackler

A safety has to be a sure tackler. As potentially the last man with a good shot at the ball carrier, the safety can give up some intensity for more certainty in his tackle. This is especially true when the running back is in open field.

At the same time, the safeties are often well placed to really level wide receivers. A few have acquired some distinction as heavy hitters. This can be intimidating to receivers entering their area, which is the point — to reduce the receiver's concentration on catching.

Consistency is the real measure of their tackling ability. The good safeties go in hard even when they will share in the punishment. Their hits aren't limited to when a receiver is reaching up and defenseless. They'll take on a big fullback rumbling downfield where the collision isn't going to be all one-sided.

Run Support

The cornerbacks and safeties work with each other to contain end runs. On every play either the cornerback or the safety (it can differ from side to side) will have primary run support responsibility. This means the responsibility to come up and force the play inside or make the tackle, once it is determined that the play is a run. When the wide receiver lines up within 8 to 10 yards of the interior line, then the <u>cornerback</u> will generally have primary run support. When the wide receiver lines up farther to the outside, the <u>safety</u> will have that responsibility. The player without this force responsibility will have deep pass responsibility. He picks up the wide receiver or drops to protect against a play action pass.

The wide receiver's alignment is used as the main determinant for good reason.

The wide receiver's alignment is used as the main determinant for good reason. If the wide receiver is split less than 10 yards, he is close enough to crackback on the safety. And if he can make that block while the corner drops to protect against the pass, there will be no one to contain an end run. Thus, the cornerback forces when the wide receiver is in close.

When the wide receiver is split wide, it's harder for the safety to get out and pick him up. If the receiver bursts off the line, he may be able to run by the safety before the safety gets over. So the cornerback defends against the pass and the safety furnishes run support when the wide receiver is split wide.

Other factors can enter into the decision. For example, if a zone defense is called, the man with the short outside zone has primary run support. Keep in mind, too, that the defensive back with this responsibility still plays the pass first. The speed with which he can break down and come up to play run is affected by the presence or absense of a pass receiver in his area. If the receivers on his side block, he can come up fast.

Strong Safety

Alignment

The strong safety is called such because he is the safety who plays opposite the strong side of the offense. In basic man-to-man coverage his role has traditionally been to cover the tight end if he releases to run a pass route. The outside linebacker, who lines up across from the tight end at the line of scrimmage, furnishes some assistance by jamming the tight end right at the snap. Since the strong safety is behind the line about 6 to 8 yards, this gives him time to key the offense and determine whether the play will be a run or a pass. He can then get in position to pick up the tight end or play the run accordingly.

The whole issue of the safety's alignment is much more important than it may appear. The way he lines up can make it easier or harder to reach his assigned area, or pick up his assigned man. For instance, if the strong safety has the deep outside in a strong side zone coverage, lining up deeper than normal would facilitate getting to the assigned area quickly. If instead he has the short outside zone in an inverted coverage, he should not be deep but rather shift out closer to the sideline.

But positioning himself in this manner makes it easy for the quarterback to read the coverage. So the strong safety tries to hide his actual assignment by mixing up his initial alignment. He may set up deep for an inverted zone or close for a deep corner zone — just the opposite of what would make things easy for him. Or he might make no adjustment from his normal man-to-man position. He could even exaggerate the situation — say, come way up and fake a blitz knowing he has a deep

. . . the strong safety tries to hide his actual assignment by mixing up his initial alignment.

zone. Then he's really gambling that the quarterback would never think that and hoping this bit of deception will throw off the quarterback's read and buy himself time to get back.

There are other considerations which put a limit on this type of tactic and, in fact, favor cheating a little in the direction of his actual assignment. Basically, it comes down to execution being more important than deception. Say the strong safety has the tight end man-to-man but lines up wider than normal, to hide the coverage. He's really vulnerable to a quick post route, and the result could be pretty damaging. So alignment of the safeties is not a trivial aspect of their play. They have to weigh the options and make a choice.

Tight End & Other Responsibilities

The tight end normally is bigger and taller than the strong safety. So the strong safety's coverage of the tight end involves a mismatch. The extent of help the strong safety gets from the outside linebacker at the line is somewhat dependent on that linebacker's assignment. If the linebacker has to pick up the fullback circling out, and the fullback starts out on the snap, the linebacker won't stay jamming the tight end as long.

The extent of help the strong safety gets from the outside linebacker ... is dependent on that linebacker's assignment.

Besides covering the tight end man-to-man, the strong safety has a variety of other pass defense assignments. He plays a deep one-third in a standard rotating zone, a short zone in an inverted coverage, and a deep one-half in a double zone. In man-to-man he may be called upon to double a wide receiver with a cornerback, while a linebacker or the free safety takes the tight end. Or he could be involved in a combination coverage. For example, if the tight end goes up the middle, the free safety takes him. If the tight end cuts outside, the strong safety picks him up.

Playing closer to the line than the free safety, the strong safety is usually characterized as the bigger and harder tackler of the two safeties.

Free Safety

Not Always Free

The free safety lines up toward the weak side of the offense. As discussed in Chapter 3, the weak side safety often has no specific receiver to cover in a man-to-man defense. So he is free to help out where needed, and hence the designation "free" safety. The extent to which the free safety is actually free varies from team to team. On some teams he may be free only five to six times a game. Whereas on others, the free safety will be free much more often. It depends on the defensive philosophy, which in turn is based on the available personnel.

If a team has an inexperienced corner or strong safety, the free safety may have to help out more, which restricts his freedom. If the defense uses a lot of different coverages — different zones, combos, etc. — the free safety is going to have many specific assignments. Often, whether he winds up free depends on what offensive play develops. For instance, with certain defenses the free safety will be free when the halfback stays in or when the split end runs an out instead of an in route.

An Opportunist

The free safety should be a ballhawk rather than a gambler. He's more of an opportunist. To be effective, the free safety has to be able to diagnose plays quickly. Here's where experience and study are important. In looking at the films, the free safety will try to pick up tendencies. He'll be more interested in overall play around his area rather than the moves of particular individual opponents.

Positioned about 8 to 10 yards from the line of scrimmage, it can be difficult to see exactly what is happening when a play begins. Something like play action with a fake handoff can momentarily disguise things. It may take a full second or so for the free safety to really decipher what's

---

The extent to which the free safety is actually free varies from team to team.

going on. In the interim, he isn't standing still. Since he plays pass first and plays run only when it is evident, the free safety will probably start backpedalling as he reads. Depending on the game situation and the defense called, he may have to move immediately toward his primary responsibility. But if he can just backpedal for a second or two, it makes it difficult for the quarterback to read. Then once the play reveals itself, he reacts.

When he has some freedom, the free safety can try to lure a throw by laying off the receiver. Then he makes his move once the ball goes up. Needless to say, he has to carefully consider his own speed, the receiver's speed, and how much ground must be covered. Under the right conditions this is how an interception can be set up. However, he can't get carried away. The free safety is usually the one his teammates are counting on for help deep.

Keys Against Pass

On a pass play, the free safety attempts to key the quarterback and the receivers. He'll try to determine what pass pattern they are running and where the quarterback will throw.

Judging distances is a big factor.

It's not simply a case of who is the likely receiver, but also how deep the ball will be thrown. Judging distances is a big factor. Different quarterbacks provide the safeties with varying amounts of information. Some of the young quarterbacks who are learning to read defenses and cope with rushing linemen do little to hide their intentions. They are mainly concerned with finding the open man and getting the ball to him. In doing so, they tend to "bird dog" the intended receiver. By keying the quarterback (which way he's looking, how his body is turned) the free safety can get a good idea where he is going to throw.

The older, more experienced quarterbacks furnish less information. They can "look off" the intended receiver until the last moment. Especially tough are the good quarterbacks with a fast release. They don't tip the direction by looking, and once they do commit themselves, the ball is in the air almost immediately. Knowing where the receivers are and who is getting open can be more informative when defending against the good quarterbacks. Sometimes it's best to just go to the deepest and fastest receiver, the one who poses the biggest threat.

Kickers

Keeping Cool

Mental attitude is a big part of kicking. About 99% of the kicker's time during a game is spent on the sideline waiting. Aside from kickoffs, he only comes in to attempt to score. He's not involved in getting yardage for his team, just kicking field goals or adding a PAT (point after touchdown). Sure, he's occasionally called upon when a field goal is improbable because of the distance. But generally he's used when the team is within range. And often the outcome of the game depends on his kick. He can win it or lose it.

Kicking the ball between the uprights requires a smooth coordinated stroke. Position, timing, motion — it all has to be exact. The mechanics are practiced until they are automatic. There are many who have it down pat. They can kick accurately and for distance.

But there is a big difference between a practice kicker and a game kicker. In a game, the pressure is on. The defensive line is crashing in. Every single kick is for keeps. The good kickers are the ones who can perform under game conditions. That's a lot different from kicking alone on the practice field. Either they make it or they don't. There is no in-between. If a kicker fails, there is nothing he can do but go to the sideline and wait for the next kick. They're not engaged in blocking, tackling, running, or any other phase of the game. With the exception of kickoffs, there are no other assignments to command their attention or vent their emotions.

To survive, the kicker has to stay cool and confident. The great kickers are even more than confident. They look forward to the challenge. When they miss, they want to go right back in and kick. The opportunity to win the game is what they want. They can handle the pressure. On the other hand, when a kicker dreads being put on the spot, his performance will reflect it.

> *... there is a big difference between a practice kicker and a game kicker.*

Soccer vs. Straightaway Style

As to the soccer versus straightaway style, the consensus seems to be that one way is not vastly superior to the other. More important is which style is best for the individual, and how good the individual is using it. Still, the soccer style with the kicking leg arcing around and across does allow the player to get more of his body into the kick, which should mean better distance. The straightaway style makes it easier to line up and may be inherently a little more accurate. But it really depends on the individual.

The kickers do note that many soccer stylists began playing soccer very young. On the other hand, straightaway kickers tend to have started kicking much later. Hence, the soccer style may reflect strong kicking legs due to years of conditioning and practice.

A study of college field goal kickers prepared by John Stanley of West Texas University provides some insights. The study covered field-goal attempts by NCAA Division I kickers in 1978. The statistics are informative in comparing the styles because they are based on a large number of kickers. A few of the overall findings are summarized below:

1978 NCAA Division I
Field Goal Attempts

	Soccer Style	Straightaway Style
Attempts (Total = 2,004)	1,243	761
% Good	59%	58%
Avg. distance (yd. line)	36	35
% Good by yardage:*		
20-29 yd. lines	74%	78%
30-39 yd. lines	67%	60%
40-49 yd. lines	43%	38%

*92% of all attempts took place between the 20- and 49-yard lines.

> **The soccer style has clearly become the dominant method for placekicks.**

The table shows that the soccer style kickers were slightly better overall. They also tended to be better at longer distances. Still, the differences throughout are small. The one place where there is an overwhelming edge is in total attempts. The straightaway style accounted for only about 38%. The soccer style has clearly become the dominant method for placekicks. In the pros, the soccer style is even more pervasive. There are only a few remaining straightaway kickers.

The Soccer Style

A kicker using the soccer style starts from a point behind and to the left of the ball (we are assuming a right-footed kicker here). Several align themselves by taking three steps back and two steps to the side from the point where the ball will be spotted. Most use basically a 2-step approach (some start with a slight stutter step which results in 3). The kicker takes a long step with his right foot, strides with his left, planting it hard, and swings the right instep through the ball. It's step, step, and kick. On that first step he twists slightly to the right, kind of winding up for the kick. After contact he follows through to the left by bringing the kicking leg up and across his body. What they hit the ball with is the high instep. The toe is out, the foot extended, and the ankle is rigid as contact is made.

Planting the left foot is critical. It should be about 6 to 12 inches to the side of the ball, depending on the size of the kicker. If the foot is planted too close or too far away, too far forward or backward it will throw the kicking motion off. This causes the ball to hook, slice, or not have a high enough trajectory to clear the linemen.

Those are the fundamentals. Each soccer kicker has his own individual style. That is, two soccer stylists may exhibit noticeably different forms. They may approach the ball at different angles and their follow-throughs might appear dissimilar. Whatever works is what counts.

The Straightaway Style

Most straightaway kickers also use a 2-step approach, but they start directly behind the ball. Again, they pace off about three normal steps from the ball in order to line up. As they begin the kick, the first step is a short one while the second is a full power stride. Unlike the soccer-style kicker who plants his left foot to the side of the ball, the straightaway kicker plants about 6 to 8 inches behind the ball. The right kicking leg is then driven straight through the ball while snapping the knee for extra leg speed. Locking the ankle, contact is made with the toe of the kicking foot. The ball is 11 inches long and the point of impact is about 3-3/4 inches from the ground. On long kicks it may be slightly higher to get more distance and less height.

Rhythm & Timing

Rhythm and timing are essential to both styles. Kicking, after all, comes down to meeting the ball just right each time. Groove the stroke and do it the same way every time. Concentrate, get down a certain rhythm, and it's all automatic. Upset the rhythm and the process works in reverse. It's not automatic, concentration is disturbed, and lack of confidence creeps in. Why a kicker starts missing is often unclear to the kicker himself. But maintaining self-confidence is crucial to finding the groove again.

When a long field goal is attempted, the kicker obviously needs more distance. But he

> **Why a kicker starts missing is often unclear to the kicker himself.**

shouldn't kick harder — that destroys the rhythm. Rather, the experts say to bring the kicking leg through quicker and keep the overall motion the same. For extra point attempts, distance is not a problem. So the kicker concentrates on getting the ball up over the defensive charge.

Kickoffs involve the same procedures except for a running start. Again the idea is not to try to overpower the ball. While overpowering the ball can lead to some real booming kicks, it can also lead to some real duds. A more deliberate technique yields consistent results.

Equipment

Soccer-style kickers use a soccer shoe with short cleats on the kicking foot. The other shoe may have longer cleats for a firm plant. They put a lot of pressure on that foot as they stop and swing through the kick. The straightaway kicker uses regular football shoes with a square toe for the kicking foot.

No tee is allowed in pro football for field goal attempts. ... A tee is permitted for kickoffs.

No tee is allowed in pro football for field goal attempts (a tee is allowed in college games). A tee is permitted for kickoffs. Given the running start, the tee eliminates the risk of scuffing the ground and is a real aid on a kickoff.

3-Man Effort

The center used in field goal situations is not always the regular one. The snap is different and the regular center may not have the ability to make it. He may not have sufficient practice time to devote to placement, or he may be so banged up and taped that he can't handle the ball well enough. In any case, whoever centers for field goal and extra-point attempts has to spiral the ball 7 yards back to the holder right on target. In addition, the laces should be up every time the holder gets the ball. This takes some trial-and-error testing and a lot of practice. The distance between the center and the holder is always the same 7 yards. So based on the number of revolutions of his snap, the center has to position the ball accordingly at the start.

The holder's job is obviously to catch the snap and place the ball on the ground straight (not tipped). He has to turn the laces to the front, away from the kicker, and hold the ball with one finger on top. While all this is happening, the kicker concentrates on the spot. Peripherally he sees the ball snapped and begins his kick.

The three have to practice together a lot. They have about 1.3 seconds to snap, catch, place, and kick the ball. Any longer and the defense will probably block it. So there's no room for error.

The kicker has to have confidence in his holder. As we said, rhythm is the important thing to the kick. A kicker expects the ball to be in place and right. If it's not positioned correctly, even the best kicker isn't going to make it.

> **They have about 1.3 seconds to snap, catch, place, and kick the ball.**

7 Yards Back

The ball is generally spotted 7 yards behind the line on field goal attempts. Placing it farther back would seem to give the kicker more time. However, it would also give the defense a better angle for blocking. At 7 yards the end men on the defense have to turn a corner in order to get around the end of the offensive line and in front of the ball. Moving the spot back eliminates the corner, or at least reduces the angle. So pro teams rarely place the ball much beyond 7 yards back for an attempted field goal.

Weather

The weather plays a bigger role than some fans might think. As the temperature drops, the air becomes denser. The kicker, with exactly the same stroke as in September, can't kick the ball as far in the frigid December weather.

Wind is an obvious problem. Even with the wind to the kicker's back, it can sometimes cause the ball to drift to one side or the other. Rain makes the ball slippery, and the air will be heavy with humidity. But an even bigger problem is footing. This is especially true for soccer stylists who have to plant that left foot hard. Just the thought of slipping can throw their concentration off and lead to problems.

Punters

Form for Consistency

On average, a punt covers more yardage than any other play from scrimmage. The object is field position and field position controls the flow of the game. An outstanding punter can take his team out of a hole and put the opposition in one. His contributions are direct and observable. His performance is immediately measurable.

Consistency is the trait which coaches look for in punters. They don't want a 55-yard kick followed by one for 30 yards. They want at least 40 yards and a 4.0-second hang time with regularity. Punting is not a matter of strength. Form, not force, is what leads to consistency.

Fact or Fancy?

Punting is one area of football that has been the subject of much opinion and analysis. Opinions are often based on everything from personal experience to mathematical equations of the physics involved. On the other hand, analysis has commonly consisted of eyeball investigation and subjective theory. Many coaches candidly admit to knowing little about the correct mechanics. At the same time there are experts who range from those convinced that "their" techniques must be followed to those who say there are no absolutes and every kicker should develop his own style.

Missing from all of this is hard scientific evidence as to what's right and what's wrong. This void will probably be filled soon since punting would seem to present a kinesiologist's dream. Those are the people in a rather new field devoted to studying the motion of the human body. Part of the mystery associated with punting is that it occurs so fast. It does, after all, come down to the foot striking the ball. And this process takes place in approximately .015 second. Translated that means take one second, cut it into one thousand equal parts, and 15 of those 1,000 would represent the interval that the punter's foot is in contact with the ball.

The Mechanics

There are four parts to the punt: the approach, drop, contact, and follow-through. From start to finish there is disagreement as to the proper technique. The approach should be anywhere from $1\frac{1}{2}$ to 3 steps, and the supporting foot either should or should not leave the ground after the kick. However, there is general agreement that the ball is to be dropped parallel with the ground, contact should be made about knee high (just as the kicking leg snaps straight), the toe should be depressed and the ankle rigid, the follow-through should be straight ahead and up.

Some high speed film studies have been made on a limited number of subjects. They have found that while foot speed is important it doesn't vary significantly between good and bad punts for the same individual. Rather than foot speed, the key is how contact is made. Hitting the ball squarely is much more important to transferring momentum than driving the foot through faster. For good contact the general rule is to hit with the arch of the foot,

From start to finish there is disagreement as to the proper technique.

right in the middle. However, there is some film-study evidence that the point of impact should be a little higher up toward the ankle, and the ball should be at a slight angle inward. Everyone agrees that hitting either end of the ball is bad (results in an end-over-end and shorter kick) and hitting the center of the ball is good (results in a tight spiral and longer kick). As to whether the kicker should leave the ground or not, one study found that the better the kick the less the kicker left the ground. They theorized that the more the leg's momentum is transferred to the ball, the less remains after impact to pull the kicker's body up off the ground.

Whether punting can be reduced to a science or not is questionable. There probably are some basic fundamentals to be followed as well as some aspects that have to be worked out by the individual. As things stand right now, professional punters, like placekickers, have their own styles. Many feel that the best punters are born, not made. Either the punter has that snap or he doesn't. Maybe, maybe not.

Getting the Punt Off

Punters stand about 13 to 15 yards behind the line. Because of the distance, the snap from center is long and sometimes off the mark. So the punter has to practice taking snaps, including some which are purposely bad.

Punters have about 2.1 seconds to get the punt off. The exact interval depends on how seriously the defense attempts to block the punt. Since the snap takes approximately 0.8 to 0.9 second, that leaves about 1.3 seconds for the kick. The punter can't fumble around with the ball. He has to be sure-handed in receiving the snap and get right into the kick.

Most punters use a 3-step approach. For a right-footed kicker it's left, right, left, and kick. Those who use a 2-step approach have a definite advantage in terms of getting the punt off quicker. They can pare the time down by a good 0.2 second. That may not sound like much, but it makes it almost impossible for a defender to reach him before the kick is away.

Many feel that the best punters are born, not made. . . . Maybe, maybe not.

If the snap is really bad or the blocking has broken down, a 3-step punter should also use a 2-step approach. The resulting kick may be shorter, but at least he'll get it off. This is another item for practice. To be comfortable and effective with the shortened approach, a punter has to work at it.

Hang Time & Distance

Hang time refers to the interval when the punted ball is in the air. Both hang time and distance are important. The punter can't emphasize one at the expense of the other. Generally, he doesn't have to. A well-punted ball will result in both. Only if his form consistently results in a kick which is too high or too low should a conscious adjustment be made.

The hang time for most kicks should be 4.0 to 4.5 seconds. And they should travel 40 to 45 yards from the line of scrimmage. Anything in excess of these benchmarks is excellent.

Accuracy

When the punting team is inside the 50-yard line the objective changes. Then the punter is expected to kick the ball out of bounds inside the 20 or hang it up around the 10. Either case will probably result in no runback and the opposition will take over deep in their own territory.

This places a premium on the punter's accuracy. These situations test his skill in tailoring the height, distance, and direction of the punt to fit the circumstances. And kicking the ball out of bounds may require a longer kick than it appears. The ball has to travel from the center of the field to the sideline (about 26 yards) as well as from the line of scrimmage to the point downfield. To be successful, the punter has to be able to take these factors into account and with one swing of the leg produce the desired result.

> ... *kicking the ball out of bounds may require a longer kick than it appears.*

Weather

Weather affects punters just as it affects placekickers. The colder it gets, the shorter the kick, all things being equal. Wind and rain create the usual problems.

When kicking into the wind, the punter will drop the ball lower, attempting to get a low driving spiral. On any punt, he will avoid hitting the laces and the valve section of the ball. These are both dead spots which absorb some of the impact and shorten the distance of the kick.

Speaking of laces, some kickers lace their kicking shoes straight across, not diagonally, and tie the knot away from the point where the foot meets the ball. They wear a thin sock and may cut off part of the shoe's tongue, all to avoid any cushioning on impact. Of course, there are a few that go all the way and just kick barefooted.

Safety Man

After the punter finishes his kick, he usually becomes a safety man on the coverage. That is, he lags back and watches the return develop in the event the runner breaks through. The teammate who blocks closest to him at the time of the kick is generally the other safety man. So they coordinate their actions accordingly.

... some kickers lace their kicking shoes straight across ...

Average Player Characteristics by Position

(based on 1981 rosters of all 28 NFL teams)

	Height	Weight	Age	Years in NFL
Center	6'3"	253	27	5
Guard	6'3"	259	27	5
Tackle	6'5"	267	26	5
Tight end	6'4"	234	25	4
Wide receiver	6'0"	188	26	4
Halfback	6'0"	199	25	4
Fullback	6'0"	219	26	4
Quarterback	6'3"	204	27	5
Nose tackle	6'3"	256	25	4
Defensive tackle	6'4"	261	28	6
Defensive end	6'4"	254	26	5
Middle linebacker	6'2"	228	25	4
Inside linebacker	6'2"	230	26	4
Outside linebacker	6'2"	225	26	4
Cornerback	6'0"	187	25	3
Safety	6'1"	194	26	4
Placekicker	5'11"	184	28	5
Punter	6'1"	199	26	4

Of all the 1,260 players, approximately:

16% were shorter than 6'0"
6% were taller than 6'5"

10% weighed less than 185 lbs.
7% weighed more than 265 lbs.

24% were under age 24
10% were over age 30

15% were rookies
12% had over 8 years' experience

CHAPTER 7

PLAY CALLS

Calling plays involves code words and numbers to designate player assignments. The quarterback is not the only one making play calls. A linebacker or safety is generally calling the defensive plays. And offensive linemen make calls at the line of scrimmage to adjust their blocking to the defense they encounter. The defense also makes adjustments after the teams line up. Moreover, as the play is unfolding defensive players are shouting to each other to coordinate their coverages. This chapter discusses play calling in general and includes some hypothetical examples.

DIFFERENT SYSTEMS

Speaking the Language

Each of the NFL teams has its own terminology and methods for calling plays. But there are some common elements in many of the systems. If a coach likes a system when he is an assistant at one team, he'll probably take it with him as head coach somewhere else. He'll make his own modifications and some changes will arise solely for purposes of secrecy. Still, the net effect is that the basic system of his former team has spread to another franchise.

So several teams may be using basically the same system, but with their own unique variations. Others have systems that are so dissimilar that they're like foreign languages when compared one to another. In any event, unless you really know what the terms and groupings mean, you can never be sure. For example, some teams designate the strong side linebacker as "Sam". On others he might be called "Stub". No big deal. However, consider a term such as "Bronco". On one team it could mean the outside linebacker <u>forces</u> an end run, while on another it may mean the outside linebacker <u>blitzes</u>.

One of the chief reasons for the terminology is simply to save time. Instead of saying "strong side linebacker" all the time, it's easier to say "Sam". When you are dealing with 11 players at one time, abbreviated designations are a lot less cumbersome. Take calling plays during the game. Deception aside, if everyone spoke in long form, it would consume just too much time. Hence, the lingo.

OFFENSIVE PLAY CALLS

Numbering Holes, Backs & Receivers

In order to identify the holes for running plays, many teams use the following system:

```
      9      7  5  3  1 0  2  4  6      8
      O      () O  O  ◇  O  O  O        O
                        O

                  O     ()    O
```

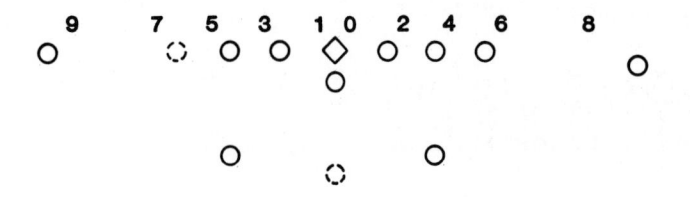

Holes in the offensive line are numbered 0 through 9.

    0 – To right side of center
    1 – To left side of center
    2 – Just outside right guard
    3 – Just outside left guard
          ...and so on.

Hole No. 7 is just outside the left tight end, or where he would be if there is no tight end on the left side (i.e., if the left side is the weak side for that play, there is no tight end on the left). Hole No. 9 relates to a wide outside run to the left. The corresponding outside numbers on the right are No. 6 and No. 8.

On other teams, the even numbers are on the left and the odd are on the right. Different numbering systems could also be used.

For running plays, the backs are numbered:

    1 – Quarterback
    2 – Left halfback
    3 – Fullback
    4 – Right halfback

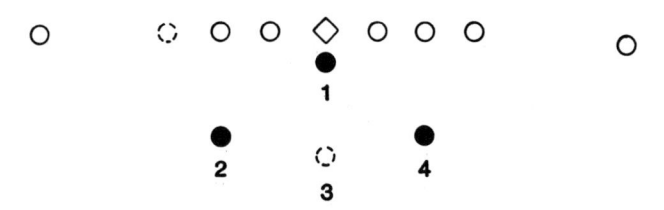

```
         O         () O  O  ◇  O  O  O            O
                              ●
                              1

                     ●        ()       ●
                     2        3        4
```

For pass plays, receivers have the following designations:

```
X - Split end
Y - Tight end
Z - Flanker
A - Halfback
B - Fullback
```

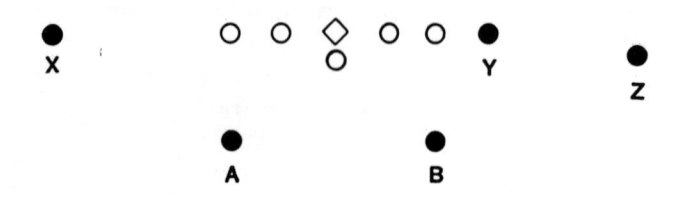

Formations

Colors are used to identify some basic formations. Descriptive words are used for other formations. (Some teams use word descriptions for all formations.)

```
Red   - Standard pro set
          (Alternatives: Full, split)
Brown - Weak side set
          (Alternatives: Far, opposite)
Blue  - Strong side set
          (Alternatives: Near, strong)
I     - I formation

Slot  - Slot formation
```

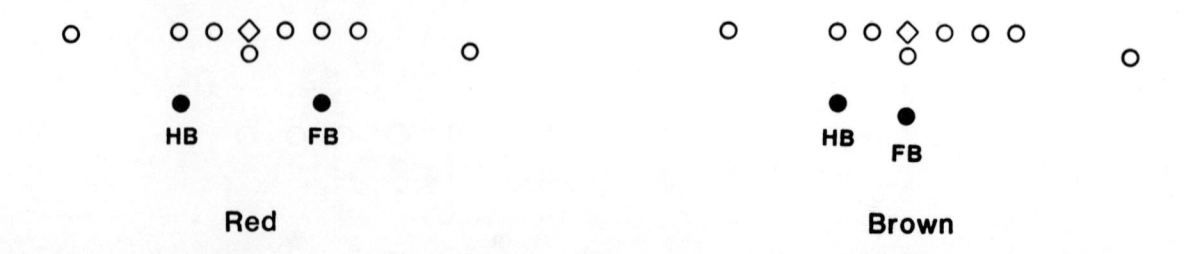

Blue

I Formation

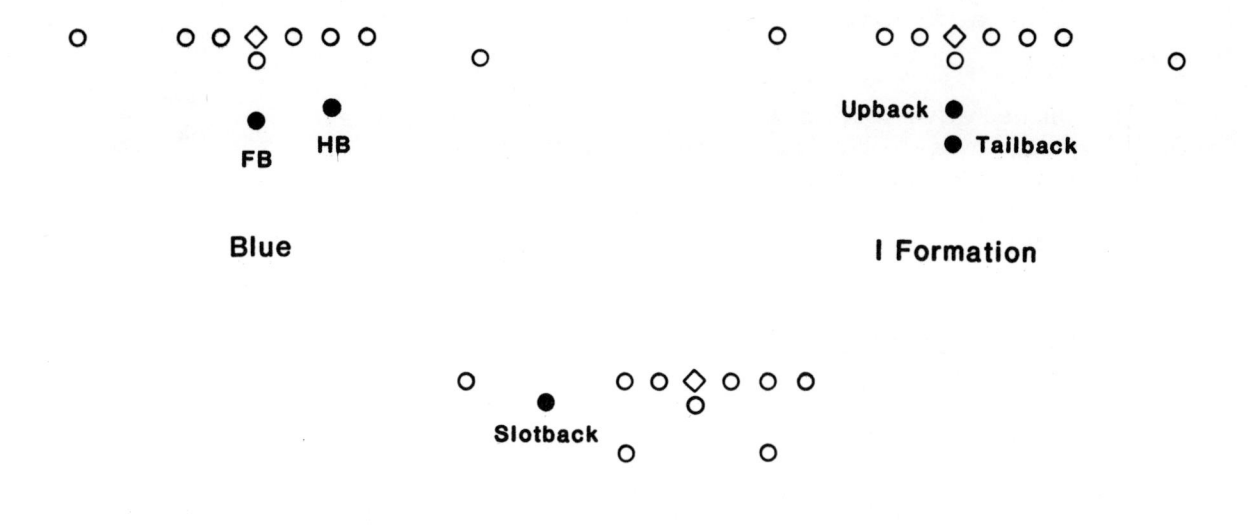

Slot

The terms "left" and "right" are added to indicate which side is the strong side (with the tight end). So, "Red Right" is a pro set with the tight end on the right side. "Brown Left" is a weak side set with the tight end on the left side.

Red Right

Brown Left

Basic Running Plays

33 Play
(No. 3 Back Thru No. 3 Hole)

After determining the formation, the basic way to call a running play is to first designate the back and then the hole. For example, "33" means the 3 back (fullback) is the ball carrier and goes through the No. 3 hole (off left guard). So a power

179

sweep by a halfback to the right side would be called 28 and a fullback slant off left tackle would be 35.

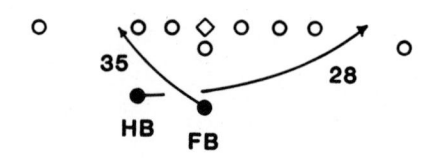

The more advanced systems used by pro teams tend to group plays by backfield action, blocking methods, or other techniques common to a number of running attacks. A hypothetical set of categories might include:

10's - Pitchouts & dive plays
20's - Halfback carrying to strong side
30's - Fullback carrying to weak side
40's - Misdirections
50's - Draws & special plays

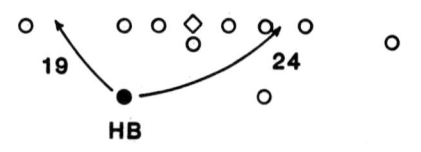

When using the series approach, the second number in a given call remains the hole to be attacked as it is in the basic method of calling running plays. Therefore, if the call is 19, it would be a pitchout to the left (10 series and No. 9 hole). Alternatively, if the call was 24, the halfback would go off right tackle (20 series and No. 4 hole).

Back & Hole
(28 & 35 Plays)

Series Plays
(19 & 24 Plays)

Calling Plays
- Quarterback vs. Coach

Whether the quarterback calls the plays or they are sent in from the sideline depends on the coach's philosophy. The points in favor of sending in the plays usually include:

- quarterback's inexperience
- vast experience of coaching staff
- enables quarterback to concentrate on execution
- enables coaches to study how play went.

The last point relates to the coaches in the press box. If they know what play is being called, they are better able to watch how the defense reacts and possibly spot why the play worked or did not work. This is especially true now that situation substitution is so prevalent and the offense is faced with so many different defenses. The coaches upstairs often take instant photos for instant analysis and later discussions with players, say, at halftime.

When the quarterback calls his own plays, the reasons include:

- quarterback has experience
- quarterback has best feel for what might work
- quarterback's decisions will generally coincide with coach's.

The last point here refers to the game plan. The game plan is based on films, a scouting report, and past encounters with the particular opponent. After spending the week discussing the opposition's tendencies, which plays may work best, and when to use them, the quarterback and coaches are in agreement as to what to call under most of the situations they are likely to encounter. (However, some coaches point out that under fire quarterbacks tend to keep going with the same plays, whereas a coach sitting in the press box will make greater use of the entire offensive scheme.)

Most coaches elect to send the plays in. Nevertheless, the quarterback normally is given authority to call a different play or to change the play at the line of scrimmage (audible).

When the coaches call the plays, some teams use hand signals from the sideline rather than employing a substitute player to relay the call to the quarterback. The feeling is that it's faster and there's less chance for error. Instead of telling the play to a substitute and hoping he understands it and repeats it correctly to the quarterback, the quarterback reads the hand signal directly. But there still is the possibility that the signal will be given incorrectly or it will be read incorrectly. In any event, teams which employ the signal system use a series of arm and hand motions. Two separate players or coaches may be giving signals at the same time. The idea is that the opposition doesn't know which one is giving the real signals at any particular point.

Calling Plays in Huddle

There are two types of huddles. Most teams use a closed huddle where the players form an elongated circle with everyone crouched over. A few teams use an open huddle with the quarterback facing the rest of the players.

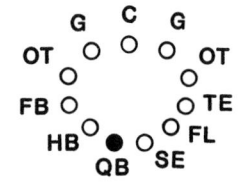

Closed Huddle

Whichever method is used, the quarterback is in charge and generally no one talks unless the quarterback asks him a question. The principal reason for this is time. The offense has only 30 seconds to call the play, line up, and snap the ball. If a player has a suggestion or the quarterback needs information, that exchange normally takes place before the huddle is formed or on the sideline.

Hypothetical Call

In the huddle, the quarterback will call a play by designating the formation, play number, blocking, and snap count. A hypothetical call could be the following:

"Red Right 20 Quick Back 0 on 3".

This is what the call means:

"Red Right" (Formation)

Pro set, strong side (tight end) on right.

"20" (Series & Hole)

20 series has halfback carry to strong side; hole he heads for is No. 0 (zero), to right of the center.

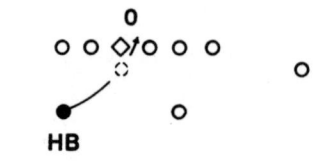

"Quick" (Onside Blocking)

"Quick" tells the offensive linemen this is a quick trap play — it designates the play side blocking as follows:

- onside guard pulls outside and lets defensive tackle across line
- offside guard pulls and traps left defensive tackle
- center blocks down on right defensive tackle
- onside offensive tackle slides off left defensive end to block on middle linebacker
- tight end blocks left defensive end.

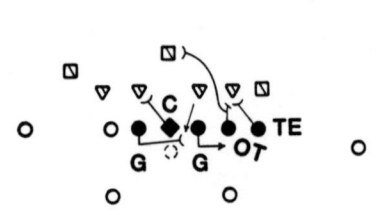

Open Huddle

"Red Right"

"20"

"Quick"

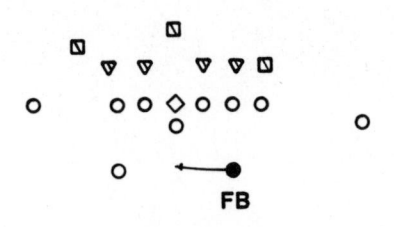

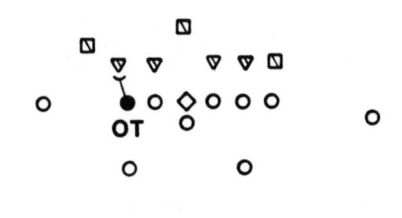

"Back" (Backfield Blocking)

"Back" instructs fullback to head toward back side (left side) in an attempt to influence middle linebacker, freeze him momentarily.

"O" (Offside Blocking)

Due to nature of play, offside blocking is straightforward; "O" has offside tackle block out on defensive end.

"on 3" (Snap Count)

Ball will be snapped on 3rd "hut".

In another system where the series are based on blocking patterns, the call might be shorter. For example, if the 50 series covered trap plays this call might be:

"Red Right 50 on 3".

Signals at Line

At the line, once everyone is in position, the quarterback will shout out signals such as the following:

"Set, Pro, Two 84, Two 84, Hut... Hut, Hut".

"Set" (Stance)

On hearing this, the players drop into their 3-point or 2-point stances.

"Pro" (Defense)

Quarterback identifies the defensive alignment; "pro" is the word for standard 4-3 defense.

"Two 84" (Potential Audible)

An audible changing the play consists of calling the snap count and then the new play; 3 is the snap count in this example, so "Two 84" is only a dummy call.

"Two 84" (Repeat Audible)

To ensure that the entire offense hears audible portion, quarterback first shouts it to one side and then repeats it to other side.

"Hut... Hut, Hut" (Snap Count)

Ball is snapped on 3rd hut; note that this quarterback is using nonrhythmic cadence (he paused between 1st and 2nd hut).

In some systems, "set" may come after the audible portion of the signals instead of at the beginning. Delaying the set call allows the linemen to position themselves after the audible (if any is called), and thus may provide for a more favorable alignment.

Calling Audible

Suppose instead of lining up in a standard 4-3, the defense goes into an overshifted 4-3. Recall that in an overshift one or more defensive linemen move toward the strong side of the offense. In this situation, suppose the right defensive tackle moves directly over the center, in the path of the intended play. Seeing this, the quarterback decides to audible, or check off, to a new play. Let's say he wants to change the play from the quick trap call explained above (Red Right 20 Quick Back 0 on 3) to a weak side slant with the fullback carrying off-tackle. If he had called that slant play in the huddle it would have been:

"Brown Right 35 Bob Man".

"Brown Right" (Formation)

Weak side set, strong side right.

"Brown Right 35 Bob Man"

"35" (Series & Hole)

30 series involves fullback carrying to weak side; hole is No. 5 (off left tackle).

"Bob" (Backfield Blocking)

Halfback blocks weak side linebacker ("bob" = back on backer).

"Man" (Line Blocking)

Linemen block straight out on men over them (man-to-man blocking).

For each game, the offense has a number of plays to which the quarterback can check off at the line of scrimmage. There is a standard formation and blocking scheme associated with each such play. The quarterback calls an audible by just giving the series and hole number of the play. When the offensive players hear a play number being audibled they know the alignment and blocking to accompany it. We will assume that the "35" audible is set up for the alignment and blocking described above. If a play has certain optional aspects, the quarterback can easily designate which one by adding a letter to the play number. For example, "35G" could tell the offside guard to pull and lead block.

Okay, back to the quarterback. In the huddle he called the quick trap play, Red Right 20 Quick Back 0 on 3. Up at the line of scrimmage he sees the defense is in an overshift. So he wants to change the play to the weak side slant, Brown Right 35 Bob Man, which as explained above is on the check-off list for that week. To call this audible (i.e., change the play) at the line the quarterback gives the following signals:

"Set, Over, Three 35, Three 35, Hut, Hut".

"Set" (Stance)

As in all quarterback calls, this signals the players to drop into their 3-point or 2-point stances.

185

"Over" (Defense)

"Over" identifies the defense as an overshifted 4-3.

"Three 35" (Audible)

Since "Three" is the same as the original snap count ("on 3"), this means the play called in the huddle is off; 35 is the new play and it means Brown Right 35 Bob Man; the snap count on all audibles automatically changes to "on 2".

"Three 35" (Repeat Audible)

As in all quarterback calls, he first shouts audible portion to one side and then repeats it to the other.

"Hut, Hut" (Snap Count)

Ball is snapped on 2nd hut since the snap count automatically becomes 2 for all plays changed at the line.

Note that the quarterback has to give the running backs time to shift from their pro set (Red Right) positions to a weak side set (Brown Right) alignment. They must be stationary for a full second after they shift before the ball is snapped.

One alternative method of calling an audible is to use a color instead of the snap count. For each game there are two or three "live" colors. If a live color is called, then the original play is off and a new play is on. Using any other color has no effect on the play called in the huddle. For instance, assume red and green are the two live colors. (These colors refer to calls made at the line of scrimmage by the quarterback and have nothing to do with colors that might be used to designate formations or anything else.) Calling "... Blue 84, Blue 84 ..." would have no effect just as was the case for "... Two 84, Two 84 ..." in the original example. On the other hand, "... Green 35, Green 35 ..." would change the play the way "... Three 35, Three 35 ..." did in the example discussed above.

Protecting Audible

If a quarterback using the color audible system thinks the defense is picking up the audibles, he can:

(1) change the live colors,
(2) make a live color "dead" for a particular play, or
(3) run a "check with me".

The last procedure means that he will call the play at the line and the players are to follow it regardless of what color precedes it (no play is called in the huddle).

Using the snap count system makes it difficult for the defense to pick up an audible because they don't know what count was called in the huddle. For this reason, as well as retaining the advantage of knowing when the play will begin, a quarterback cannot fall into a pattern on his snap counts. To make sure this doesn't happen, some teams have a reserve on the sideline keep track of the snap count the quarterback uses on every play.

Defensive Shift After Audible

The defense may start shifting after the quarterback gets through the audible portion of his signals. To counteract this, the quarterback may instruct the players in the huddle that the snap will occur early, before he completes the audible portion. For example, the ball could be snapped as the quarterback begins to repeat the dummy audible. When a quarterback does this he usually calls a basic play in the huddle since he'll be locked in with no opportunity to change it at the line.

On a given call, if a defensive shift negates the play and the quarterback is too far along, he may go through with the play and just take the loss. However, if it's a crucial down, he might call time out or restart the signals and check off. This should not occur often.

Pass Plays

Calling a pass play involves a slightly different procedure. In that case, the call has to instruct each of the potential receivers what route to run. To accomplish this, many of the pass routes are numbered. The passing trees for X, Y, and Z illustrate routes 1 through 9 for each. The routes for X and Z are the same (the trees are reversed to keep the inside routes inside and the outside routes outside in both cases). Some of the numbered routes for Y are different.

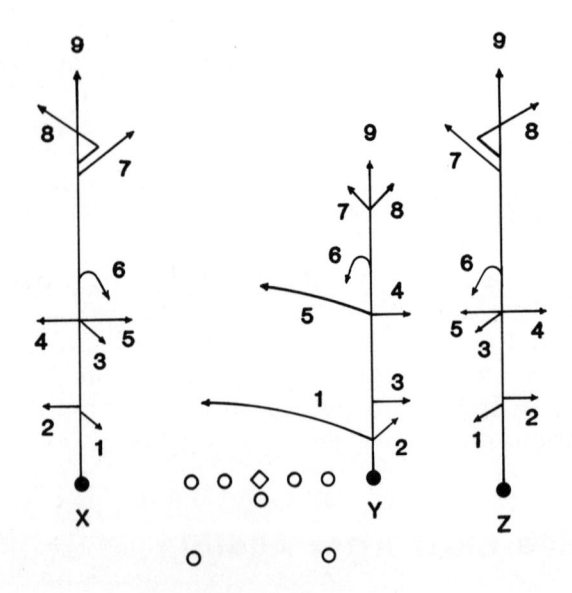

Numbered Pass Routes

for X (Split End)

Y (Tight End)

Z (Flanker)

A possible pass play would be:

"Red Right 439 Flare Check on 1".

"Red Right" (Formation)

Pro set, strong side right.

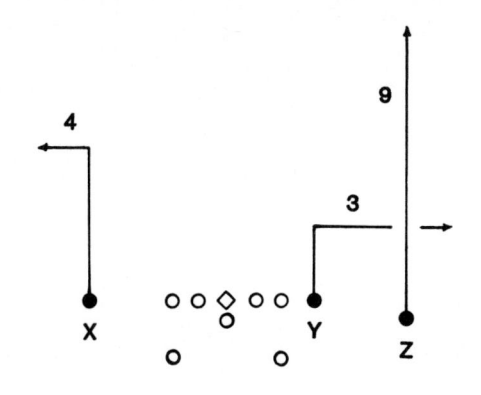

"Red Right 439"

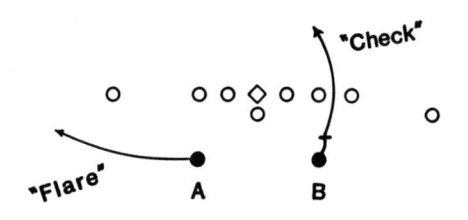

"Flare Check"

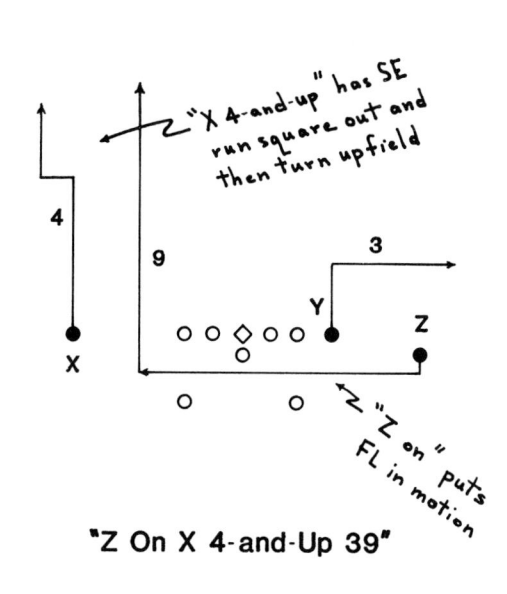

"Z On X 4-and-Up 39"

"439" (XYZ Routes)

"439" designates the routes of X, Y, and Z in that order —

- 4: X runs a square-out
- 3: Y runs a short-out
- 9: Z runs a streak or fly.

"Flare" (A's Route)

After giving routes for X, Y, and Z, the route of the A back (halfback) is called; "Flare" instructs halfback to flare to outside.

"Check" (B's Route)

Route for B back (fullback) follows that for A back; "Check" tells fullback to run a check pass route (momentary block and circle out thru the line).

"on 1" (Snap Count)

Ball is snapped on 1st "hut".

Routes 1 through 9 don't include all the possibilities for the receivers. In many cases the quarterback may want to modify one of the basic routes or add a different one. Suppose he wants X, the split end, to turn upfield after making his break to the outside (i.e., change from a square-out to an out-and-up). In that case, he calls out the receiver whose route he is modifying (X) and then calls the route as desired (4-and-up).

If the quarterback wants to put a man in motion, he can do this by indicating which man (X, Y, or Z) along with the word "on" right after he calls the formation. So if he wanted the flanker in motion, he would say "Z on".

The whole call with the flanker in motion and the split end's route modified would now be:

"Red Right Z on X 4-and-Up 39 Flare Check on 1".

Note that if the formation is called with the strong side left, that puts Z and Y on the left side and X on the right side. The quarterback still calls the routes for X,Y, and Z in that order.

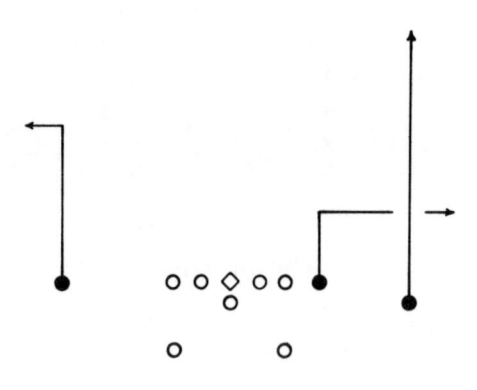

Alternative Method

Some teams group pass plays in series, somewhat like running plays. For instance, the 70 series would include plays where X is the primary receiver, the 80 series has Y as the main receiver, and the 90 series focuses on Z. So a 99 call has Z as the primary receiver running a streak or fly route.

For each such call, the other two receivers have a designated complementary pattern to run. If the quarterback wanted to modify a route, he would specify the change in the manner used above. Similarly, the routes of both running backs could be designated by a single letter preceded by the term "Flare". Flare A could be one combination, Flare B another, and so on.

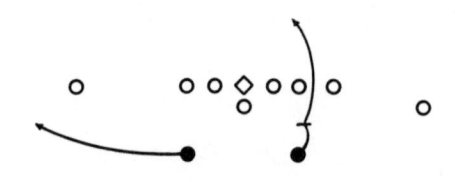

Pass Pattern 99

Using this type of system, the original pass play in the example above would be called:

"Red Right 99 Flare G on 1".

Flare Pattern G

LINE CALLS

Reason For

When a play is called in the huddle, the offense does not know what defensive alignment it will encounter. That alignment has a direct effect on the offensive linemen because the defensive linemen are right across from them. In some cases the blocking for the play called in the huddle won't work because of how the defensive linemen have positioned themselves. In other cases, a change in blocking would give one or more of the offensive linemen a better blocking angle.

It is true that with the use of rule blocking there are rules for each lineman to employ in the event the situation isn't the same as in the playbook. But teams don't want to fall back on rule blocking all the time. The linemen have to vary their blocks in order to keep the defense off balance.

For these reasons, the offensive linemen make line calls. These are calls at the line of scrimmage which identify a particular blocking pattern or change specific blocks. Line blocking for a specific play could be even or odd depending on how the defense lines up. **Even blocking** would be straight ahead, everyone blocks the defensive man over him. Or it could be blocking in accord with the way the play was diagrammed. **Odd blocking** would entail angle blocking, cross blocking, or some alternative pattern to the basic scheme for the given play.

After they break the huddle and set up at the line, the center will call even or odd using code words or numbers. Additional calls may be made to switch assignments or to enable the offense to pick up a possible blitz or stunt, based on how the defense men have positioned themselves.

Making the Calls

Not all teams use line calls to the same extent. Some rely more on blocking rules to carry out overall patterns. Others use a lot of line calls to fit the blocking to the exact alignment encountered. The more reliance is placed on calls, the more the linemen have to think and communicate on the line before the snap. Moreover, some teams have very complicated blocking systems which can lead to rather complex terminology.

Most calls are directed to the onside or play side blocking since that is where the hole has to be opened. Offside or back side blocking is less complicated. It usually involves sealing off the inside gap and cutting off pursuit.

To make line calls, teams use numbers, colors, names, objects — whatever integrates well with their play calling signals. They might use words like "Fire" to indicate even blocking and "Nail" to designate odd blocking. That relates to patterns. To signal specific combinations for two linemen, names such as "Charlie" (cross block), "Frank" (fold block), and "Curt" (co-op or momentary double-team) can be used.

In order to identify defenders some systems number them 3,2,1,0,1,2,3 where the man over the center (nose tackle or middle linebacker) is zero, man over each guard is 1 and so on. A "2" call could then be used to double-team the defensive end on the play side.

The center makes most of the overall calls and ensures that players on both sides are alerted to any adjustments affecting them. The guards and tackles can generally make calls which relate to their own particular assignments. On each play they will make a call so the defense can't tell which are the line calls and which are the dummies.

Examples

As an example, assume an off-tackle play to the right side has been called. Against a standard 3-4 defense the center blocks the nose tackle, the onside guard cuts off the inside linebacker, and the tackle and tight end double-team the defensive end. As the offense and defense set, the center gives the "Fire" call along with some meaningless signals to alert the linemen that the standard blocking scheme will be used.

However, suppose instead of lining up in a standard 3-4, the nose tackle and inside linebacker line up in a gap stack toward the play side. In this situation, the center gives a "Nail" call which has the onside guard block down on the nose tackle, the center release for the offside linebacker, and the tackle slide off the double-team for the onside inside linebacker.

As a second example, assume a dive play off right guard. In the huddle, the quarterback calls for straight man blocking against a 4-3. As they line up, the defense fits so the center freezes the blocking called in the huddle by an "Ice" call. But suppose the defensive end then shifts in just a little. It's not much, but the offensive tackle is no

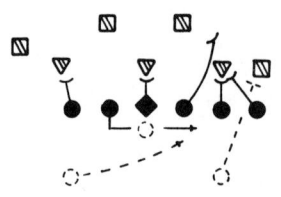

3-4 Defense

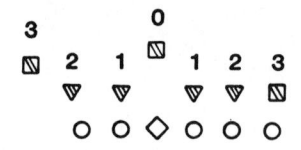

4-3 Defense

Numbering Defensive Front for Blocking

"Fire" (Standard Blocking)

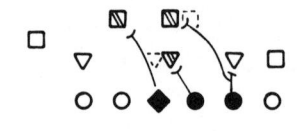

"Nail" (Odd Blocking)

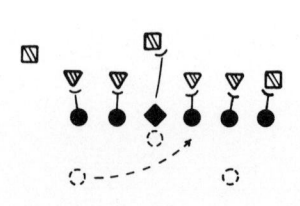

"Ice" (Freezes blocking called – Man Blocking)

"Charlie" (Changes blocking – OT & G Cross Block)

longer sure he can block out that end to open the hole. So he makes a "Charlie" call. This alerts the guard next to him that he wants to cross block on the defensive tackle and end. Since the offensive tackle made the call, he blocks first and the guard crosses behind him.

Keep in mind that the center and any other players making line calls have to coordinate them with the signals being given by the quarterback. If the quarterback checks off to a new play at the line, the center may have to change the blocking to match it.

DEFENSIVE CALLS

In General

Defensive calls specify the overall alignment, the pass coverage, and any stunts or blitzes to be used on the play. Defensive calls are signalled into one player who relays them to the remaining players in the huddle. In the past, the middle linebacker was generally used because of his central location after the huddle broke and the players lined up. He was well situated to make adjustments. Now many teams don't have a middle linebacker, and those that do often take him out in passing situations. Consequently, several teams have as a signal caller an outside linebacker or safety who is an experienced defender and plays in all formations.

The defensive calls are generally sent in with arm and hand signals. The signal caller and one other defensive player will both read the signals. The purpose is to make sure that they are read properly, especially in the event the one calling the signals got banged in the head on the previous play. At the same time, someone else will check the down and distance.

Making Changes

As is the case with the offense, the defense doesn't know what alignment it will face when the huddle breaks. Consequently, the signal caller is given authority to change the call or make adjustments at that time. For instance, if the defense called is strong against the run and the offense comes out in a passing formation, the coverage has to be changed.

The defensive linemen are not subject to a prohibition against movement like the offensive linemen are. Therefore, they can change their positions after the offense is set to try to take advantage of how the opposing linemen are positioned. The linebackers and secondary may be forced to adjust if the running backs shift or a receiver goes in motion.

Terminology

The defense assigns a name to each player, stunt, and blitz. Coverages are numbered but also have code words to enable changes while the teams are lined up. An example of some of the defensive terms that might be used by a particular team follows:

Defensive Linemen

Nose tackle:	Nose
Left end:	Lou
Right end:	Ron

Linebackers

Strong side	
– outside:	Sam
– inside:	Stu
Weak side	
– outside:	Will
– inside:	Walt

Cornerbacks

Strong side:	Sue
Weak side:	Wanda

Safeties

Strong side:	Jack
Weak side:	Jill

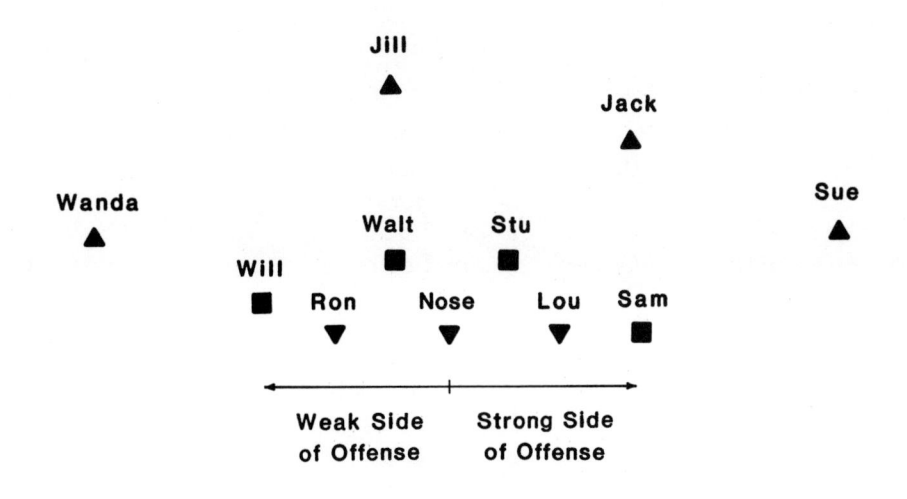

Designations for Defensive Players

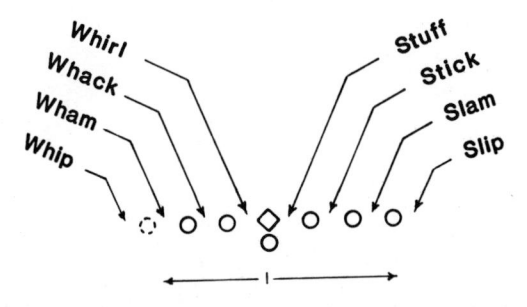

Diagram positions:
- Jill (triangle, deep middle)
- Jack (triangle)
- Wanda (triangle, weak side)
- Sue (triangle, strong side)
- Walt (square), Stu (square) — linebackers
- Will (square) — weak side outside linebacker
- Sam (square) — strong side outside linebacker
- Ron (▽), Nose (▽), Lou (▽) — down linemen

← Weak Side of Offense | Strong Side of Offense →

Blitz Hole Designations

Weak Side of Offense: Whirl, Whack, Wham, Whip
Strong Side of Offense: Stuff, Stick, Slam, Slip

Gaps for Blitzes

Strong side
- outside center: Stuff
- outside guard: Stick
- outside tackle: Slam
- outside tight end: Slip

Weak Side
- outside center: Whirl
- outside guard: Whack
- outside tackle: Wham
- outside tight end: Whip

Sample Blitzes

Strong side outside linebacker blitzes tackle-tight end gap:	Sam Slam
Strong side inside linebacker blitzes guard-tackle gap:	Stu Stick
Weak side inside linebacker blitzes strong side center-guard gap:	Walt Stuff
Weak side outside linebacker blitzes outside tight end (2-tight end offense):	Will Whip

Note: This illustrates how code words can shorten terminology.

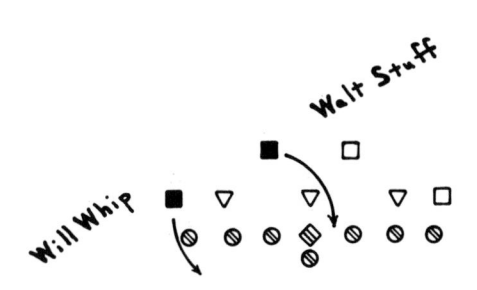

Will Whip & Walt Stuff Blitzes

195

Sample Coverages

Basic man-to-man	Cover 1	or Raleigh
– same with Stu Stick	Cover 2	or Reno
Double cover split end	Cover 3	or Tulsa
– same with Sam Slip	Cover 4	or Tahoe
Double both wide rec'rs	Cover 5	or Flint
– same with Stu Stick	Cover 6	or Frisco
Strong side zone	Cover 7	or Salem
– inverted zone	Cover 8	or St. Joe
Weak side zone	Cover 9	or Wausau
– inverted zone	Cover 10	or Waco

Force Responsibility (on end runs)

Cornerback: Cloud
Safety: Sky
Linebacker: Bomber

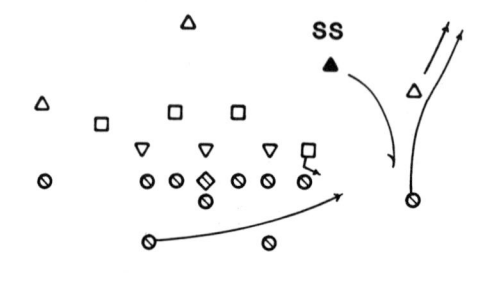

Sky Force

Example Calls

Assume that one of the inside linebackers is relaying the defensive signals. In the huddle he might make the following call:

"30 Sam Slam Walt Whack Cover 1".

"30" (Formation)

Standard 3-4.

"Sam Slam" (Blitz)

Strong side outside linebacker blitzes thru tackle-tight end gap.

"Walt Whack" (Blitz)

Weak side inside linebacker blitzes thru guard-tackle gap.

"Cover 1" (Pass Coverage)

Basic man-to-man.

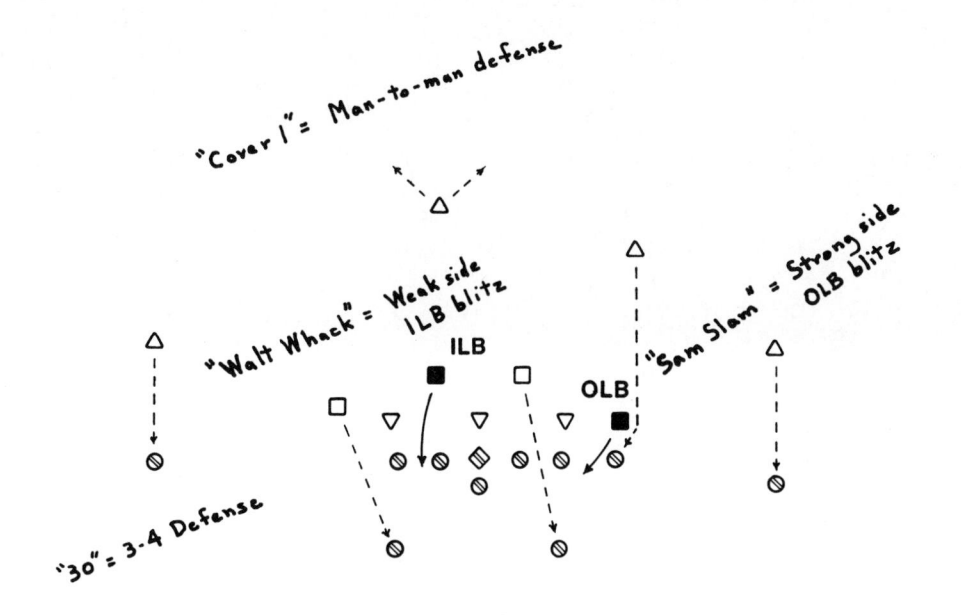

"30 Sam Slam Walt Whack Cover 1"

As the offense lines up, the signal caller yells out which side is the strong side as well as any other pertinent information to identify the formation. In this example, he might just yell out "Y Left" to indicate the tight end is on the left side (when viewed from the defense).

Now assume the offense puts the flanker in motion heading to the weak side. Based on his knowledge of the opponent's tendencies, the game situation, and the motion, the inside linebacker may change the defense by yelling:

"Frisco, Frisco, Frisco".

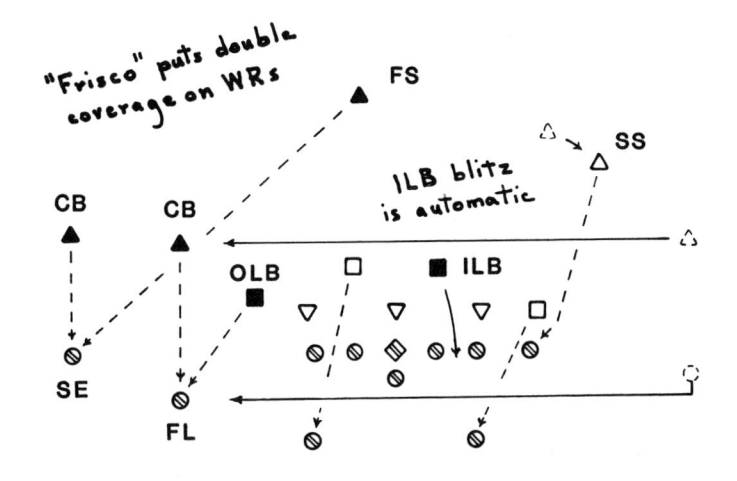

"Frisco, Frisco, Frisco"

"Frisco"

This changes the pass coverage from basic man-to-man to man-to-man with double coverage of the wide receivers. Because the Frisco call carries its own blitz (Stu Stick) the blitzes originally called are superseded.

Next, the free safety may call "Bomber" informing the weak side linebacker he has the force responsibility on that side if the play turns into an end run. The strong safety will make the same call on his side since he is now the only deep back to protect against a pass over there.

This is a rather simple example. Defensive play calls can include other aspects such as player positioning. A nickel back, for instance, could line up in one of several different locations on certain coverages. So the defensive call would specify where he should start on the play involved. Also, like the offense, the defense uses a lot of dummy calls to conceal the real ones.

Shouting in Secondary

As the play unfolds, there is likely to be some shouting by the linebackers and defensive backs. The purpose is to help one another out. Once a linebacker or defensive back determines the play is a run, he yells "run, run, run". Or if he sees that play action is going to be a pass, he calls "pass, pass, pass". The reason for the two repeat calls is to make sure that as many defense men as possible hear it. With the noise of the crowd and everyone moving on his assignment, a single call, or even one repeat, might not be heard.

There are other calls made as defenders switch coverage of receivers, position themselves in zone areas, spot screens and draws, and so on. "Ball, ball, ball" is sometimes used to let a cornerback playing man-to-man on a receiver know that the ball is in the air. And these types of calls have to be timed right. It can't be made too soon, or the cornerback will look up and lose his man. Too late, and the receiver will make the catch.

CHAPTER 8

IN MOTION

The first part of this chapter covers a few of the keys that players look at, adjustments they make, and techniques they use as they line up and run through certain plays. The second part deals with matching defenses against offensive play calls. Ten different offensive plays are used and a defense appropriate for each is given. The discussion throughout is brief in order to touch on a number of topics.

[After the Friday practice session, the defensive coordinator gets a few of the players together to show Joe how to spot and read keys. In the dialogue below the players involved in the discussion are designated as follows:

    OG. = Offensive guard
    OT. = Offensive tackle
    WR. = Wide receiver
    QB. = Quarterback
    DT. = Defensive tackle
    DE. = Defensive end
    OLB. = Outside linebacker
    CB. = Cornerback

"C" and "F" refer to the coach and the fan as in prior chapters.]

Is He Leaning?

C.   Okay, we don't have much time. Show Joe how an offensive tackle can tip the play.

[The offensive tackle gets down into what appears to be a normal 3-point stance.]

C.   Joe, what would you guess the play would be?

F.   I don't know. I haven't seen any offensive tackles line up close.

C.   Take a look at his down hand. See all the pressure on it. And you can see how he's leaning a little bit forward. This means he's going to fire out across the line and the play is going to be a run.

[The offensive tackle resets himself.]

C.   Now see how he adjusted. There's no real pressure on the hand. His feet are more underneath him; he's kind of back on his haunches. This indicates he's ready to set up for a pass block. He sure isn't going to blow anybody back out of that stance.

[Again, the offensive tackle comes up and goes back into his stance.]

C. Okay, now he's kind of intermediate. No exaggeration one way or the other, so you can't really tell. That's the way he should line up every time.

DE. But during a game, people lose their concentration. Or they become emotional now and then, and you can pick up these little leans. And they can help.

Line Splits

C. Now let's have a center, guard, and tackle line up.

The spacing between the offensive linemen is usually about 3 feet. The tackle normally splits a little more from the guard than the guard splits from the center. Now, if the guard is going to pull to the outside, the guard may split wider from the center by about a foot. That means one less step to get to the end of the line. Also see how he's back over his legs — both his body lean and the split signal a pull.

[The guard now moves over closer to the center and leans forward.]

C. Here, he's a little closer than normal to the center and ready to fire out. There's a good chance he's headed for the middle linebacker. He's closer to the center in order to get by the defensive tackle and block the linebacker.

Another thing they may do is widen the split somewhere in the line simply to increase the gap there.

[The guard returns to almost a normal split from the center, but the offensive tackle positions himself about 4 feet outside the guard.]

C. You can see the hole between the guard and tackle is about ½ yard wider than normal. That may mean the ball carrier is headed there.

2½ ft   3 ft

O   O   ◇   O   O
OT G   C   G   OT

Approximate Normal Alignment

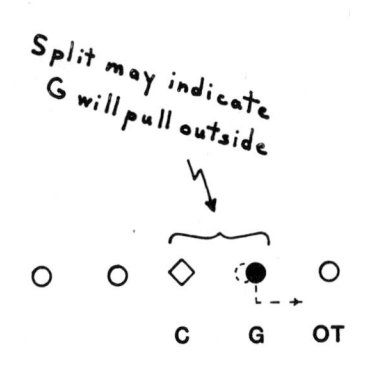

Split may indicate G will pull outside

O   O   ◇   ●   O
        C   G   OT

Wide Split by Guard

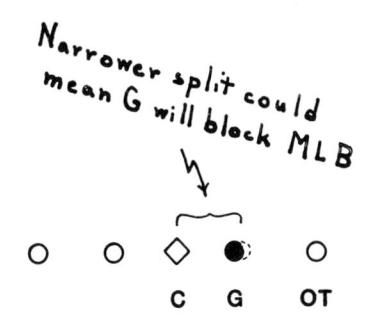

Narrower split could mean G will block MLB

O   O   ◇   ●   O
        C   G   OT

Narrow Split by Guard

F. Couldn't the defensive linemen stay in their normal positions and plug up the hole?

DT. Sure we can. In fact, if the hole is wide enough and the defensive man fast enough, he can shoot right through the gap. But not shifting out with the offense will put the offensive linemen to one side of the defensive linemen. That gives the offensive linemen good blocking angles.

C. Standard splits are used on most plays. The spacing is changed on some in order to get the defensive linemen to change their spacing, or if they don't, then, as Bill said, to develop blocking angles.

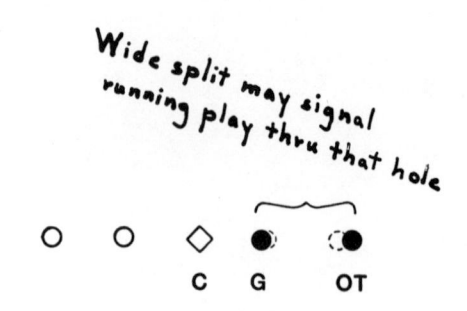

Wide split may signal running play thru that hole

Wide Split Between G & OT

Running Backs & Tight Ends

OLB. Running backs can provide similar infomation. If a running back is leaning hard on his down hand, he may be coming out fast. If it's a running play and he has a block to make, he may cheat up a foot or two so he can make that block.

DE. The same with the tight end. If he splits 2 to 3 yards, then he's not going to down block on me. At that distance, it wouldn't be very effective. So I don't have to be concerned about that and can concentrate on other things.

OLB. A wide split by the tight end usually means he'll release for a pass. But not always.

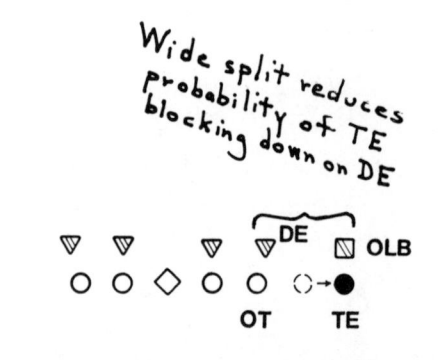

Wide split reduces probability of TE blocking down on DE

Wide Split by Tight End

How Informative Are Keys?

F. With all this information, is it pretty easy to spot plays?

OLB. Whoa, wait a minute. What we're talking about is stuff you <u>may</u> pick up. The offense knows the kinds of things the defense is looking for. Ideally, everyone lines up the same way each time — no lean or other noticeable difference. But as someone said, as the game progresses there are lapses. A player doesn't concentrate or becomes a little overanxious about his assignment.

DE. Or they may try to give you false keys, what they call key breakers. They make it look like they are going to pull outside or run inside or whatever. But actually they're going to go the other way.

C. I think the big thing is that you have to coordinate this type of information with the tendencies you've studied in the films and scouting report.

Formation recognition is a big thing. When they line up in a certain formation you know what they've done out of that formation in the past. So if the offense gets into a strong side set, the defensive tackle may know that he won't be trapped. He may also know that out of that formation the guard over him will either man block (straight ahead) or pull out leaving the tackle to angle block on him. So with that background information as well as the game situation, down, and distance, he can look for these little things like how the guard is leaning and it becomes much more meaningful.

It's pretty hard for the offense to have different players giving off false keys that all coordinate as well as jive with their overall tendencies from the formation.

Sure, in a big game they can do something new from a given formation. But the odds are 50-50. The play works, or they screw it up themselves.

Offensive Keys

F. How about the defensive linemen? Do they show anything?

DT. We don't have to worry about leaning forward or anything like that. The offense knows we're coming whether it's pass or run.

Now if I line up about a foot back, it might mean that I'm going to stunt with the defensive end. Let him charge inside first, while I loop around behind him and go outside. But I'm pretty much aware of that, and I'll try to cross them up occasionally so they can't be sure.

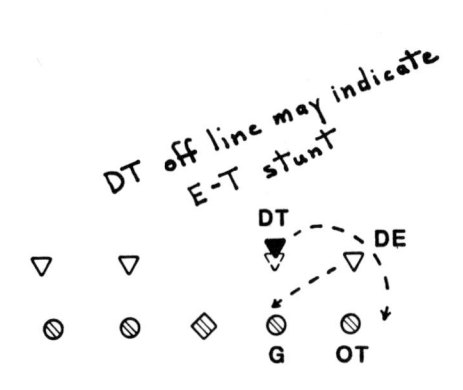

DT off line may indicate E-T stunt

Defensive Tackle Off Line

C. That's what they all say. Nobody ever thinks he's the one that's tipping.

QB. Outside linebackers can give you some clues. If an outside linebacker is cheating out and back, it can mean zone coverage where he has the short outside zone.

If the middle linebacker in a 4-3 is off the line an extra yard or two, and he has been pursuing well to the outside, he's more or less giving you some running room in the middle so he can pursue. In a situation like that, we might run some inside plays to tighten him up and then go back outside.

C. But that's more of a tactical decision on the middle linebacker's part, rather than giving you a key.

QB. Yeah, I guess you could say that.

Checking on the free safety is probably more in line with our discussion here. If the free safety is deep at the snap, the chances are he will be free or covering the deep middle zone. Up close, and he may be blitzing or going to cover for a linebacker who is blitzing. If the free safety is cheating to the outside, it can mean double coverage of the split end. If he's cheating outside and is closer in than normal, he may have the short zone on an inverted coverage. Finally, if he's edging toward the strong safety, he might be covering the tight end, thus leaving the strong safety free to double on the flanker or to blitz.

C. How the free safety declares himself after the snap is also important.

QB. That's for sure.

C. Suppose the free safety does have the deep middle to cover. When the ball is snapped he can simply turn and run to that area, which makes his assignment apparent to the quarterback. On the other hand, if he just floats as he watches the play unfold, the quarterback isn't sure where he's going. The safety has to declare himself in time to do his job, but the longer he can hold off the tougher he makes it on the quarterback.

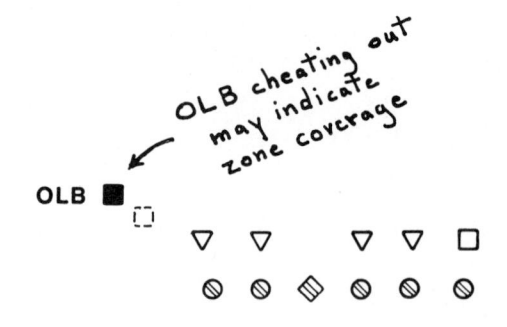

Linebacker Cheating Out

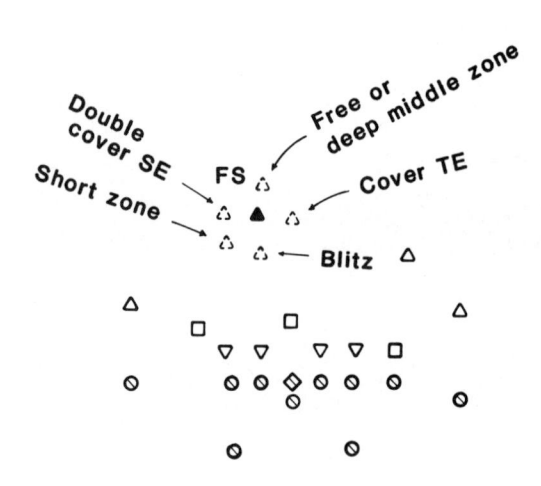

Free Safety Alignments

Personal Traits

F. Do you ever spot something like the quarterback licking his fingers before a pass?

C. That stuff is pretty rare. If someone has a habit like that it won't take too long to spot it. Keep in mind that everybody is watching films — coaches, the players themselves. In addition, we're looking at them in practice, and the coaches in the press box are trying to spot anything that's obvious during the game. Of course, like anything else, somebody may be doing something and nobody catches it. And then someone says, "My Lord, look at that", and then everybody tries to figure out how long the guy has been doing it. But, as I said, that stuff is pretty rare.

DT. Sometimes there are some subtle things that can tip you off. Things that rookies or young players may do. Coming out of a huddle, a running back may glance at the hole or check where the linebacker is. A little thing like that.

It's over in a flash, so you have to watch them real close. Some of them do the opposite. When they're going to carry, they won't look at you at all, to make sure they don't tip — but you're picking it up. You just look at what they do and then see how the play turns out, and start putting things together.

Other Keys

OLB. Don't get the wrong impression, we don't spend all our time looking for tipoffs as the opponent lines up. Most of the real keys are the ones that occur right after the snap — say, when somebody blocks down instead of straight out. The uncovered offensive linemen (the guards versus a 3-4 defense, the center versus a 4-3 defense) are a good key for a pass play. They can't come out beyond the line and they have no one in front to block. So you can see right away if they're setting up for a pass.

As a play begins, most players are keying certain other players to determine what the offense or defense is doing. But sometimes your opponents don't try to hide anything. They go right ahead and cheat out or lean forward or whatever. You know, and they know you know. Then it's purely a matter of execution.

DE. Speaking of that, I remember in my rookie year, late in the season I was working against this offensive tackle. It was near halftime and the game was close, and everybody was really putting out. So they break the huddle and this guy comes up to the line. Then, as casually as can be, he says, "It's a sweep this way on two". In all my football — park district, high school, college — I never had that happen before — somebody come up and tell me the play! So I figured this guy's jivin' me, and I start looking for something else.

OG. So what happened?

DE. Hut-one, hut-two, here comes the sweep and they took me right out of the play. Exactly what he said.

So late in the second half, he comes up again and says, "Off-tackle on two". Now he's really got me thinking. So I'm going to check it out real close. They set up and boom! It's off-tackle right at me and I get blown out. They went on the first sound by the quarterback — didn't go through any count. Then he says he's sorry he missed the count, but, gee, he gave me the play — what more did I need?

After the game, one of our old pros told me not to pay any attention to that stuff. Just don't even listen. You never know whether it's true or not. It's a distraction.

Adjusting to Counter a Blitz

C. Why don't you show Joe how to counter a blitz with a slant-in.

QB. Well, obviously we don't have a complete offense or defense, but you can get the idea.

[The left side of the offense along with the corresponding players on defense line up.]

QB. Assume the split end is supposed to run a square-out at about 15 yards, but on the snap the weak side linebacker blitzes.

[The quarterback calls a quick count. As he backs up, the halfback shouts "blitz" and blocks the blitzing weak side linebacker. The split end, instead of going downfield, slants in to where the outside linebacker normally covers, and the quarterback fires the ball to him.]

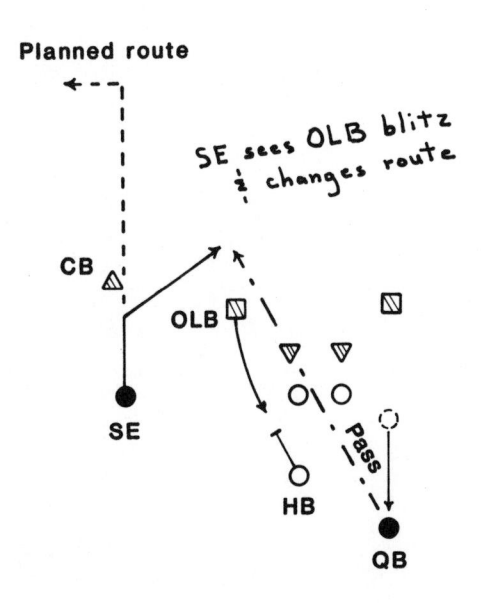

Planned route

SE sees OLB blitz & changes route

Countering a Blitz

QB. This was pretty obvious, but that's one way to handle the blitz. It's an illustration of how a receiver and a quarterback both have to adjust to make it work. Instead of heading downfield on the route called, the split end saw the outside linebacker blitzing and cut right into the area the linebacker vacated. I have to know the split end is going to slant in and then throw right away.

WR. In a game it's not easy for the wide receiver to see a linebacker blitzing. I have to get off fast on the snap, so I can't watch to see what the linebackers are doing. It's easier to see a safety blitzing. But if I have some indication that a linebacker will, then I can glance over. And if I hear "blitz" shouted, I'll break off my route and cut in.

CB. From a defensive standpoint, the cornerback knows when a blitz is on. So he may play the receiver tight against short moves on the theory that the receiver will never reach the long cuts before the quarterback has to throw.

Finding Best Opening

QB. Let me show you something else that might not be obvious to the fans. This time the wide receiver will run a square-in about 16 yards deep. And the defense will be in a weak side zone.

207

[They set up as before, the quarterback does a quick count and the split end heads downfield. In this type of coverage the cornerback has the short outside zone and the two linebackers cover the short inside zones. When the split end reaches the back end of the short zones he breaks inside. The quarterback doesn't throw. The split end comes into the first inside zone and the outside linebacker now has him covered. Just as he passes that linebacker heading for the next zone, the quarterback cocks and fires, leading the receiver slightly so he catches the ball when he's right between the two linebackers.]

QB. These guys on defense played it pretty straight for me, so it worked out better than it might in a game. Anyway, what I wanted to illustrate is that when a receiver is going into the middle, it's usually not a timing pass like on a short-out or a hitch where you throw even before the receiver makes his break. Going into the middle there are a lot of people around, and you throw when and if the receiver is open.

You'll notice I didn't throw when the receiver was first open, right after his break inside. The reason is the lane between the cornerback and the first linebacker was narrower than the lane between the first linebacker and the second linebacker. So rather than trying to force it in the first opening, I waited for the second.

F. Does that mean that if you find a man open, you'll check on other receivers to see if they are more open?

QB. No, you don't have time. Based on the defense you see, you can usually narrow your choice down to 1 or 2 receivers as you're backing away from the line. Who the primary receiver is changes with the defensive coverage you're facing. Normally, if I see a man is open or is going to be open, I throw to him. I don't wait for someone else, unless the purpose of the play is to go long. By the time you check another receiver and come back, the man who was open will probably be covered.

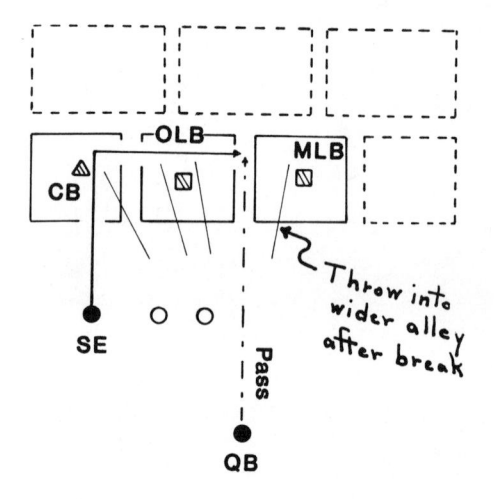

Finding Best Opening

Throws into the Middle

WR. Let me add something about throws into the middle. One thing you find out real fast is whether the quarterback likes you. If he wants to, he can really hang you out to dry. By that I mean, if he throws it high and a little behind, you're just hanging in mid-air for all those linebackers and safeties to crunch you — and they do it. Some receivers are so concerned about getting hit in there, they really don't go for the ball. We call that short-arming it. In fact, some guys just don't run routes in the middle at all.

The good ones are willing to go in there, make the catch, and take their punishment. Coaches say you're going to get hit anyway, so you might as well concentrate on catching it. That's fine, but there's a limit to how much the body can take.

QB. He's right, and I think most quarterbacks are aware of this. You don't want to lose your best receiver for one catch on a crossing pattern. If he goes out with a concussion or ribs or something like that, it's just not worth it. A good receiver is too valuable to the quarterback and the team. So the quarterback's going to do all he can not to jeopardize the receiver.

WR. Another thing is that throws into the middle should be from the neck down if possible. High throws risk a tipped ball. If it goes off your hands, the ball's in slow motion. And with all those people around, there's a good chance it will be intercepted. If a throw is off target, it should be a little in front rather than a little behind the receiver. It's easier to adjust going forward than backward, especially if you have a step on the defender.

F. How do you know where all the defenders are when you're supposed to be concentrating on the catch?

WR. Well, you don't. But here's where a good quarterback helps a lot. I can tell by the way the quarterback throws about where the defenders are. If he makes a good solid throw right on the number, I know that they are close, but not on top of me. If he fires it in low, then somebody is going to hit me right away. If he kinda leads me a little, then I've got some running room.

But at the same time, I have to factor in the quarterback's situation. If somebody is crashing in on him, I know he's unloading as best he can. So I don't rely on the pass to tell me where the defenders are.

Altering a Pass Route

F. How about where you have to alter your route as you're running? Can you give me an example?

WR. Basically, what happens is the receivers read the defense and according to what they do, there are two or three options. The thing is, each team wants the receivers to break off their routes a little differently.

As for an example, suppose I'm to run a quick hitch about 6 yards out. But the corner comes up to play bump-and-run. When he does that, the short route is off and my job is to go deep after I beat the press. In other words, the route has changed from a quick hitch to a fly. And the quarterback knows this because he sees what the corner is doing.

Okay, let's say I release from the line without getting knocked off course and I'm heading deep. On a fly, you are supposed to just outrun your man. But looking downfield I see the defense rotating into a 2-deep zone. Well, there's no way I'm going to outrun that. The strong safety is going to head deep and keep me in front of him.

So once I get past the cornerback's short zone and I'm heading into the strong safety's deep zone, I'll curl in. Now the quarterback, who is also reading the defense, knows that given the situation I'm going to turn into the seam between the deep and short zones. So if he is going to throw to me, that is where he'll do it. This illustrates how I might adjust my

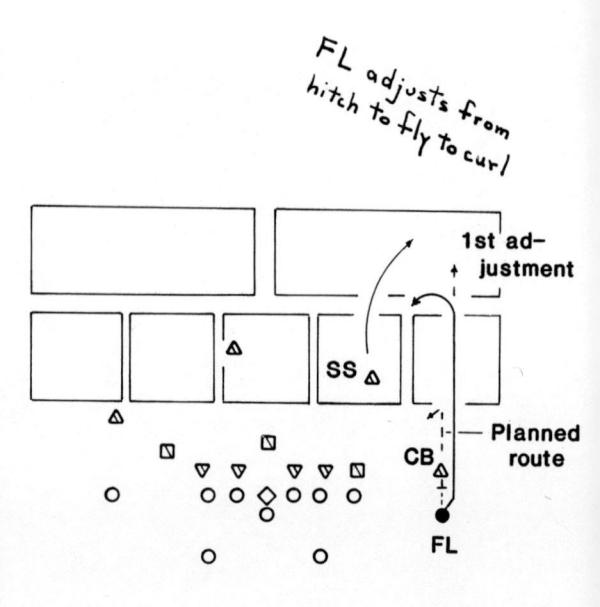

Adjusting a Pass Route

route from a quick hitch to a fly to a curl based on what the defense does.

That's just one example. There are many other things that can happen or techniques to use. For instance, if you're working against a corner who plays tough bump-and-run, your route may depend on how you bounce off his chuck. If it's inside, you go inside. If it's outside, you go outside. Downfield, if you're on a post, but they force you too far outside, then maybe you just go to the corner. The one thing you can't do is fool your quarterback. That's why it's important to work together so he can anticipate how you'll adjust. That's vital.

Looking into Backfield

CB. I'll tell you something else that's not always apparent, especially to someone watching the game on TV. That's these pump fakes by the quarterback. What you can't see on TV is that the fake is timed with the receiver's break.

Let's say I'm covering someone with real good moves, and he and his quarterback can do a real number on timing passes. You know, before he cuts, the ball is in the air, right where he's headed. Well, if they somehow manage to complete a couple of out patterns on you, you have to be real careful. If you're backpedalling on this guy and catch sight of the quarterback cocking his arm and starting forward, your natural inclination is to get ready for a pass. As the receiver breaks outside you may go with him and then realize it was a fake. If you committed a little too hard to that break, the receiver can shake you by cutting upfield or back inside. You've got to be careful about looking into the backfield.

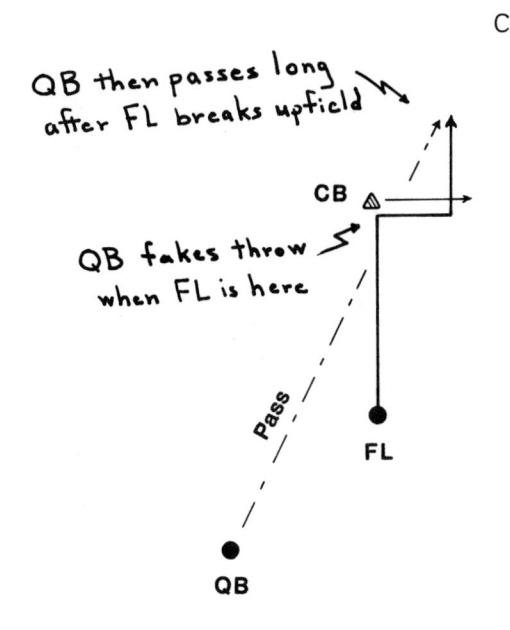

Looking Downfield

QB. The quarterback has the opposite problem. He has to be careful about looking downfield. If you start watching whom you're going to throw to, those linebackers and defensive backs will pick it up fast. You really have to

Pump Fake on Break

read the defense and determine who has the best chance of getting free or at least just single coverage. Remember, you know where the receivers are heading. So you read and look away from your main target. Then when the receiver should be making his break, you look back and hope he's there and the defense is what you anticipated it would be. If it's not, you'll try to just throw it away or dump it off.

WR. A young quarterback who bird dogs his primary target makes life a lot tougher for his receivers. The defense just converges on them. The longer the pattern, the worse it is.

Blocking for Short Passes

OT. And let me tell you, the longer the pattern, the more pressure it puts on the offensive line. That's because we have to hold up the pass rush longer.

On a quick pass, it's a different situation and we use a different block. What the offensive line tries to do then is hit hard and low. Bring those defensive linemen down. The quarterback isn't going to take his normal drop of about 7 yards. He just goes back about 3 and throws. So we have to get the defensive line and all those big paws down as fast as we can. Holding them off isn't the problem like it is on the long pass, because the quarterback is going to throw right away.

Scrambling & Blocking

OG. The other extreme is probably where the quarterback can't find anybody open and he starts to scramble. This poses a real problem for the offensive linemen. When the quarterback is in the pocket, we know where he is even though our backs are to him. We know what angle to take in blocking whether the defender comes inside or outside. But once the quarterback starts scrambling, we don't know where he is. And that's why it generally starts to look like a fox hunt with all the defensive linemen running madly after the quarterback.

C. Talk about scrambling, we better start moving before the equipment men shut down the locker room.

DEFENSIVE COUNTERS

[Later that afternoon Joe made arrangements to meet with the team's All-Pro linebacker. Joe hopes to discuss different defenses and when they would be utilized. He meets the linebacker at the training center as the last few players are leaving. While Joe and the linebacker head for the main classroom, Joe relates the things he has gone over with other people during the week. After entering the classroom, they go up to the large blackboard that spans most of the front wall. There they talk for a while about different defenses.]

LB. Why don't I name some offensive plays, and you can tell me what a good defense for each would be. It doesn't have to be anything fancy, just stick with the basic ones you've mentioned to me. And we'll also forget about the fact that if the offense saw the defense, they probably wouldn't go through with the play, or at least they would alter it. This should help you get a feel for matching defenses against offenses.

Weak Side Run

LB. Let's start with a run outside the weak side guard. What would be a good defense against this?

F. How about using a 4-3 with an undershifted line? That would shift the defensive linemen toward the weak side, in the direction of the play.

LB. Okay. I might add that the weak side defensive end and defensive tackle shouldn't be stunting, but playing straight ahead. But I'm not going to get into a lot of possibilities, or we won't cover much ground. An under is okay.

Undershift concentrates linemen on weak side

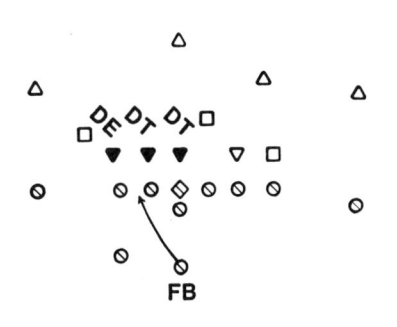

Weak Side Run

Long Trap

LB. Now suppose the offense tries a long trap, against the strong side defensive end.

F. Ah... I'm drawing a blank.

LB. Well, what's the theory behind a trap?

F. To let the defender across and block him from the side.

LB. And who is the best kind of target?

F. Okay, I'm catching on. It works best against someone who is charging hard. So the defensive end should be reading rather than blasting across the line.

LB. This time, I'd use a 3-4. Without a defensive tackle next to him it's easier for the defensive end to see the trap coming. Ideally, he would be slanting inside which makes it easy for him to turn into the trapping guard and plug up the hole the guard is trying to open.

DE is harder to trap in 3-4 defense, especially if DE is reading, not charging

Long Trap

Flanker Reverse

LB. Suppose the offense ran a flanker reverse. The quarterback hands off to the halfback heading to the strong side, who in turn hands off to the flanker going toward the weak side.

F. I'm not sure. One thing, you wouldn't want everybody pursuing the halfback.

LB. Think of something basic. Look at where all the action is — in the backfield.

F. So we want defenders in the backfield. How about a blitz? Blitz both outside linebackers.

LB. Right. That should stop the reverse cold.

Blitzing OLBs should shut off reverse

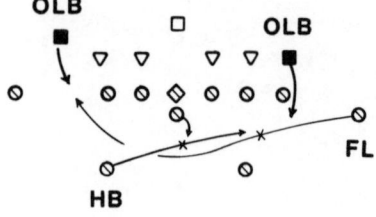

Flanker Reverse

Sweep Weak

LB. Consider a sweep to the weak side.

3-4 linebackers flow to smother end runs

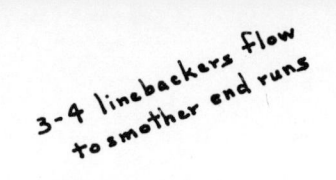

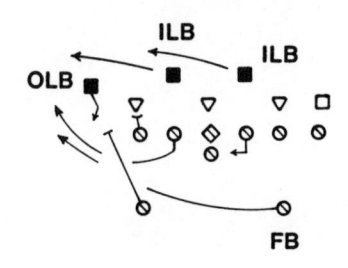

Sweep to Weak Side

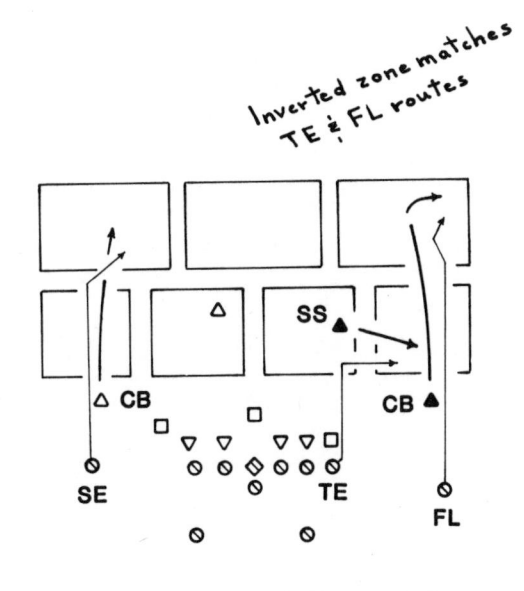

Inverted zone matches TE & FL routes

Flanker Corner, Tight End Out

Inverted zone would be bad coverage

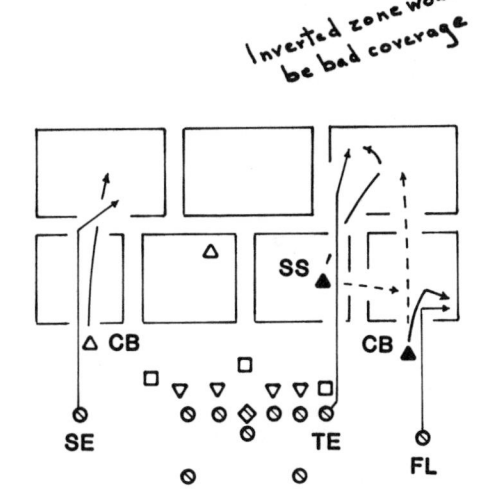

— Strong Side Zone
---- Inverted Zone

Flanker Out, Tight End Corner

F. I guess I'd use a 3-4. Let all those linebackers swarm to the outside to string it out and choke it off.

LB. I agree, a 3-4 provides good pursuit against runs to the outside. You'd also want your force man coming up fast.

Flanker Corner, Tight End Out

LB. Now, let's assume the flanker runs a corner route and the tight end runs a short-out. The split end is on a post route. Let's also assume that for these pass plays you employ four down linemen in order to get a rush.

F. Use a strong side rotating zone out of a 4-3 defense. That puts the emphasis over there on the strong side. And the deep middle would be protected against the split end.

LB. A strong side zone would be all right, but this is a good pattern to use an inverted zone against. The strong safety will be moving outside right where the tight end's route will take him. And the cornerback is better able to cover against the flanker on a corner route since the safety would have to get both deep and over to the sideline.

Flanker Out, Tight End Corner

LB. Now, what if the flanker runs a short-out and the tight end runs a corner? The split end again goes to the post.

F. This is the same as the last pattern except the flanker and tight end have exchanged routes. Would an inverted coverage still work?

LB. No. That would lead to trouble. The safety could not get over to cover the flanker on that out route, and the tight end could get wide open at the inside seam.

F. So, use a strong side zone?

LB. Yes, that would be much better.

3 Wide Receivers & Tight End

LB. Suppose they line up with 3 wide receivers, a tight end, and a single set back. The third receiver is in the slot to the left. Let's say the tight end can catch but he's not fast and so no deep threat.

F. Who should be assigned to cover the slotback? I guess that means we have to go to a nickel defense.

LB. Not necessarily, depending on how fast the slotback is and what kind of routes he runs, you can line up with a linebacker over him and then go into zone coverage. But I agree, using a nickel back is usually the way to go.

F. Man-to-man coverage would probably be best. A cornerback on each wide out and the nickel back on the slot man. The strong safety takes the tight end and the free safety is free. I'd take the middle linebacker out and have one of the outside linebackers pick up the set back if he releases to that linebacker's side.

LB. Well, let me make a couple of suggestions. First, if the two remaining linebackers play outside, you're inviting a run up the middle, so you many want to pull the free safety up a little. Next, if the tight end is no deep threat, you can leave the linebacker man-to-man on him. That would allow you to use the safeties in a 2-deep zone. Then you would have help deep for the man-to-man defenders underneath.

F. What about the set back?

LB. I'd stack the right linebacker inside so he'd be better able to pick up the set back if he went to the far side. Or you could make the coverage contingent on the set back's release, but let's not get into that.

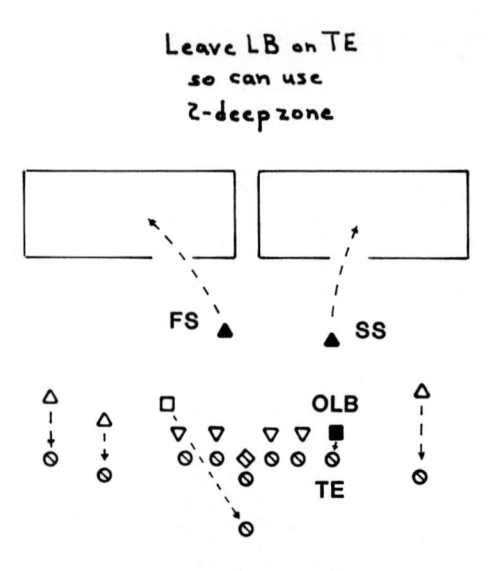

Leave LB on TE so can use 2-deep zone

3 WRs & TE vs. Nickel (TE not deep threat)

Use combo on TE & LB zones to help

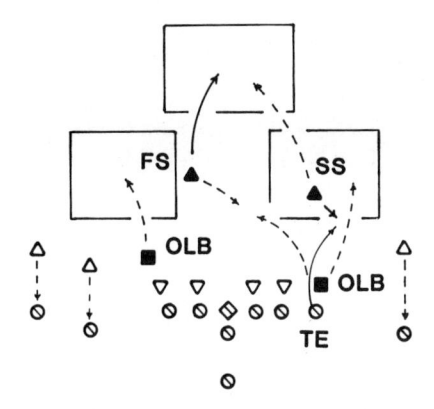

**3 WRs & TE vs. Nickel
(TE is deep threat)**

Zone coverage avoids isolating RB on LB

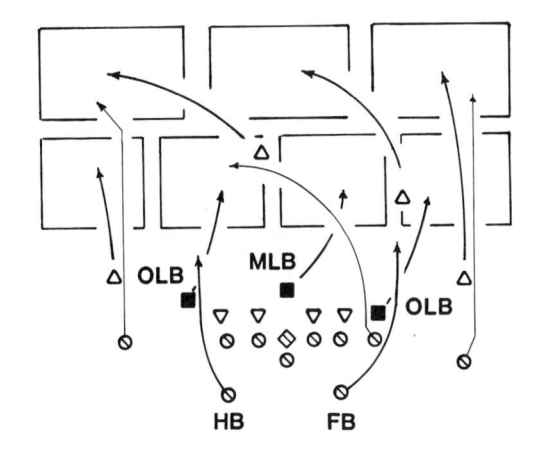

RBs Release Downfield

Tight End Deep Threat

LB. Take the same situation as the last one, but now assume that the tight end _is_ a deep threat.

F. In that case you would want the strong safety covering him, wouldn't you? And the free safety could centerfield against the deep threat.

LB. You could put a combo coverage on the tight end. If he goes outside, the strong safety takes him. If he goes inside, the free safety picks him up. The safety without the tight end could still go to the center and then help out against the deepest threat. Depending on what the set back does, the linebackers would help out underneath by covering the hook/curl zone on their respective sides.

Backs Release Downfield

LB. Suppose you're facing a standard pro set and the backs both release straight downfield. The tight end runs a crossing route, the flanker streaks down the right side and the split end goes for the left corner.

F. It looks like the middle is getting flooded. That could be bad for zone coverage. But I wouldn't want linebackers covering the running backs. So I guess I'd use a weak side zone.

LB. That's the point I was trying to make. You don't want slow linebackers covering running backs streaking out of the backfield. Zone coverage is okay here.

Fullback Sideline (Play Action)

LB. Finally, consider a play action pass. Let's say the fullback starts out as if to lead block for an end run. The halfback fakes a run to the strong side and then pass blocks. The tight end runs a delayed crossing route, meaning he first blocks out on the linebacker and then releases. The flanker goes to the post and the split end runs a curl. The fullback heads for the deep sideline. And assume he's a real pass threat.

F. Well I guess you could use a strong side zone again. You wouldn't have a linebacker on the fullback.

LB. That's true, but playing straight zone can leave a lot of holes. In this case you could use zone on the strong side and middle, and man-to-man on the weak side. If you invert so the strong safety covers the short zone, he'd have force responsibility to start with. So he'll be looking for the run and can come right off the play fake and pick up the fullback heading out. At the same time you'll have the flanker covered deep. On the other side the cornerback can stick with the split end.

F. What about the weak side linebacker?

LB. I'd blitz him. With play action its very hard for the quarterback to pick up a blitz. He's faking a hand off and has his back turned. A blitz can really pressure him.

[Their discussion ends and Joe gets set to leave.]

LB. You know what we went over here was pretty basic. We could have come up with better defenses in some cases and added a lot of refinements. But if you got some general ideas from this type of exercise, it's worthwhile.

One thing you have to keep in mind is that plays don't always work the way they're drawn up. If they did, every offensive play would gain good yardage and every defensive play would stop them cold. So it really comes down to execution. Which group of players can carry out their assignments better.

At the same time, I hope that what you take away from our discussion is an appreciation of how calling the right defense can help. It positions your players to meet the offense at the point of attack and makes execution that much easier. On the other hand, if you're in the wrong defense, your job of stopping them is that much harder.

Man-to-man/zone coverage mixes defense on QB

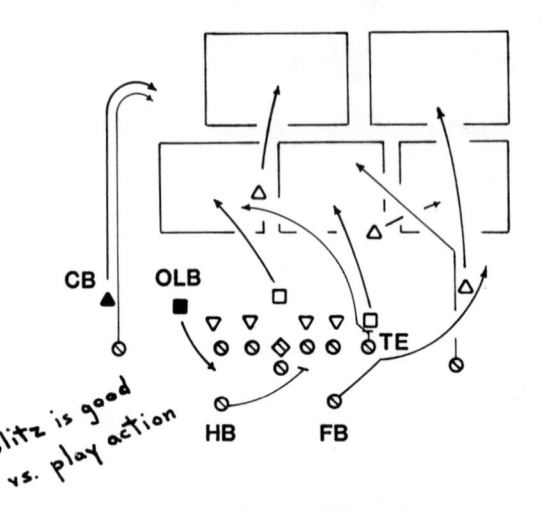

Blitz is good vs. play action

FB Sideline (Play Action)

CHAPTER 9

SPECIAL TEAMS

The special teams carry out the kicking game — kickoffs, punts, field goals, and extra points. About one out of every six plays (including kickoffs and extra point attempts) involves special teams. Their importance rests not only on the number of plays, but also on how they affect field position and the crucial points they can score. This chapter discusses a few aspects of special teams play.

KICKOFFS

Rules

The kickoff is one type of free kick (kicks after a safety or a fair catch are the other types). Kickoffs are made from the 35-yard line of the kicking team. Because it is a free kick, the receiving team cannot have any players within 10 yards of that 35-yard line.

The receiving team must attempt to take possession of the ball. Once a kick travels at least 10 yards or is touched by a member of the receiving team, the ball is live and can be recovered by the kicking team. However, the kicking team may not advance the ball unless the receiving team took possession and then fumbled.

If the kicked ball goes out of the end zone between the sidelines, it's a touchback, and the receiving team gets possession out at their 20-yard line. If the receiving team takes possession in the end zone and downs the ball, it's a touchback. If the kicking team takes possession in the end zone, it's a touchdown.

Kicking Team

The positions on the kicking team are designated as L1 through L5 and R1 through R5, depending on whether they are to the left or the right of the kicker. The assignments for the players vary somewhat from team to team. The following is representative:

- The 4 inside men (L1, L2, R1, and R2) are generally "wedgebusters". Their assignment is to go downfield and hurl their bodies through the wedge protecting the return man.

- The 4 middle men (L3, L4, R3, and R4) attempt to get behind the wedge by closing in from the sides. Often the No. 4 man will cross inside the No. 3 man on his side. Their main goal is to make the tackle.

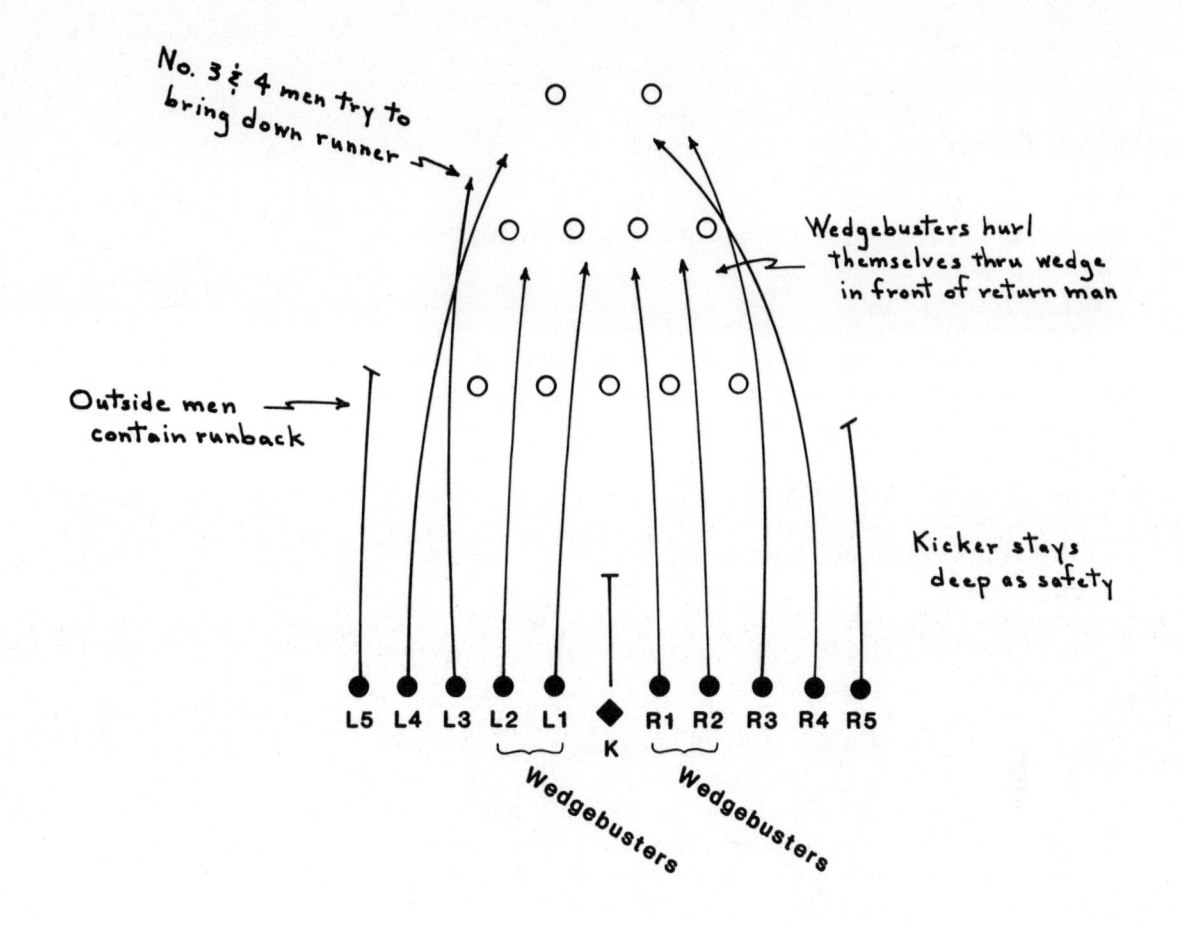

Kickoff Team

- The 2 outside men (L5 and R5) have containment responsibility. They cannot let the ball carrier get to the outside. They must force him inside toward the other covering players.
- The kicker usually stays deep and acts as a safety.

In operation, these players have to be in tiers. If they came as one big wave of tacklers and the return man broke through at any point, the kicking team would be in big trouble. (This also applies to punt coverage.)

For an onside kick, the kicker will usually attempt to kick the ball at least 2 lanes over to one side. Members of the kickoff team on the other side will fall back and behind the resulting scramble to protect against a runback.

Receiving Team

There are typically three groups of players on the receiving team.

- The front 5 are stationed around midfield. Their job is to block out the wedgebusters and maybe pick off the first middle man on each side. They sometimes cross over and block on the opposite side of their respective initial alignments.

- A 4-man wedge forms about 10 yards in front of the return man with the ball. The purpose is to shield the ball carrier from the initial onslaught of potential tacklers who make it downfield.

- Two return men stand inside their own 10-yard line. If the ball goes into the end zone, one will field it and the other will call whether to run the ball out or down it for a touchback. The return man without the ball then supports the wedge men.

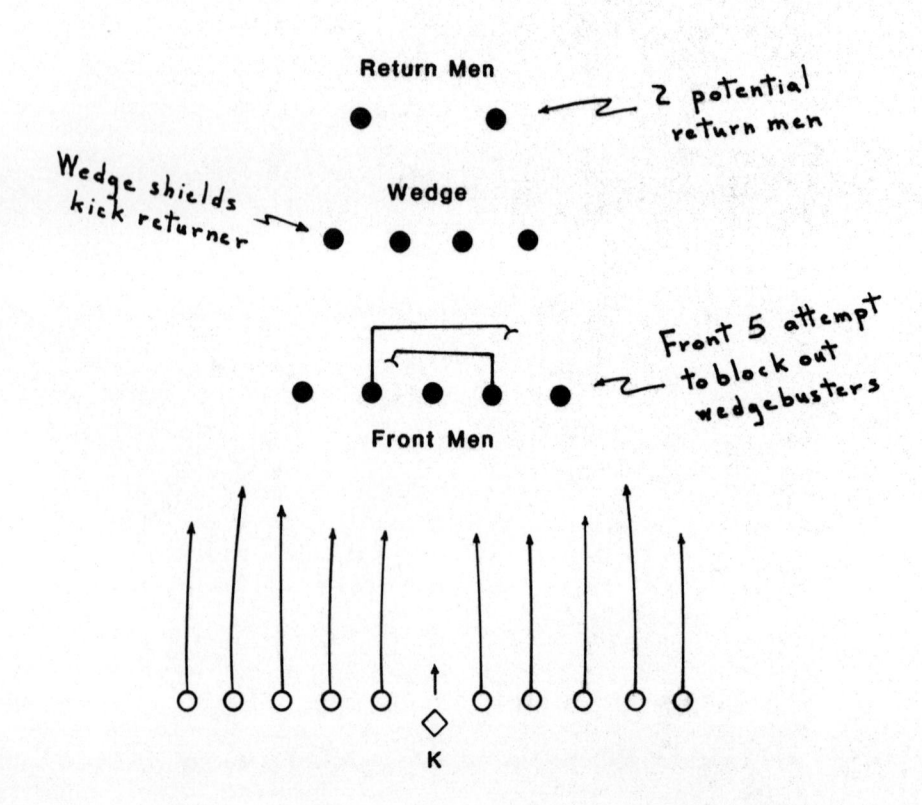

Return Men — 2 potential return men

Wedge — Wedge shields kick returner

Front Men — Front 5 attempt to block out wedgebusters

Kick Return Team

Basically, the return can go up the middle or along either side of the field. The direction of the return is determined before the kickoff (it changes if the actual kick is too far to the opposite side of the one called). The front men, after their initial blocks, fall back to form a wall on the appropriate side or to block for a middle return. The runner stays behind the wedge until he sees an opening and then breaks away. To a great extent, the distance of the runback depends on the individual effort of the return man.

PUNTS

Rules

Unlike a kickoff, a punted ball cannot be recovered beyond the line of scrimmage by the kicking team unless it was first touched by the receiving team. Thus, the receiving team can let the ball roll dead if they wish. Only the outside eligible receivers on the kicking team can go downfield before the ball is actually punted. Since a punt is not a free kick, the defense can line up close and attempt to block it.

A defender may make contact with the punter: (1) if it's incidental to (and after) his blocking the kick, (2) if the punter first runs with the ball or otherwise breaks his natural kicking rhythm, or (3) if the punter muffs the snap or the snap hits the ground. A punt that is blocked and does not cross the line of scrimmage can be recovered and advanced by either team. If the kicking team recovers the ball, it must still make enough yardage for the first down to retain possession.

Punting Team

Teams use basically two types of punt formation. One is the **tight punt formation**. This positions the front linemen close together, except for the 2 ends who are split out about 5 yards each. There are 3 blocking backs — 2 to the kicking side of the punter and 1 to the offside. The punter stands back about 10 to 12 yards deep. The formation is only employed where protection of the

Tight Punt Formation

punter is important (usually deep in his own territory). Because of the tight positioning, it does not facilitate a quick release of the players for good punt coverage.

The other formation is the **spread punt formation**. The interior linemen take wider splits than in the tight formation. Two blocking backs are positioned behind the gaps on each side of the center. These are the most direct rush routes to the punter, and thus require extra protection. A third blocking back (sometimes called the "personal protector") is about 5 to 6 yards behind the line. As the last blocker in front of the punter, he picks up anyone who penetrates that far. Because the spread formation provides less protection, the punter stands farther behind the line — 13 to 15 yards — which also necessitates a longer snap.

The center has a particularly difficult job. He has to spiral the ball back 15 yards through his legs, knowing he's going to get blasted as he starts to recover. And a bad snap is a costly mistake. As a result, the center is allowed to snap when he is ready. The punter will shout "down" for the players to position themselves and then "set" to indicate he is ready to punt. It's then up to the center to go when he's ready.

The split ends, having no blocking assignments, release immediately and sprint to the ball, making sure the ball carrier stays to their inside. The linemen must hold their blocks until the ball is punted and then get into their lanes (which are about 5 yards apart) as quickly as possible. They don't take an angle directly to the ball. Each one must cover his respective area and pursue properly. The punter and personal protector usually stay back as safeties on each side of the field.

Punt Return Team

The receiving team may concentrate on either blocking or returning the punt. If the punter is even a little bit slow in getting his kicks off, the center has been having problems with the snap, or the defense sees some other aspect they can exploit, they will be inclined to go for the block. Otherwise, the rush will only be sufficient to put some pressure on the punter, and most of the effort will be directed to the return.

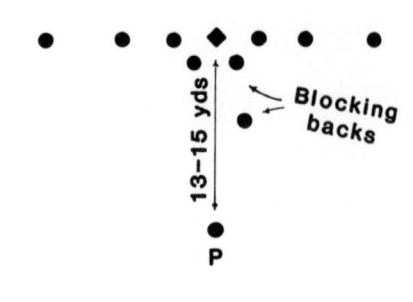

Spread Punt Formation

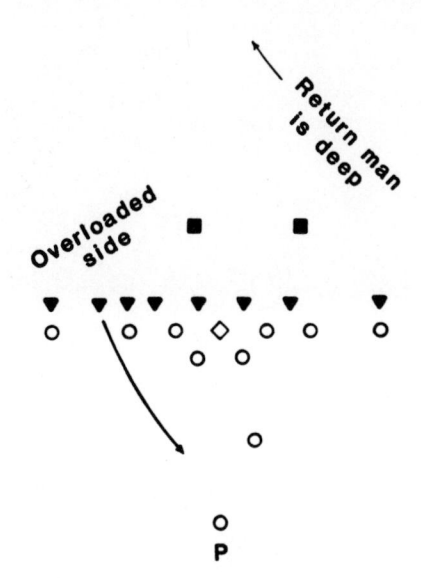

Punt Defense

A commonly used technique for blocking a punt is to overload one side of the line with more rushers than offensive blockers. The idea is to try to get one man around the end of the line. That man has to estimate where the punter's 2- or 3-step approach will take him and aim for that spot. And he has to cross in front of the punter, not head directly for the punter or he'll surely make illegal contact.

Another technique involves the middle. Since the most direct route is up the middle, rushers coordinate their actions in order to pull the center and blocking backs out of position. In some cases, a defensive lineman will actually try to grab an offensive lineman and pull him across the line. Then another defender will rush through the vacant hole.

When attempting to set up a return, many teams put two defenders over each split end. Since the ends are the only players who can release immediately, holding them up can buy time for the return man.

Returning Punts

Generally, it's easier to set up a return wall to one side than to establish blocking for a return up the middle. If two men are back, one catches the ball while the other watches the defense and calls to him whether to fair catch or not. Since blocking below the waist is no longer allowed on punt returns, blocking consists mainly of getting the proper position on the opponent and screening him off from the ball carrier. These blocks are difficult to maintain and have to be timed right.

On a runback, the safety without the ball takes the first man of the kicking team downfield. The other players peel back from the line of scrimmage and form a wall on the designated side of the field. They must space themselves appropriately and avoid double-teaming tacklers, so that they can block out the maximum number possible. However, their efforts are only productive if the return man can avoid the first potential tacklers downfield and get to the outside. In this regard, one determinant is how long the receiving team can hold up the kicking team at the line.

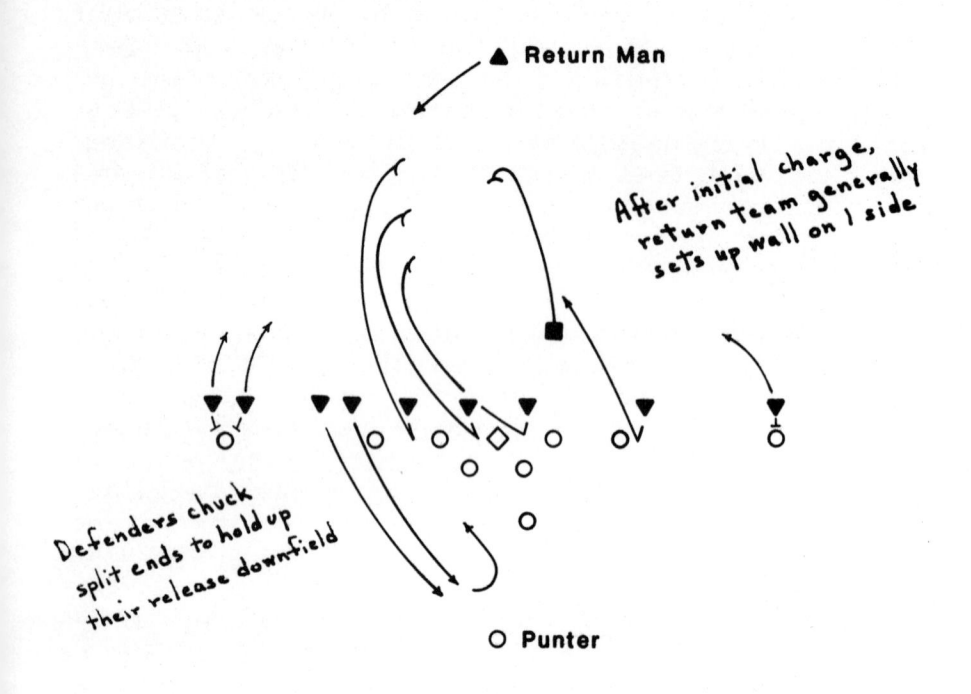

Punt Return

The return men are usually instructed not to back up beyond their own 10-yard line. It is likely that any punt beyond that point will go into the end zone. If the punt is received inside the 10-yard line, the odds are against a return that will get beyond the 20-yard line. So the percentages favor playing for a touchback.

FIELD GOALS & EXTRA POINTS

Rules

A field goal may be attempted using only a placekick or the outmoded dropkick. The dropkick is performed by dropping the ball to the ground and kicking it on the bounce. The dropkick was used when the ball was more pumpkin-shaped. In the 1930s the ball was made narrower to facilitate a better grip for passing. It resulted in more pointed ends thus making the dropkick obsolete.

Like the punt, the field goal is considered a kick from scrimmage and many of the same rules apply. The defensive team may advance an unsuccessful field goal attempt. Otherwise, the defense takes possession at the line of scrimmage. If the line of scrimmage during the unsuccessful attempt was inside the 20-yard line, the defense automatically takes possession out at the 20-yard line.

An extra point attempt commences with the ball spotted between the hashmarks and at least 2 yards from the goal line. The offense may elect to have the ball spotted outside the 2-yard line because of field conditions or for some other reason. The defense cannot score on a try for point. Once the defense gets possession or blocks the kick, the ball is dead.

Kicking Team

The kicking team generally uses a tight 7-man line with two blocking backs (often linebackers) protecting the wings. The front line's objective is just to seal inside and stop penetration. The holder spots the ball (no tee) about 7 yards behind the line. Against a team with a record of blocks up the middle, the ball might be spotted an extra yard back. But this is rarely done because it gives the outside rushers a better angle and it throws the timing off among the center, holder, and kicker.

The blockers on the wings sometimes are confronted by an overload of rushers. The blocker may have to hit two defenders, one to his inside and then one to his outside (called a "double bump"). In order to get around the blocker on the end and reach the kicker, a defense man has to turn a sharp corner. Because of the sharp angle, a good bump by the blocker should be sufficient to throw that charging defender off course long enough for the kick to clear the line. The key is getting the kick off fast. It has to be done in 1.3 seconds or it probably will be blocked.

Defending Team

The methods used to block placekicks are tailored to fit a team's personnel. Placekicks are blocked from the outside or up the middle. To do it from the outside requires speed. To do it from the middle requires penetration and height. As in the case of defending against a punt, one end of the line is often overloaded in an attempt to get one of the two outside men around the corner. Tall, strong rushers are used in the middle. Some of them may line up directly opposite offensive linemen. The purpose is to penetrate, push the opposing blocker back. Other rushers line up opposite gaps in the offense. They will try to slide through and block the kick. By lining up in a gap, a defender may attract two blockers, possibly allowing another rusher to get through. In some cases, two defenders attempt to wedge an opening which a third defender, just behind the line, can rush into.

The extent to which the defending team suspects a fake field-goal attempt determines the number of rushers versus the number of safety men. Two or three men (cornerbacks/safeties) are positioned off the line to protect against a pass or run when a fake is possible.

On extra-point attempts no safety men are employed, since the kicking team has no reason to fake the attempt. One or two jumpers are often used. They stand behind the line at the snap. They do not make contact with the blockers, but rather run up and leap as high as possible as the kick is made. The rules do not permit them to climb on, or otherwise use, their teammates to heighten their jumps. Thus, their effectiveness is dependent on good penetration by the defensive line, pushing the blockers back so the jumpers can get close.

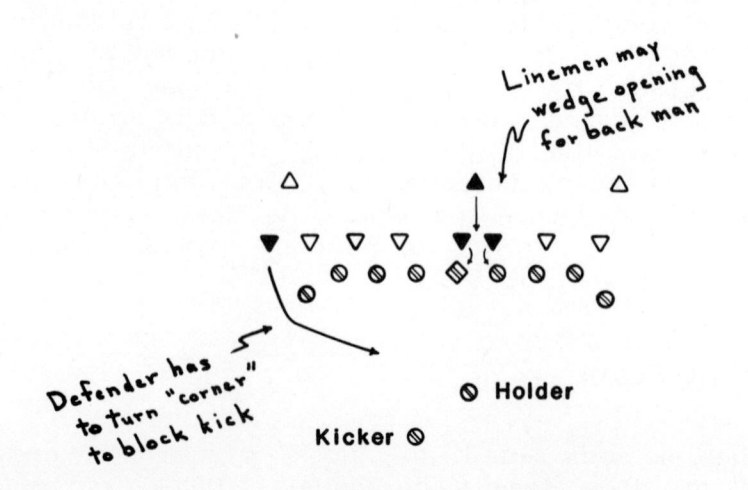

Field Goal Attempt

CHAPTER 10

STATISTICS

This chapter discusses various football statistics. Some statistics provide insight into the strategies being used, while others help one to evaluate the performance of specific teams or players. Certain statistics are meaningful. Others are not. The purpose of the chapter is to consider some statistics that may provide useful or interesting information for the fan.

Why Statistics?

Statistics are for losers. The only thing that counts is the final score. Or so the saying goes. Overkill? We think so. Some statistics provide meaningful information, and other statistics are just plain interesting. But they can be deceptive, and analysis of them can become interminable. Except for the statistic addicts, it probably doesn't take long to exceed the average fan's limit to care. We'll try not to let our discussion get out of hand.

In general, we'll limit our comments to overall statistics as they relate to one or two past seasons. More specifically, we'll briefly discuss three areas. First, some overall statistics of general interest. Second, a look at how a few of the common performance standards correlate with the teams having the best won-lost records in 1980 and 1981. Third, a brief overview of statistics related to individual player positions.

LEAGUE STATS

Offensive Plays

How many offensive plays does an NFL team have on average in a single game? Based on the 1981 regular NFL season, the answer is about 73 (72 in 1980). That is, on average a team has about 73 opportunities in which to run, pass, punt, or attempt a field goal. (Kickoffs and extra point attempts are excluded from this total.)

The following is a breakdown of what the 28 NFL teams decided to do with those opportunities:

	1980	1981
Pass	46%	47%
Run	45	44
Punt	7	7
Attempt FG	2	2
	100%	100%

Emphasis on Passing

As previously discussed, there were two rule changes adopted in 1978 which made passing easier. The first allowed the offensive linemen to open their hands and extend their arms when pass blocking. The second prohibited defenders from contacting potential receivers except once within 5 yards of the line of scrimmage. The following comparison of passing statistics shows the resulting change from 1977, the last season prior to the new rules:

	1977	1980	1981
Pass plays (vs. run)	42%	51%	51%
Avg. total yards*	286 yds	323 yds	335 yds
Avg. passing yards*	142 yds	196 yds	204 yds
TDs by pass	48%	54%	54%

*Average yards per game for <u>one</u> team.

As you can see, in the pass versus run category passing has increased to the point where it is now used slightly more than running plays. <u>Total</u> yards per game rose by 49 yards from 1977 to 1981, but <u>passing</u> yards per game increased by 62 yards. Thus the number of yards gained by running has decreased even though total yards have increased. Finally, the majority of touchdowns are now scored on passing plays. In 1981 only about 40% of the touchdowns were made on running plays with the remainder coming on kick returns, fumble recoveries, and interceptions.

Number of Rushes

Despite the recent emphasis on passing, running remains important. Running plays are important not only for gaining yardage but also for maintaining control of the ball. By simply determining which team ran the ball more times, you will generally know the winner. That doesn't mean which team gained more rushing (running) yardage, or had a better rushing average. It means just count the number of times they ran the ball, and the team with the higher number usually wins.

Box scores list the number of rushes for each team. So for anyone reading the sports section of a

Monday newspaper this is easy to check out. During the 1981 regular season, the team that rushed more won 82% of the time. During the 1980 regular season, that figure was also 82%.

Running vs. Passing

Getting back to the running versus passing aspects, consider the following 1981 figures:

   40 or more rushes: team won 90% (86% in 1980)
   40 or more passes: team won 20% (24% in 1980).

In other words, the teams that ran at least 40 times in a game almost always won. And teams that attempted to pass at least 40 times in a game generally lost.

To a great extent this just indicates that when a team falls behind, they have to start passing in an effort to catch up. On the other hand, when a team gets ahead, they may try to run out the clock. However, a significant portion (40%) of the 1981 regular season games (48% in 1980) were decided by 7 points or fewer. So in a lot of games one team is not that far ahead of the other.

Home Field, etc.

A few other overall 1981 statistics that might be of interest involve the home field advantage, type of playing surface, and effect of having less time to prepare after playing on Monday night.

Home Field Advantage

- Home team won 62% (54% in 1980).

Playing Surface

- 50% of the playing fields used by NFL teams in 1981 had artificial turf.
- Grass* teams playing on turf won 37% (48% in 1980).
- Turf* teams playing on grass won 34% (43% in 1980).

*Surface used on home field.

Monday Night Effect

- Teams which played the preceding Monday night won 47% (50% in 1980).

Thus, there seems to be some advantage to playing at home. It also seems that a team is at somewhat of a disadvantage when playing on a surface different from that of its home field. Grass teams appear to be slightly better at adapting than turf teams. Over the years, teams playing on Monday night have won more games (54% for 1970 thru 1981) the following week than they have lost. This is in spite of the fact that they have one day less in which to prepare. However, in recent years this has not been the case.

We recognize that using overall numbers makes for a rather simplistic analysis. For example, it doesn't take into account that some teams are better than others, and it doesn't attempt to determine how that quality difference affects the overall results. But a sophisticated analysis isn't what we are trying to present.

TEAM STATS

What Winners Do

The 10 teams with the best won-lost records during the 1981 regular season were:

Team	Record	Opponents' Record
San Francisco*	13-3	
Cincinnati	12-4	
Dallas	12-4	
Miami	11-4-1	
New York Jets	10-5-1	
Buffalo	10-6	
Denver	10-6	
Philadelphia	10-6	
San Diego	10-6	
New York Giants	9-7	(136-119-1)
Kansas City	9-7	(124-131-1)
Tampa Bay	9-7	(122-134)

*Super Bowl winner

What we are going to do is look at a few of the common performance indicators and see how they correlate with the top 10 teams in terms of won-lost records. Because there were three 9-7 teams, 12 teams are listed above. To limit our analysis to the 10 with the best records, only one 9-7 team (the New York Giants) will be included on the basis of its opponents' overall record.

Offense vs. Defense

One of the continuing controversies among many fans is whether defense is more important than offense or vice versa. Without getting into that one, let's just look at the results for 1981. At the end of the season, the NFL teams are ranked offensively on the basis of average yards gained per game. Similarly, teams are ranked defensively on the basis of average yards given up per game. Another way of gauging offensive or defensive performance is based on average yards gained or given up **per play** (rather than per game). We will use those statistics in the analysis that follows.

 Of the 10 teams with the best W-L records:
  5 were among the top 10 offensive teams
  6 were among the top 10 defensive teams
   (7 and 6 in 1980, respectively).

So there isn't a preponderance one way or the other. There are about an equal number of the top offensive and the top defensive teams included among those with the best records.

Running vs. Passing - Offense

Now consider the running vs. passing aspect —

 Of the 10 teams with the best W-L records:
  only 3 were among the top 10 rushing teams
  but 6 were among the top 10 passing teams
   (4 and 8 in 1980, respectively).

Thus, here the results favor a team with a strong passing attack over ones with a strong running game. (Note that this does not contradict the earlier comment that the team with the greater number of rushes in a given game usually wins. As was pointed out, it is the <u>number</u> of running plays, not the total rushing yards or rushing average, which counts.)

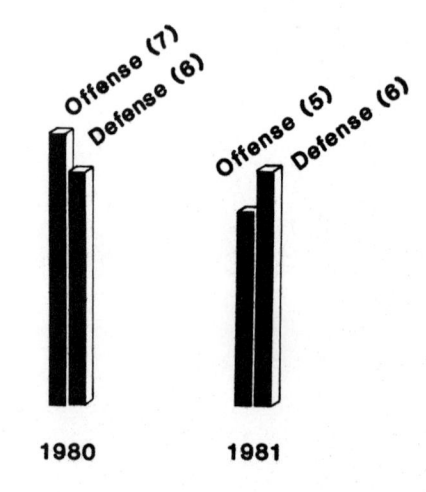

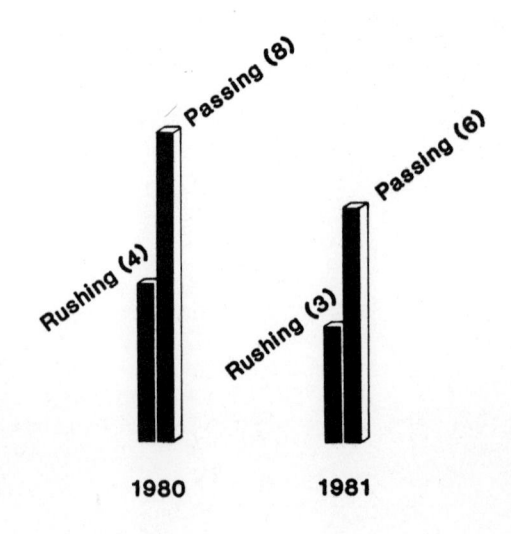

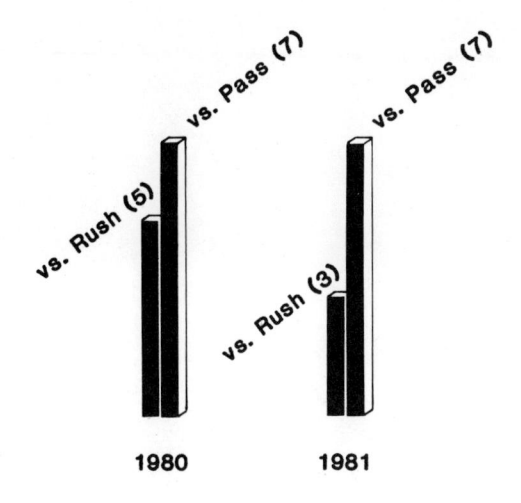

Running vs. Passing - Defense

On the defensive side —

Of the 10 teams with the best W-L records:
  3 were among the top 10 defenders vs. rush
  7 were among the top 10 defenders vs. pass
    (5 and 7 in 1980, respectively).

So defensively, the preference is again toward the passing game. In fact, the majority of teams with the best pass defenses comprised the majority of the teams with the best won-lost records.

Running vs. Passing - Play Selection

Excluding punts and field goal attempts, a team's offensive plays are either runs or passes. Here we are considering those teams which percentage-wise either ran the most or passed the most.

Of the 10 teams with the best W-L records:
  4 were among the top 10 in running %
  3 were among the top 10 in passing %
    (8 and 2 in 1980, respectively).

Although the figures are not as heavily weighted in 1981 as in 1980, there was still a bias toward teams which ran the most among those with the best records. To some extent this reflects the fact that good teams get ahead and then run to kill the clock. But it also shows that the teams which pass the most generally don't have the best records.

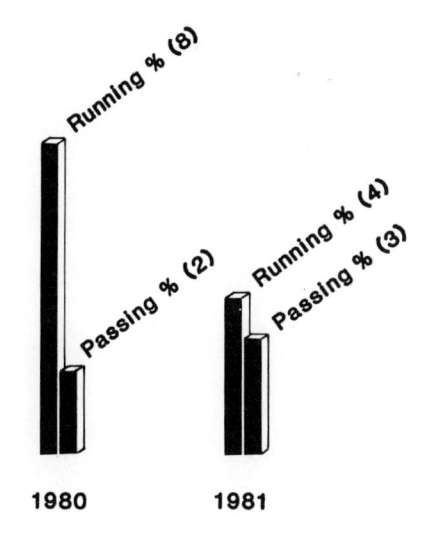

TD per Pass Percentage

The percentage of pass plays resulting in touchdowns has become an important statistic because of the emphasis on passing. As an example of the stat, in the 1981 regular season the San Diego Chargers scored 34 TDs on 648 pass plays (including quarterback sacks). So the Chargers scored on 5.3% of their attempted passes — the highest percentage in the league.

Turning to the top 10 winning teams:
  7 were among the top 10 teams in
    TD per pass play percentage
    (8 in 1980).

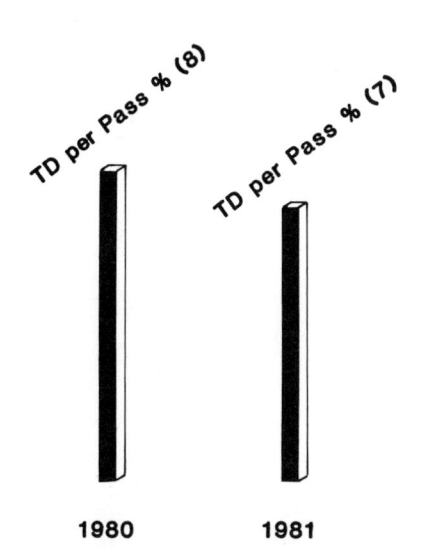

So the results seem to bear out the importance of that stat.

Net Turnovers

Turnovers are another common statistic used in evaluating teams. Turnovers consist of fumbles and pass interceptions where possession of the ball is, in effect, turned over by one team to the other team. Turnovers are commonly summarized on a net basis. In other words, the number of fumbles recovered and passes intercepted by a team are added together as positive numbers. From that total is subtracted the number of fumbles lost to and passes intercepted by the opposition. The net result is either a positive or negative number (or zero).

Suppose a team recovered 15 fumbles, intercepted 20 passes, lost 10 fumbles, and had 12 of its passes intercepted; it would have a net turnover total of +13 (15 + 20 - 10 - 12 = 13). If another team recovered 10 fumbles, intercepted 15 passes, lost 20 fumbles, and had 9 of its passes intercepted, that team would have a net turnover total of -4 (10 + 15 - 20 - 9 = -4). Obviously, the more positive the number, the better the performance.

> Of the 10 teams with the best W-L records:
> 6 were among the top 10 teams with
> a positive turnover record
> (6 in 1980).

Interceptions = Recoveries?

Breaking down the net turnover total into its components brings out the following:

> Of the 10 teams with the best W-L records:
> 6 were among the top 10 teams in
> net fumble recoveries
> 6 were among the top 10 teams in
> net interceptions
> (4 and 7 in 1980, respectively).

The difference between the 1980 and 1981 results might be somewhat attributable to the fact that interceptions far outnumbered fumble recoveries in 1980 (627 vs. 412) whereas the difference was much smaller for the 1981 season (609 vs. 507).

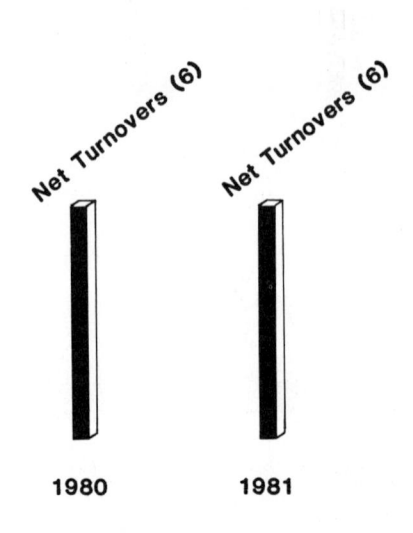

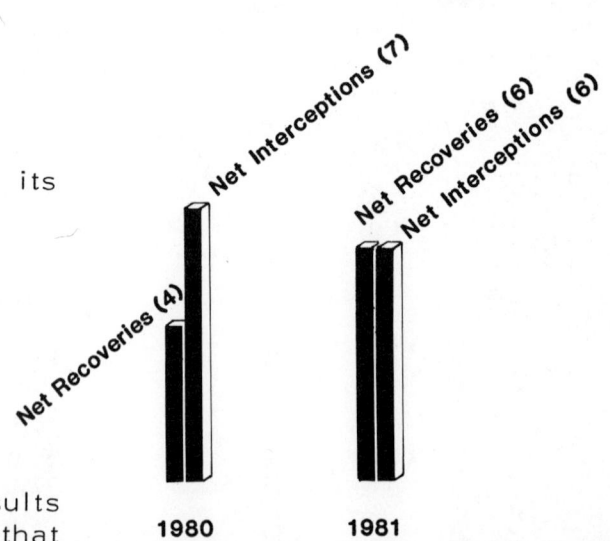

Quarterback Sacks

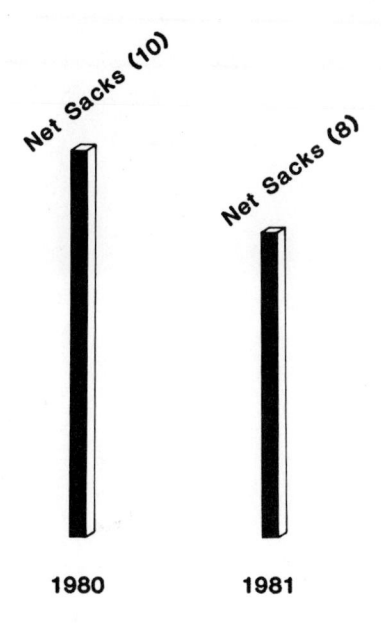

Quarterback sacks is the last team statistic we'll consider. A sack occurs when the quarterback is tackled before he can get a pass off. Sacks, like other statistics, can be summarized on a net basis (sacks made, less sacks given up).

Of the 10 teams with the best W-L records:
8 were among the top 10 teams in
net sacks (10 in 1980).

Of all the stats discussed here, the net sack total is the one which has the highest correlation with the best won-lost records for both 1980 and 1981. This just indicates how important pass blocking and pass rushing are to the outcome of games.

Table (Statistical Rankings of Top Teams)

The accompanying table summarizes the above discussion. It shows how the teams with the best won-lost records rank in the various statistical categories covered.

1981 Ranking in Various Categories Among All NFL Teams

	1981 W-L-T	Average Off.	Average Def.	Offense Rush	Offense Pass	Defense Rush	Defense Pass	Play Selection Run %	Play Selection Pass %	TD per Pass Play	Net Turn-overs	Net Fum-bles	Net Inter-cept's	Net Sacks
SF	13-3	–	3	–	9	–	3	10	–	–	1	1	3	8 t
Cin	12-4	2	–	–	3	–	10	–	7	2	4	3	5 t	8 t
Dal	12-4	8	–	4	6	–	–	2	–	4	2	–	1	6
Mia	11-4-1	–	–	–	–	–	–	–	–	–	–	4 t	–	7
NYJ	10-5-1	–	4	–	–	–	4	8	–	8	10	–	5 t	1
Buff	10-6	6	6	–	5	–	6	–	–	9	–	–	–	2
Den	10-6	–	9	–	10	–	5	–	–	7	8	4 t	–	–
Phil	10-6	9	2	2	–	6	1	7	–	5	7	7 t	10 t	4
SD	10-6	1	–	10	1	7	–	–	3	1	–	–	9	3
NYG	9-7	–	1	–	–	1	2	–	10	–	–	10 t	–	–
No. in category		5	6	3	6	3	7	4	3	7	6	6	6	8

t – tied for ranking

Note: Where no ranking is shown, team was not in top 10 for that category.

INDIVIDUAL PLAYER STATS

Rating Quarterbacks

Rating quarterbacks is difficult. The quarterback's assignments are many and his role pivotal. His intangible qualities directly affect his teammates in their performance.

The system used by the NFL to rate a quarterback concentrates on his passing abilities. For the 1981 season the quarterback with the highest rating was Cincinnati's Ken Anderson who had a 98.5 rating. The formula for deriving the rating is rather complex mathematically. What makes the meaning of the actual rating number somewhat ambiguous is that a quarterback can score over 100. For example, in 1976 Oakland's Ken Stabler attained a rating of 103.7.

Without getting into a lot of detail, here's how the quarterback rating system works from a conceptual standpoint. The current system was established in 1973 in an attempt to provide ratings that could be compared between years. So now the performance of Quarterback X in any given year can be compared with the performance of Quarterback Y in any prior year. Previously, the NFL had used different systems, some of which rated quarterbacks each year in relation to how their peers performed in that particular year. Thus no comparison between years was possible.

Four categories provide the bases for the new rating:

(1) Completions
(2) Interceptions
(3) Touchdowns
(4) Yards gained.

All of the four categories are figured on a per attempt basis. In other words, the quarterback's performance is analyzed by determining the percentage of his pass attempts completed, the percentage intercepted, the percentage thrown for a touchdown, and the average yards gained per attempt.

The quarterback is then given a score for each category. There is a set score or point value for each actual percentage or average attained for a given category. For example, if a quarterback's completion percentage is 35%, his score in that category is 0.250. If his completion percentage is 50%, his score is 1.000.

These category scores can each range from 0 to 2.375. The scoring system is designed so that a score of 1.000 equals about an average performance, whereas a score of 2.000 would about equal or exceed the existing NFL record in that category. For instance, a score of 2.000 in the percentage completion category would require a 70% completion average. The all-time record is 70.3% held by Sammy Baugh for Washington in 1945.

The four category scores are then added up and converted to an overall score on the basis of 6.000 points = 100. A rating of 67 is thus equivalent to an average performance in all four categories (total score of 4.000 ÷ 6.000 points × 100 = 67, if you care about the math). A rating of over 100 is truly exceptional. In fact, the NFL has gone back and calculated the figures for prior years; only 9 NFL players have ever exceeded 100.

The rating is pretty comprehensive regarding a quarterback's passing ability. It doesn't put too much weight on just one aspect like, say, completion percentage. A quarterback could attain a very high completion percentage by simply throwing short passes, where the running backs have to earn most of the yardage on their own.

However, the rating system doesn't touch on other aspects of the quarterback's performance that are vital to his team's success. What kind of leadership does he provide? Does he call good audibles and take advantage of situations that arise during the games? Is he a running threat? Is he tough enough to absorb the pounding quarterbacks receive?

Rating Offensive Linemen

Other than sacks surrendered, there aren't any published statistics for the offensive linemen.

If it were possible, one of the most meaningful stats would be how much time they allow the quarterback to get off a pass. Even the best passers can't be effective if their linemen don't hold off the defense.

If a quarterback is not passing well, consider the offensive line. Check on the number of sacks surrendered, and determine whether the quarterback is being continually pressured. On the other hand, if the quarterback is having a good year, note the number of sacks per pass attempt. You're likely to find he's getting good protection and the offensive line has a lot to do with his success.

The same goes for run blocking. If a runner is having an exceptional year, his offensive line must be doing something. But if a great runner is not having a great year, his line is probably partially to blame.

Another stat that would be at least interesting, and probably somewhat meaningful, is the number of holding penalties the individual linemen have accumulated. Such penalties often have the effect of thwarting crucial drives in many games.

Rating Running Backs

Running backs are ranked according to total yards gained. This is probably the best overall indicator, but average yards per carry and total touchdowns scored are other stats which provide meaningful information. Unfortunately, there are no published statistics which deal with the running back's success in short-yardage situations. If a player can consistently come up with the yard or two needed for a first down, it will bring down his overall average. But success in these situations demonstrates his effectiveness as a runner.

When evaluating a running back, the team's overall offense should be taken into account. If a team has a weak passing attack, it can make running more difficult. The defense doesn't have to worry as much about the pass, so they can key on the running backs. The yards-gained stats also ignore the running back's blocking and pass catching abilities.

In the future, the combined total of rushing and receiving yards will probably become a more common criterion than it is currently. On this basis, only one player exceeded 2,000 yards in 1981 (Atlanta's William Andrews). Moreover, he was only the sixth player in NFL history to accomplish this.

Rating Receivers

Receivers are ranked in terms of number of pass receptions. However, many feel that total yards gained is a more meaningful criterion than just the number caught. Average yards per reception, and the number of touchdowns scored are also published for receivers and provide useful info. Some have suggested a rating system which would take into account all four of these categories.

One stat that isn't compiled, but would be interesting, is the number of balls dropped. This would involve some judgment as only catchable passes should be counted. The stat would tell a lot about a receiver, as well as something about the passer. Some of the so-called mediocre quarterbacks are victims of poor receivers and/or poor offensive lines.

Other informative stats would include the number of passes caught in the middle, where the receiver is likely to get hit hard. And the number of receptions made on third down or in other critical situations would help to highlight the clutch performers.

Rating Defensive Linemen

Finding statistics on individual defensive linemen is difficult. Teams keep track of things like tackles, sacks, and fumbles caused, but they are seldom published. Sportscasters will sometimes supply this type of information in the case of an individual lineman who has accumulated a number of sacks during the year or made many tackles during a game. But the information supplied is pretty skimpy. The number of holding penalties caused and passes hurried by a defensive lineman would also be informative.

Actually, individual statistics could be misleading in some cases. An exceptional defensive lineman may not have many sacks because he is constantly being double-teamed. Several of his teammates' sacks could be attributable to the fact that the offensive linemen are doubling on him, thus leaving them opposed by only one blocker. That's why the defense's sack total as a team is meaningful in evaluating the unit as a whole.

Sacks aren't the only criteria. In a particular game a good defense may have trouble getting to the quarterback, but that doesn't mean they're not applying pressure. If the offense is continually holding in running backs and tight ends to block, the number of potential receivers is reduced and the linemen are doing their job.

Rating Defensive Backs

Interceptions are the principal published statistic covering defensive backs and linebackers. That leaves all the other aspects of their play unaccounted for. Even the number of interceptions must be interpreted when comparing two players. If a cornerback is particularly good, the opposition will throw away from him. The number of chances for him to intercept thus dwindles, yet it is directly attributable to his effectiveness.

The type of defense employed also affects the number of interceptions. The free safety who is "free" most of the time will have more opportunities to make interceptions than the safety or cornerback who covers an assigned receiver or area on almost every play.

As in the case of receivers, the number of dropped (potential) interceptions would be an interesting statistic.

Rating Placekickers

There is a rather complete array of statistics available on placekickers. Extra points attempted and made, field goals attempted and made, field goal percentage, average yards of those attempted, made, and missed as well as breakdowns for different distances are all available. Using total points scored to rate kickers is meaningful in terms of direct contribution to the final outcome. On the other hand, a kicker on a high-scoring team will have more opportunities to score, and regardless of the team, kicking a lot of points is easy if given a lot of chances. Consequently, many feel that accuracy is the best measure of performance.

Even overall accuracy can be misleading. If one kicker attempts almost all his field goals within 40 yards of the goal posts, his percentage successful should be greater than another kicker who has been frequently asked to try from longer distances. (The distance for a field goal is measured from the point where the ball is spotted, normally 7 yards behind the line of scrimmage, to the goal post, which is 10 yards behind the goal line.)

Pressure is another aspect. There is a big difference between kicking a field goal in the last few minutes when the game is on the line, and kicking one in a lop-sided contest. Because of all these different factors there have been suggestions that a rating system be established which would take several into account and roll them into one overall number. For placekickers, this has not yet been done.

Rating Punters

Punters are rated in terms of both gross and net average punting yards. We will close this discussion by considering how those averages are determined. While gross yards are straightforward, net yards take into account the gross yardage of the punts, the distance they were returned, the effect of touchbacks, and the number blocked.

In general, gross yards are measured from the line of scrimmage to the point where the ball stops or is taken by the receiving team. Since the punter normally stands about 15 yards behind the line, the ball actually travels farther than the gross number calculated. Cincinnati's Pat McInally had the highest average gross yards per punt for 1981 — 45.4 yards. Adding roughly 15 yards means his average kick travelled about 60 yards total.

Hang time (the time the ball is in the air) is important in allowing the kicking team to get downfield and stop the return. However, punts are not officially timed and recorded. To take this aspect into account, the actual return yardage is subtracted from the total gross yards of all punts.

If a ball goes into the end zone, it results in a touchback and the offense gets possession out at their own 20-yard line. This is factored into the punter's rating by multiplying the number of touchbacks he kicked by 20 yards and subtracting that total from his gross yardage less return yardage.

The resulting net yards (gross yards minus return yards minus touchback yards) are then divided by his total punts plus the number that were blocked. The number of blocked punts are not counted in determining the punter's average gross yards per kick. But they are included in arriving at his overall <u>net</u> average. By counting the blocked kicks the punter is, in effect, getting zero yardage for those attempts. That may or may not be fair, depending on whether he flubbed it or his protection broke down.

As an example of how the system works, assume a punter punted 100 times and also had one punt blocked. His gross yardage was 4,000 yards and the punts were returned a total of 500 yards. Ten of his punts resulted in touchbacks. His rating would be determined as follows:

Gross yards	4,000
Less: Return yards	− 500
	3,500
Less: Touchback yards (10 × 20 yards)	− 200
	3,300
Divided by total punts plus no. blocked	÷ 101
Net average	32.7 yards

There's one other statistic kept for punters which is significant. That is the number of punts which ended up (after any return by the receiving team) inside the 20-yard line. The figure is important because the overall net rating doesn't take this into account. Getting good field position for his defense is the punter's goal. So the number of times he puts the opposition inside its 20 tells something about his performance.

CHAPTER 11

WATCHING & KEEPING SCORE

In this chapter a few suggestions about how to watch a game are made. They are aimed at the fan who is interested in gaining some understanding of what different players do by observing them in action. A method of keeping track of the plays is also outlined. The procedure is relatively simple, yet it enables one to quickly evaluate the overall strategy of each team as the game progresses.

You Can't Watch Everything

Most people watching a football game watch the player with the ball. Of the 22 players on the field they zero right in on him. That's only natural since where the ball goes is what counts. Trying to take in all the action is impossible. Even coaches can't do that. It's one reason teams take movies of each game using wide angle lenses so that all the players are visible. Cameras are stationed high up at both the 50-yard line and one end zone to provide two perspectives. Then the coaches and the players study the films taken at their own games and the three most recent games of each week's opponent.

Regarding the films of the opponent, the defensive coaches will concentrate on watching the offense, and the offensive coaches will do the same with respect to the opponent's defense. They work in groups with one coach calling out formations, etc., and another writing the information down for subsequent analysis of tendencies. The films are run back and forth until all the details have been studied. They are also shown to the players so they can see the tactics employed by the opposition. And many players study them on their own to analyze the particular individuals they must deal with.

Even practice sessions are filmed to some extent. This enables the coaches to review the techniques of individual players as well as analyze team play. This is especially true when practicing against the offensive and defensive maneuvers employed by next week's opponent and when the coaches install new plays of their own.

Action Away from the Ball

For the average fan, watching the ball and the player who has it may be the easiest method of following a game. However, by watching some of the action away from the ball, the observer can gain a little insight into what the various other players are doing.

Suppose a fan concentrates on watching the center. After several plays, he or she will see how the center handles the nose tackle over him, goes out and blocks on a linebacker, angle blocks on a lineman, or helps a guard in pass blocking. In short, the observer will start to get some idea of what the center does after snapping the ball.

Moving to the guards, they usually provide the first indication of where the play is going. If they block straight ahead, it will probably be an inside run. If they pull to one side, the running back generally heads in that direction. If the guards drop back, it will be a pass play. Thus, by observing the guards one sees not only their varied assignments, but also how the plays begin to unfold.

The same holds true for running backs. See how they line up before the snap. Then watch who takes the handoff and how the other back blocks. Or maybe they'll both stay in and pass block, or release on a delayed basis into pass routes.

Regarding the defense, one can watch each defensive lineman and see how he charges the line and what kind of moves he uses. On a pass play, observe how the linebackers all drop back if they are in zone coverage. One can also check which receivers or areas the various cornerbacks and safeties are covering.

Problems for the Viewer

It's surprising how much action there is that fans never look at. There are several reasons for this. First, it's actually hard to look away from the ball. Second, many people don't really know what the other players are trying to do. Third, even if you do look at the other action, it's often difficult to see.

Regarding the first point, looking at other players initially requires a little effort. After a while it's easier to do and one can change the point of focus as the play develops. As to the second point, it is hoped that this book has given the reader some idea as to what the various players are trying to accomplish. The final point does raise a problem.

For the fan with not the best seat in the stadium or the viewer at home, it's hard to see what some of the players are doing. In fact, TV cameras do just the opposite of what is being suggested — they follow the ball. So the viewer is limited to watching the action on the periphery of the screen if he or she wants to observe players other than the quarterback or the running back with the ball. There's no question it limits the possible subjects for watching. Moreover, to keep the ball in view the camera will often cut away from the lineman or linebacker whom the fan has decided to follow. Nevertheless, there is a lot of action being shown. And if you look for it you can learn a lot.

Don't Make It a Chore

This discussion is not intended to suggest that there is a right way and a wrong way to watch a football game. To the contrary, people watch football games for enjoyment. There's no point in making a chore out of it.

What is being suggested here is that devoting a little time to watching certain players can be both interesting and informative. Since there are a number of pro football games on TV each weekend, one way to do this is to turn on a game not involving your favorite team, just to concentrate on a few players. At first it may seem futile — everything happens so fast and there is a lot of congestion in certain areas. But if you're interested, give it a chance and you'll soon start seeing things you've never noticed before. This isn't a process where you have to sit through entire games. Do it for a while and then switch back to watching the ball. Over a period of time you'll develop a better understanding of the game and actually spot more things when you _are_ following the ball.

Scoring Method

If you're so inclined, we're going to outline a method of keeping score. In following the suggested approach, one can go to the extent desired. Just the basics will suffice for most. An avid watcher may want to do more.

Two points before going further. First, there is no set way to do this — you are free to come up with your own variations. Second, this is for your enjoyment — if you miss a play, don't worry.

This particular method involves the following steps:

(1) Using lined paper, draw in several columns on the right-hand side.

(2) Over each column write the names of the running backs, wide receivers, and tight ends who are likely to play for one team (leave one or two columns blank to write in occasional subs).

(3) Number the lines at the left side consecutively from top to bottom.

(4) On another piece of paper do the same for the opposing team.

(5) For each play, note the down and distance, e.g., 1st and 10 (1/10), 2nd and 8 (2/8), etc.; on 1st downs also jot down the approximate field position (yard line).

(6) For each play, indicate who ran with the ball, who caught it, or who was the intended receiver; use the following code:

R = ran with ball
C = caught pass
I = incomplete pass

Use the left side, right side, and center of each column to indicate the left side, right side, and center of the field, respectively.

249

Example: Assume RB Smith runs to left for 3 yards.
RB Jones runs to right for 2 yards.
QB throws incomplete pass to TE Brown on right side.
Punter kicks ball to opponent's 15-yard line with no runback.

		RBs		WRs		TE
		Smith	Jones	Wilson	Adams	Brown
①	1/10 at (own) 35	R				
②	2/7		R			
③	3/5					(Short) I Dropped
④	4/5 Punt to 15, no return					
⑤						
⑥						

The rest is up to you. You can add any notes you think are pertinent — penalties, timeouts, whatever. For instance, on the sample scoring sheet above we noted the incomplete pass was a short one which the tight end should have caught, but dropped.

When the ball goes over to the other team, use the scoring sheet for the opposition.

The method of scoring is simple and gives a running record of what is happening from an offensive standpoint. For the average fan, the real benefit is derived from scanning up and down the columns rather than reading each line. Is the team mainly running or passing? Are they favoring one side or the other? Is a particular receiver not being used? As the game progresses it's easy to answer these kinds of questions. One can get a pretty good idea of how varied the attack has been with a quick look. It doesn't take a lot of study or analysis.

The scoring sheet also tells something about the defense. If the opposition is mainly running to the right, they may think that side of the defense is weak. If they've thrown deep a couple of times on one side, they probably feel the cornerback covering that area is vulnerable.

For the interested fan it's really somewhat amazing how much information this simple scoring method provides. It affords a complete record of the entire game as it progresses. No more guessing at how many times they passed on 1st down, how many balls have been dropped, which way are they running, how well are they mixing their plays. It's all there along with the yardage for each play.

Example: NFC Championship (January, 1982)

The National Football Conference championship game played in January, 1982, involved the Dallas Cowboys and the San Francisco 49ers. This game was close throughout with the lead changing six times. Its outcome wasn't clear until the final seconds. The following two pages show how the results of the 4th quarter are reflected using the scoring method discussed.

The quarter opened with Dallas behind 17-21, but having the ball 2nd and 10 at San Francisco's 12-yard line. Note that with its first two possessions Dallas scored both times. On the other hand, San Francisco turned the ball over twice to end its first two series.

With a 27-21 lead, Dallas mainly ran the ball using Tony Dorsett and then punted. Starting at their own 11-yard line, with 4:54 left, San Francisco mixed runs and passes to score the go-ahead TD. Six of the first seven plays in that

NFC Championship (January, 1982)

Dallas Cowboys
(4th Quarter)

#	Play	Dorsett (RB)	Springs (RB)	Hill (WR)	Pearson (WR)	Johnson (WR)	DuPree (TE)	Cosbie (TE)	Saldi (TE)	Notes
61	2/10 at +12						C			
62	3/3						I			Wright broke up in EZ
63	4/3 FG good [20-21]									
64	1/10 at -49	R								
65	1/10 at +40		C							at 37
66	1/10 at 27	R								
67	2/4							C TD		play action, good throw
68	PAT good [27-21]									
69	1/10 at -27	R								
70	2/10	R								good tackle Williamson
71	3/8								C	
72	1/10 at 38		C							Jones caught screen pass
73	2/6	R								
74	3/1		R							
75	1/10 at 48	R								
76	2/8	R								
77	3/5			I						thrown behind & high; off WR Donley's hands
78	4/5 Punt to 11; Solomon fair catch									
79	KO to 11; Newsome ret. to 25									
80	1/10 at -25				C					good throw betw 3 def'rs
81	1/10 at +44 QB [Fumble] Dallas TO 0:39	Pillers hit Stuckey recovered								
82										

▼ — Indicates start of series (when team took possession of ball)

252

NFC Championship (January, 1982)

S.F. 49ers
(4th Quarter)

		RBs		WRs				TEs	
		Elliott	Cooper	Clark	Solomon	Wilson	Schumann	Young	Ramson
61	KO to 2; Lawrence ret. to 19								
62	1/10 at -19					I overthrown at +40 (had def'r beat)			
63	2/10			C (wide open)					at 34
64	1/10 at 40	R							
65	2/6			R Fumble Breunig caused					at 49 Easley carrying good tackle by Newhouse
66	KO to 1; Ring ret. to 17								
67	1/10 at -17		I good def. (Breunig)						at 35
68	2/10			C					at 23
69	1/10 at 35					I Interception by Walls			at +27 underthrown
70	1/10 at -11 4:54 left	I low & behind							off RB's hands
71	2/10	R							
72	3/4				C good adjustment by Solomon				
73	1/10 at 23		R						
74	1/10 at 34	R							
75	2/3 2:50	I thrown behind							
76	3/3 Penalty Dallas offside		R had 1st down						
77	1/10 at 46		C						
78	2/5 2:00				R Reverse				
79	1/10 at +36			C stayed in bounds					good throw
80	1/10 at 25				C				pick play
81	1/10 at 13 S.F. Time Out 1:15				I overthrown in EZ (had def'r beat)				
82	2/10	R good block by Ayers							
83	3/3 S.F. Time Out 0:58			C TD good adjustment & great catch					QB under heavy rush
84	PAT good 27-28								
85	1/10 at +48 QB fell on								
86	2/15 Dal. Time Out 0:27 QB fell on			End of Game					

253

drive involved Lenvil Elliott. Six of the last seven plays involved Freddie Solomon, Dwight Clark, and Earl Cooper.

Note that Dallas threw only twice to wide receivers, but four times to tight ends. San Francisco threw nine times to wide receivers, but none to a tight end (however, Clark lined up in a tight end position several times).

There was only one penalty in the 4th quarter and it had no significant effect. But the three turnovers were important, especially the first and the last. Dallas scored and went ahead after San Francisco's fumble. But later, with the ball on San Francisco's 46-yard line, Dallas also fumbled to effectively end the game. This was especially costly since Dallas had one of the best field goal kickers in the league. A pass completion could have put him in range with a chance to win the game.

Well, enough about this particular contest. The point is that with a few simple notations it is easy to keep track of what strategies are being used and when the critical points occurred. One could talk at length about possible ways to evaluate the information. For example, focusing on 1st down performance, utilization of players, play selection, and so on. Suffice it to say that the scoring method provides a lot of raw data for analysis.

It might also be mentioned that the example includes some notations about player performance. This is optional. It's up to the individual fan as to how much or how little to write down.

CHAPTER 12

CONCLUSION

What Have We Done?

As originally stated, the aim has been to provide some generalized insights into pro football tactics, techniques, and overall strategy. By now you should have an increased knowledge of different formations, how plays work, the way they are called, and the specific responsibilities of the players. No attempt has been made to cover everything. Nor did we deal with all the variations utilized by different teams. However, based on what has been presented, you should be able to compare what your favorite team does — spot tactics they employ and understand why they are used.

Strategy Should Fit the Players

We trust that the material presented has brought out the close connection between overall strategy and the abilities of the specific players on a given team. If a cornerback runs a 4.7 40, he shouldn't be given assignments designed for someone with 4.5 speed. If the team is going with a young quarterback, the offensive scheme better not require the judgment of a veteran. If one inside linebacker is experienced but the other is not, their responsibilities have to be juggled between savvy and raw talent. In short, the strategies employed must exploit the strengths and compensate for the weaknesses of each individual player on the field. And if the strengths don't outweigh the weaknesses, you're in for a long season.

The emphasis on each player is important. It doesn't take the opposition long to find a weak link. They analyze your team, player by player. Kind of like Santa Claus, they know when a player's been good and when he's been bad. But, unlike St. Nick, if the opposing coaching staff sees that someone is vulnerable, they'll take advantage. It's either assault or entrapment — they openly attack him or surreptitiously set him up. In any case it's just a matter of time.

The coach's job is to look over his entire roster of players and determine how the best result can be achieved with that group. The fact that some team in the other league won the Super Bowl with a particular philosophy and the home town fans are clamoring for a similar strategy really has no relevance if it doesn't fit the players involved. Trying to force players that don't belong into a specific offensive or defensive scheme is like pounding the old square peg into a round hole.

That doesn't mean that coaches don't have their own overall philosophies. They do. But if a coach wants to use that philosophy he has to have the players who can carry it out. So the players he drafts and those he keeps are the ones that best match the roles they will be given. After that, it's up to the coach to develop those players and make adjustments to his system to yield the best result. In a lot of cases this is fine tuning. The adjustments aren't readily apparent. But when the veterans start leaving and the replacements have different skills, then the changes have to be more significant.

Importance of Team Play

So the strategy used should be the one which yields the best overall result from the particular players on the roster. So what else is new? That's obvious. Or is it? Sometimes that requires compromise. You can't always accentuate the individual abilities of 11 players at the same time. Football is still a team game. For the success of the team, it may not be wise to favor formations and plays which feature certain players. Many championships have been won by teams which played well together, rather than emphasizing the role of one or two superstars.

So don't forget teamwork. As diagrammed, every offensive play will gain yardage and every defensive play will stop them dead. Execution really is the key. And execution is a team concept.

Evaluating the Strategy

The perceptive fans seem to recognize that there is more than one way to win in the NFL. Once the roster is fixed, looking covetously at players on other teams doesn't help. The real question is whether the strategy being used is the best, given the circumstances. If it's not working, why isn't it? That can be a tough question to answer without studying game films, watching practice, and knowing exactly how the plays are supposed to work.

At the same time, a situation can be overanalyzed. The margin of difference between the majority of NFL teams isn't that great. In a lot of games it boils down to breaks and mistakes. Like the old saying — there are usually two or three big plays that determine the outcome and they can come at any time, on any down. On the other hand, well-coached teams don't make a lot of costly mistakes. And teams which have confidence in themselves and in what they are doing seem to be able to make their own breaks.

Best Wishes

We hope that what you have gained from this book will make watching football games more enjoyable. It's a uniquely interesting sport with an element of strategy behind every play.

INDEX

A

Angles,20
Anderson, Ken,238
Andrews, William,241
Area blocking,65
Audible (see calls)

B

Backfield,22
Backpedalling,151
Backs release downfield,217
Back side,48
Backup unit,60-61
Baugh,Sammy,239
Bench route,70
Blast (charge),58
  play,53
Blitz,40,41,63,73,134,218
  control man,66
  counter,206-207
  delay,66
  heavy (3-4 def.),77
Blocking,101-102
  area,65
  bob,106
  center,98
  check,70
  crab,102
  crackback,10
  cross,102
  cut,102
  cutoff,102
  double-team,47,102,139
  down,58
  even/odd,191
  fill,106
  fold,102
  hook,58,102
  influence,102
  isolation,54
  kick out,47,102

  man,64-65
    vs. even def.,66
    vs. odd def.,67
  option,12,105,139
  pass,40,64-67,99-100,101
    short pass,212
  punt return,225
  rule,12,101-102,190-191
  run,101-102
  running back,106-107
  scramble,102
  shoulder,101-102
  vs. stunt,67
  tight end,117
  trap,50,136,139
  zone,65
Bubble,56
Buffalo,233
Bump-and-run,38

C

Calls
  audible,181,184-187
  backs,177
  cadence,105
  defensive,193-198
  examples,182-186,188-190,192-193,194-198
  formations,178-179
  hand signals,181
  holes,176-177
  huddle,181-182
  line,12,190-193
  pass play,188-190
  play,175-198
  quarterback vs. coach,180-181
  receivers,178
  running plays,179-180,182-183
  series approach,180,190
  signals at line,183-184
  strong side,179
  terminology,176,194-196
Center,48,51,54,64,66,97-98,167,
  192,193,224,247

Charge
    blast,58
    inside,57
    outside,57
    vs. reading,133,214
Check block,70
Check thru,71-72
Cincinnati,233
Circle route,71-72
Clark, Dwight,254
Clearing route,87
Clip,10
Close line play,10
Combination
    coverages,81-82,218
    pass defenses,73
    pattern,87-89
Combo,82,217
Comeback,69
Contain man,13 (see force man)
    responsibility,63
Containment,13,59,78,140,148
Contain unit,60-61
Cooper, Earl, 254
Corner,69
Cornerback,38,59,75-76,77,78,79,80,
    81,82,111,149-154,247
Coverage
    combination,81-82,218
    combo,217
    double,76
    man-to-man,74-77
    mombo,82
    zone,74,78-81
Crackback
    block,10
    zone,10
Crossing route,70
Curl,68-69,72
    zone,74,75,81

D

Dallas Cowboys,42,233,251,252,254
Deals,61
Deception,21
    vs. execution,36
Defense
    combination,73,81-82
    dime,44
    double nickel,44
    even,11,39
    field goal,227-228
    flex,42-43
        strong,42
        weak,42
    4-3 (see 4-3 defense)
    free safety,75-76
    gap,11,41
    goal line,41,44
    key,57
    man-to-man,73,74-77,90-91,216
    nickel (see nickel defense)
    numbering,192
    odd,11,39,41
    pass,73-82
    prevent,38,44
    reading,110,119-120,125-129
    6-5,44
    6-2,44
    stack,11,41-42
    3-4 (see 3-4 defense)
    zone (see zone)
Defensive
    back,198
        rating,242
    calls,193-198
    end,37,58,62,63,138-140
    formations,35-44
    line,37
    lineman,56,57-58,131-140,203,247
        rating,241
    plays,56-63
        secondary,37,149
    tackles,37,57,62,134-138
Delay route,70
Denver,233
Diagrams,4,6-7
    explanation,6
Dime defense,44
Dive plays,124
Dorsett, Tony,251
Double bump,227
Double coverage
    on split end,76
    vs. tight end,91
    on wide recrs.,76
Double-double zone,80
Double nickel,44
Double slot,88
Double-team block,47,102,139
Double tight,31
Double wing,30

259

Double zone (5 under, 2 deep), 80
Down block, 58
Down lineman, 36
Drag route, 70
Draw play, 58, 138
Drive man, 47
Dropkick, 226

E

Eligible receiver, 9, 13, 14, 22, 23-24, 30, 223
Elliott, Lenvil, 254
End
   defensive (see defensive end)
   end-tackle stunt, 62
   split (see split end)
   tackle-end stunt, 62
   tight (see tight end)
Even defense, 11, 39
   man blocking vs., 66
Examples
   audible, 184-186
   defensive calls, 194-198
   line calls, 192-193
   pass blocking, 66-67
   pass defense, 74
   pass play, 188-190
   running play, 182-183
   signals at line, 183-184
Extra point (see field goal)

F

Fair catch, 14
Fakes, 12, 89, 107, 211
Fan, hypothetical, 4
Field, 11
Field goal, 226-228
   attempts by NCAA Div. I kickers, 164-165
   defending team, 227-228
   rules, 226
Fight the pressure, 136
Fill, 48
   block, 106
Films, 246
5 under, 2 deep zone, 80
5 under, 3 deep strong side zone, 81
Flag route, 13, 69
Flanker, 24, 48, 52, 55
   corner, tight end out, 215
   out, tight end corner, 215
   reverse, 214

Flare, 71-72, 108
   control man, 66
Flat, 74
   route, 71-72
Flex defense, 42-43
   strong defense, 42
   weak defense, 42
Flooding zones, 86
Fly (or go or streak), 69
Force, 60, 221
   man, 13, 59, 60, 78
   responsibility, 79, 198
   unit, 60-61
Formations, 9, 15-44
   defensive, 35-44
   double slot, 88
   offensive, 21-35
   punt, 223-224
   recognition, 34, 203
4-man line, 40, 43-44, 62, 74, 136-137
4-point stance, 36
4-3 defense, 36-40, 56, 74, 213
   linebackers, 144
   variations, 41-44
4 under, 3 deep zone, 78-79
Free kick, 14, 220
Free safety, 9, 38, 63, 75, 76, 77, 78, 81, 82, 90-91, 160-162, 204
   defense, 75-76
   throw away from, 90
Front, 36
Front side, 48
Fullback, 27, 47, 49, 52
   deep sideline, 217
Fumble, 14

G

Games, 61
Gap defense, 11, 41
Gap stack, 57
Go route, 69, 72
Goal line defense, 41, 44
Guard, 48-49, 50-51, 54, 64, 67, 98-100, 192, 201, 247
   middle, 39
   nose, 39

H

Halfback, 27, 47, 49, 51-52, 207
Handoff, 20, 89, 105

Hands, use of,13
Hang time,169,172,243-244
Hashmarks,11
Head linesman,10
Hitch,68-69
  & go,70
Holder,167-168,227
Holding,12,141-142
Hook
  block,58,102
  pass route,68,69
  zones,74,76,81
Huddle,181-182

I

I formation,28-29
Ineligible receiver,11
Influence block,102
Injury, risk of,108
Inside charge,57
Inside linebacker,39,77,146-147
Interior
  line,31
  lineman,34
Inverted zone,78,215
Isolation block,54

J

Judge
  field,10
  line,10
Jumper,228

K

Kansas City,233
Keys,18,202,205
  against pass,161
  defense,57
  multiple,146
  offensive,203-204
  read,58,145
Kicker,163-168,221
  field goal attempts by NCAA
    Div.I kickers,164-165
  rating,242-243
  soccer,165-166
  soccer vs. straightaway,164-165
  straight away,166-167

Kicking team,220-221,227
Kickoff,14,220-223
  rules,220
Kick out,47,102
Kicks
  free,14,220
  onside,221

L

Lanes
  rushing,137
Linebacker,56-57,62-63,74,78,80,81,
    82,84,143-148,198,247
  controlling,89
  inside (see inside linebacker)
  middle (see middle linebacker)
  outside (see outside linebacker)
  short zones,74
  strong side,37,75,76,77,78,79-80
    linebacker zone,79-80
  weak side,37,76,77,78,84
Line calls,12,98,190-193
Line judge,10
Linemen & linebackers,58-59
Line splits,23,201-202
Look-in route,68,70

M

McInally, Pat,243
Man blocking,64-65
  vs. even/odd defense,66-67
Man under 2-deep zone,81,216
Man-in-motion,33,189
Man-to-man defense,73,74-77,90-91,216
Miami,233
Middle guard,39
Middle linebacker,37,57,58,62,75-76,
    78,146-147,193
Misdirection play,21,52-55
Mombo,82
Motion,33,111,189
Muff,14,223

N

New York Jets,233
New York Giants,233-234
Nickel back,77,81,82
Nickel defense,43-44,77,82,216
  w/designated chaser,82

double nickel,44
  vs. 3 wide recrs.,81
Nose guard,39
Nose tackle,39,62,134-135
Numbers
  backs,177
  defenders,192
  holes,176-177
  jersey,14
  receivers,178
  series approach,180,190

O

Odd defense,11,39,41
  man blocking vs.,67
Offensive formations,21-35
Offensive guard (see guard)
Offensive keys,203
Offensive line,92,212
Offensive lineman,65,66,67,95-100
  rating,239-240
Offensive running plays,46-55
Offensive shifts,34-35
Offensive tackle,47-48,51-52,54,64,
    100,192,200-201
Officials,10
  field judge,10
  head linesman,10
  line judge,10
  referee,10
  umpire,10
Offside,48
Off-tackle power play,46-50
One-chuck rule,13,73
Onside,47
Onside kick,221
Open set,23
Option blocking,12,105,139
Out-and-up,70
Outside charge,57
Outside linebacker,39,59,75-76,147-148,
    193,204
Overshift,41

P

Pass
  attacks,83-92
  blocking,40,64-67,99-100,101,212
  defenses,73-82
  plays,64-72,188-190
  routes,68-72,210-211 (see routes)
  rules,73
  trees,188
Pass patterns,64,72
  choice,72
  combination,87-89
  timing,72,111
PAT,163
Personal protector,224
Philadelphia,233
Pick play,12,88
Pinch,56,61
Pivots,123-125
Play action pass,21,65,66,89,
    129-130,140,217
Players,93-173
  stats,238-244
Plays,45-82
  blast,53
  calls,175-198
  defensive,56-63
  dive,124
  draw,58,138
  misdirection,52-55
  offensive running,46-55
  offensive, stats,230
  off-tackle power play,46-50
  pass,64-72
  pick,12,88
  recognition,145
  running,179-180
  tipping,200-205
  trap,9,50,139
Pocket
  handoff,105
  passing,64,137,140
Post man,47
Post route,13,68-69
Prevent defense,38,44
Pro set,6,22-25,27,28
  strong side,26-28
  variations,25-27
  weak side,26-28
Pro slot,30
Pulling,99
Pump fake,211
Punt,14,223-226
  spread formation,224
  team,223-224
  tight formation,223-224
Punter,169-173,223,224
  rating,243-244

Punt return team,224-226
  rules,223
Pursuit,13,20,59,60-61

Q

Quarterback,49,55,121-130,207,211-212
  sacks,237
  stats,238-239
Quick post,68-69
Quick trap,50-53,139

R

Read,34,79
  vs. charging,133,214
  defenses,110,119-120,125-129
  keys,58,145
  offenses,156
Receiver
  eligible,9,13,14,22,23-24,30,223
  ineligible,11
  rating,241
  wide (see wide receiver)
  3 wide recrs.,31-33,81,216
Receiving,107-108
  team,222-223
Recognition
  formation,34,203
  play,17-18,145
Recoveries,236
Referee,10
Releasing from line,117-118
Return man,222-223,225-226
Reverse,21,214
Rotation
  throw away from,84-85
  zone,78,80,90
Routes
  adjusting,110,119-120,210-211
  bench,70
  check thru,71-72
  circle,71-72
  clearing,87
  comeback,69
  corner,69
  crossing,70
  curl,68-69,72
  delay,70
  drag,70
  fast-glide-fly,70
  flag,13,25,69
  flare,71-72,108
  flat,71-72
  fly (or go or streak),69
  go,72
  hitch,68-69
  hitch-and-go,70
  hook,68,69
  look-in,68,70
  out-and-up,70
  post,13,69
  quick post,13,68-69
  running back,71-72
  shoot,71-72
  short-out,68-69
  slant,68-69
  square-out/in,68-69
  tight end,70
  wide receiver,68-70
  zig-out,70
Rule blocking,12,101-102,190-191
Rules,35
  changes,16,134,231
  kickoff,220
  one-chuck,13,73
  pass blocking,73
  punts,223
Run blocking,101-102
Run support,49,59,60,90,157
Run to daylight,49,105
Running back,25,27,91,103-108,202,
    205,247
  pass blocking,66
  pass routes,71-72
  rating,240-241
Running vs. passing,232,234-235
Rushing
  lanes,137
  statistics,231-232

S

Safety,59,76,80,155-162,173,193,221,
    224,225,247
  free (see free safety)
  strong (see strong safety)
  weak,9,38
San Diego Chargers,233,235
San Francisco 49ers,233,251,253,254
Scoring method,249-254
Scrambling,212
Scrapes,48
Seams,85-86
Secondary, defensive,37,149

Shifts
  offensive,34-35
  overshift,41
  undershift,41,213
Shoot,71-72
Short out,68-69
Short-yardage situations,27,41
Shotgun,32,129
Signals
  at line,183-184
  hand,181,193
Single set back,30-31
Situation substitution,16
6-5 defense,44
6-2 defense,44
Slant,56,61
  pass route,68-69
Slot formation,29-30
  double slot,88
  I,30
  pro,30
  slot,29,31-33,87
  slotback,29
  using,87-89
Snap,32,97,129
Soccer kicker,165-166
Soccer style vs. straightaway,164-165
Solomon, Freddie,254
Special teams,219-228
Split backs,26,28
Split end,24,49,52,55,224
  double coverage,76
Splits, line,23,201-202
Square-out or -in,68-69
Stabler, Ken,238
Stack defense,11,41-42,57
  gap,57
Stance,99
  2-point,29,37
  3-point,29,34,36,44,104
  4-point,36
Stanley, John,164
Sweep weak,214
Sweet spots,36
Statistics,229-244
  defense,234,235
  home field,232-233
  interceptions,236
  league,230-233
  Monday night,233
  offense vs. defense,234
  offensive plays,230

passing,231
players,238-244
playing surface,232-233
recoveries,236
running vs. passing — offense,232-234
running vs. passing — defense,235
running vs. passing — play selection,235
rushes,231-232
sacks,237
team,233-237
  ranking,237
TD per pass percentage,235-236
turnovers,236
Straightaway kicker,166-167
Streak route,69
Strong safety,9,38,63,75-76,77,78,
  79,81,82,158-159
  X zone,78
Strong side,9,24,31,52,179
  linebacker,37,75,76,77,78,79-80
    zone,79-80
  set,26-28
  zone,78-79,84,215
    5 under, 3 deep,81
    inverted,78,215
Substitution,16
Stunts,61-63,134
  & blitzes,134
  blocking vs.,67
  end-tackle,62
  tackle-end,62
  tackles w/linebacker,62

T

Tackle
  defensive (see defensive tackle)
  end-tackle stunt,62
  nose,39,62,134-135
  offensive (see offensive tackle)
  stunt, w/linebacker,62
  tackle-end stunt,62
Tackling,12
Tailback,28-29,53,55
Tampa Bay,233
TD per pass percentage,235
Teams
  field goal,227
    defending,227-228
  kicking,220-221,227
  punt returns,224-226
  punting,223-224

    receiving,222-223
    special,219-228
    stats,233-237
Tee,167,227
Tendencies,17
Terminology,74,176,194-196
3-4 defense,6,36,39-40,56,74,214,215
    blitz,77
    linebackers,144
    variations,41-44
    5 under, 3 deep strong
        side zone,81
3-man line,43-44,62,81
3-point stance,29,34,36,44,104
3 wide receivers,31-33,81,216
Throw
    away from free safety,90-91
    away from rotation,84-85
    into the middle,208-210
    underneath,89
Tight end,24,31,47,49,50,52,55,91,
    115-120,202
    deep threat,217
    vs. double coverage,91
    double tight,31
    pass blocking,66
    pass routes,70
    & 3 wide recrs.,216
Time
    hang,169,172,243-244
    of the essence,19
    official,10
    stadium clock,10
    30-second clock,10
    timing patterns,72,111
Tipping play,200-205
Touchback,220
Trap
    block,50,136,139
    long,139,214
    play,9
    quick,50-53,139
Trends,16
Triple wing,30
Twists,61
2-point stance,29,37
2 tight ends,31

U

Umpire,10
Undershift,41,213
Upback,28-29,53-54

W

Watching & keeping score,245-254
Weak safety,9,38
Weak side,9,24,31
    linebacker,37,76,77,78,84
    run,213
    set,26,28
    sweep,214
    zone,80,217
Weather,168,172
Wedge,220,222,223
Wedgebusters,220,222
Wide receiver,27,31-33,109-114,207,210
    double coverage,76
    pass routes,68-70
    3 wide recrs. vs. nickel defense,81
    3 wide recrs. & tight end,216
Wing
    double,30
    triple,30
Wingback,30-31,33

Z

Zig-out,70
Zone
    blocking,65
    coverage,74,78-81
    crackback,10
    curl,74,75,81
    defense,73,84-87
    w/designated chaser (nickel
        defense),82
    double (5 under, 2 deep),80
    double-double,80
    5 under, 3 deep,81
    flat area,74
    flooding,86
    4 under, 3 deep,78-79
    hook,74,76,81
    linebacker,74
    man under 2-deep zone,81,216
    rotation,90
    stretching,85-86
    strong safety X zone,78
    strong side,78-79,84,215
    strong side inverted,78,215
    strong side linebacker,79-80
    terminology,74
    weak side,80,217

265